Realistic Cost Estimating For Manufacturing: Second Edition

William Winchell

Alfred University

Richard Perich

Publications Administrato

Published by

Society of Manufacturing Engineers
Publications Development Department
One SME Drive
P.O. Box 930
Dearborn, Michigan .8121

Realistic Cost Estimating For Manufacturing

Society of Manufacturing Engineers
Dearborn, Michigan 48121

Second Edition
First Printing

Library of Congress Catalog Card Number: 89-61736

International Standard Book Number: 0-87263-364-0

Manufactured in the United States of America

PREFACE

Never before has there been a greater need for accurate product cost estimating in manufacturing than now. With today's production costs increasing, competition getting stiffer and the marketplace changing continually, a manufacturing strategy lacking a sharp examination of material, labor, and tooling costs is headed toward failure. Today's complex manufacturing environment is no place for the "guess-timate" or the estimator's "little black book." Carefully prepared and detailed analyses of what a product will cost have taken their place.

Twenty-one years ago, when this book first appeared, it took a comprehensive approach to discussing the cost estimating function. Succeeding years, however, brought about advancements in technology, which inevitably had an impact on manufacturing. For example, it is possible today to obtain computer software to assist in virtually any phase of production—and that certainly includes cost estimating.

Realistic Cost Estimating for Manufacturing, Second Edition has been revised with up-to-date figures, costs and concepts. It also now includes a chapter on computer applications as well as information on estimating multipurpose jigs and fixtures. The book contains illustrations and examples of estimating forms used by many manufacturers, which should serve as models and examples to the estimator.

The Society of Manufacturing Engineers wishes to thank Ivan R. Vernon, Editor of the first edition of this book.

Dr. Vernon's work in the first edition is classic both to the many students who used it as a textbook as well as to estimators working in the field. The work from the first edition formed a strong foundation for this edition.

A special acknowledgement should go to those who acted as reviewers for Dr. Vernon's book. They include William J. Van Dyke, Desmond Douglas, Joseph Seman and Maurice Collin. I also wish to thank Ed Neimeier and Dwane Hartmann, students at Alfred University, for their valuable assistance in preparing the second edition.

William Winchell
Alfred University
Alfred, New York
July, 1989

TABLE OF CONTENTS

1

THE ESTIMATING FUNCTION

Cost estimating is critical to the success of any company that competes in today's marketplace. It provides information about what products in the future may cost. This contrasts to cost accounting which keeps track of what current products cost.

One major use of cost estimating is in providing prices of future products to other companies. Selling prices are sensitive to market competition. If the price is competitive, future business will be gained. But if the actual costs to produce the product are higher than estimated, there may not be an adequate profit. Even worse, a loss may result. On the other hand, if the estimated costs are higher than necessary to make the product, the selling price may be established too high to gain needed business.

Another major use of cost estimating is in deciding if investments should be made to produce a product for many customers. This may be for the consumer market where a commitment for buying the product in advance is not possible. Studies of the market by the sales department will reveal what price range will be competitive. The cost estimate provides information that is used to decide if the investment will be profitable and provide an adequate return on the capital needed. If the cost estimate does not reflect the real cost, a wrong decision may be made. If it is too high, the company may not undertake a needed business venture. In contrast, if the estimated cost is low, the company may embark on a venture that is doomed to financial failure.

Other uses for cost estimating include comparing alternative product designs, or deciding whether to make or buy a part. Most companies in the United States make less than five percent profit on sales. With this slender margin, the cost estimate has little room for error. This is compounded by off-shore competition which make products perceived to be good quality at much lower labor costs. To remain competitive worldwide, a company must project lower costs in the estimate by incorporating needed improvements in quality and productivity.

Cost estimating is the prediction of expenses and investments that will be made to design, manufacture and market a product. The expenses, in general, consist of direct labor, direct material, factory burden, product design, general and administrative, and selling costs. The investments consist of tooling, equipment, and facilities. The combination of these projected costs and investments for a product is called a *product cost estimate*. The management of a company adds an amount to the estimate for profit establishing the selling price. This book concentrates on discussing those costs and investments associated with manufacturing—direct labor, direct material, factory burden, tooling, equipment and facilities.

Estimating is a staff function in a company. This process may be shared among several departments. In small companies and some large ones it is still done by a single entity. Often, the reason it is shared is it is difficult for a single entity to have the expertise necessary to do this critical task. However, this restraint may disappear with the advent of more sophisticated computerized cost estimating packages discussed in Chapter Five.

If the product cost estimate is in response to a request for quotation from another company, the process may be coordinated by the sales department. Key details of the estimate are typically completed by manufacturing engineering, industrial engineering, product engineering, and accounting. Usually, operating personnel and management review appropriate details to encourage other insights and gain concurrence in the approach taken. A committee made up of top management reviews the completed estimate and establishes the desired profit and selling price. The sales department presents the completed Product Cost Estimate as part of a quote to the company that may buy the product. Other parts of the quote may include product drawings, quality standards and the time schedule. Each of the functions mentioned and their relationship to cost estimating will be discussed later in this chapter.

EXPLANATION OF TERMS

Estimates used for product costing may be classified in several ways. The term *product cost estimate* generally refers to any estimate of the costs in making a part, subassembly, or entire product. The term *part estimate* refers to the estimate of the cost of manufacturing a product subassembly or part. Also, the term *product estimate* is sometimes used to emphasize the fact that an entire product, rather than a subassembly or part, is being estimated.

The term *part* refers to the smallest component of a product or product subassembly. A *subassembly* is composed of two or more parts. An automobile exhaust system, for example, is a subassembly. The tailpipe and the clamps and bolts attaching the tailpipe to the automobile are parts. A product usually consists of a number of parts and one or more subassemblies.

The product cost estimate has various cost categories. When necessary to distinguish between major costs, the terms *material cost estimate*, *labor cost estimate*, and *tooling estimate* are useful. In recent years, tooling costs have increased to such an extent, many companies specify tooling cost separately rather than include it as part of factory burden.

Estimating is necessary in areas other than product costing. A *facilities cost estimate*, *project cost estimate*, and *construction cost estimate* are all used for estimating other manufacturing needs. Such planning is usually done by a facilities group.

IMPORTANCE OF LIFE OF PRODUCT

Suppliers to larger companies are seeing a trend towards long-term contractual relationships. This is in reverse to past practices of being assured of the production of a part for a year at a time. For the supplying companies, this means they can plan processes that are more specialized and automated. The long-term contract assures that massive investments for automation, the kind that must be used for several years to justify the expense, can be adopted. The larger companies awarding the contracts expect lower prices and long-term commitment to quality and productivity improvement. In fact, many of them are using the *target cost* concepts discussed in this chapter to assure competitive product prices. Suppliers are asked to compete against each other for these contracts. For the suppliers, this means cost estimating must take a much longer range focus. Specific annual reductions in cost and improvement of quality must be predicted over the life of the contract. The affects of inflation over the term of the contract must also be understood and off-setting improvements planned. This must be done with a commitment from the entire organization.

NEED FOR BUSINESS

A company, whether new or established, is fighting for survival. The life cycle of the production of products is short. New products and new customers must be constantly added to replace those products for which there is little or no demand. One example of this is the computer industry. In less than a decade, IBM has introduced four major product changes—PC, XT, AT and PS-2 and still lost market share. Even the computer is becoming a commodity with purchase decisions based upon price since customers perceive quality of different brands alike. Another example can be found by looking at the companies comprising the Dow Jones Index in the 1920s and comparing with the companies comprising that same index today. Only some of the companies survive.

The key to adding new products and customers is providing products that are competitive in price, perceived of good quality and delivered on time. A product cost estimate identifying the resources to do this is critical to the future profitability of any company.

TARGET COST

Target cost recognizes that there is a fundamental difference between traditional product cost and selling price. Except for some government "cost-plus" contracts, selling price is determined largely by the competition in the marketplace. On the other hand, product costs are traditionally determined internally in the company and relate to product design, procedures, wage rates, and manufacturing processes. In most companies, there is no direct relationship between the selling price and product cost. But, selling prices must be greater than costs or the company will not survive. There will be no profit to sustain the business.

Target costs can be defined as those product costs that must not be exceeded for a product to make a profit in the competitive marketplace. Development of a target cost starts with analyzing the competitive selling price, perceived quality, and desired attributes for the product in the marketplace. Marketing studies bench marking products made by other companies could help determine this. The next step is finding out what the maximum product cost would be to make a profit at the competitive selling price. This cost is the target cost. A comparison between the traditional estimated cost and the target cost provides insight into improvements required. These improvements are likely gained through enhanced product designs and manufacturing processes. If the target cost can be achieved, the detailed Product Cost Estimate is finished. If it cannot, future plans for the product are stopped. The concept of target cost illustrates the importance of a supplier having strong product design capabilities. For many products there is a strong relationship between the product design and "manufacturability."

PRODUCT COSTS

Types of Cost

Understanding the product cost structure is critical to comprehending the process of estimating. This structure is illustrated in *Figure 1-1*. On a macro basis, product costs are of two types—*direct costs* and *indirect costs*.

Direct costs are the costs that can be traced to a specific product. For many companies, only direct labor and direct material are included in this category. These two costs combined are known as *prime cost*.

Direct labor involves the wages of people that do tasks in the manufacturing process for a specific product. The wages paid to a press operator to form a bracket is an example of this. So is money spent to pay for a person to drive a fastener to hold a bracket onto another part.

Direct material is the cost to purchase material or parts that will ultimately be part of a specific product. This is the cost of the metal purchased to form a bracket. Cost for fasteners purchased from a supplier to assemble a bracket would also be in this category.

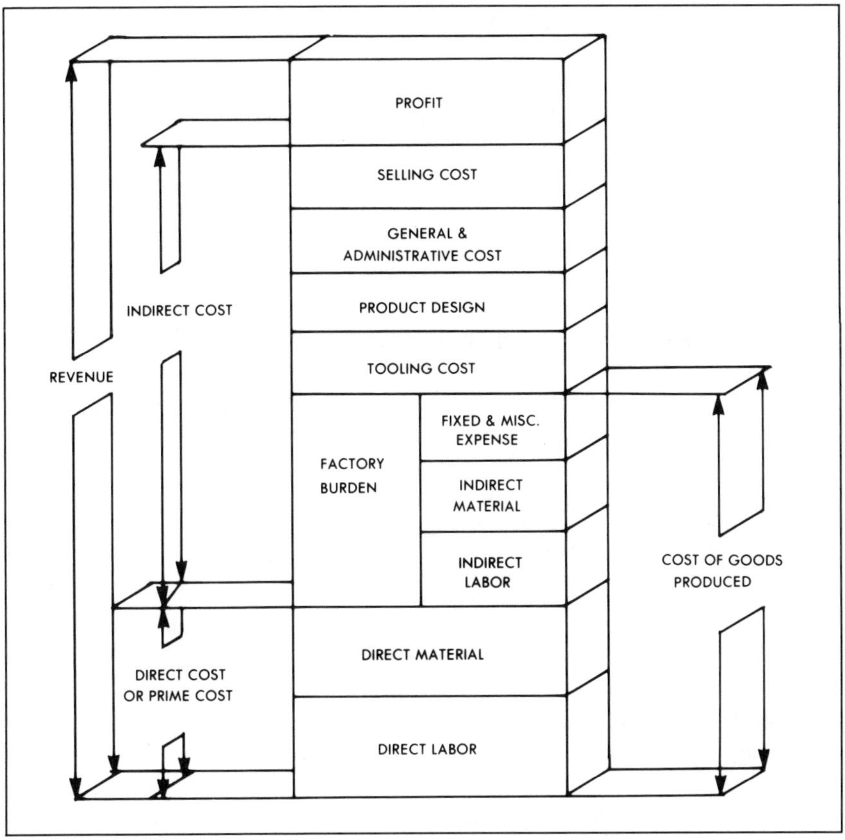

Figure 1-1. Product cost structure.

For the same manufacturing process, these costs should be directly proportional to the quantity produced. For example, the cost for wages, purchased metal and fasteners to produce and assemble 100,000 brackets should be ten times the cost for 10,000 brackets using the same manufacturing process. Often costs, which may otherwise be proportional, are considered too small to be worthwhile to keep track of as direct cost. An example may be the minute cost of the cleaning solution to wash a bracket prior to assembly. In this case, it is included as part of the indirect costs.

Indirect costs are costs that are "considered" as *not* being traceable to a specific product but are still required to run the company. These costs, unlike direct costs, are also *not* directly proportional to the quantity of a specific product produced. The categories comprising indirect costs vary greatly among companies. A representative grouping of categories is *factory burden*, *tooling*, *product design*, *general* and *administrative costs*, and *selling costs*. The combination of direct costs and factory burden are known as *cost of goods produced*.

Factory burden includes all costs associated with the operation of the plant considered *not* directly related to a specific product. Sub-categories include indirect labor, indirect material, and fixed and miscellaneous expense.

Indirect labor refers to the wages of people that do tasks *not* considered directly related to the manufacturing process for a specific product. The costs of janitorial services, forklift operators, maintenance people, inspectors, and machine set-up people are examples. A practice in companies that process batches is to separately estimate the wages involved in setting-up the tools and equipment to run each batch. This is used to quote a lump-sum set-up charge each time an order is processed.

Indirect material is the cost to purchase material that will *not* ultimately be part of a specific product. This may include such items as cutting or grinding fluids.

Fixed or *miscellaneous expense* is defined as salaries of people, *not* considered directly related to the manufacturing process for a specific product, such as telephone bills, energy bills, taxes, cost of perishable tools, and depreciation of equipment. This category also includes the salaries of industrial engineers, manufacturing engineers, production supervision, buyers and material engineers. Unusual expenses sometimes are absorbed by the supplier and charged to this category without an offsetting charge to the buying company. Examples include premium freight, overtime costs, depreciation of new facilities, and launch or debugging costs. There is a growing trend among suppliers to recognize these added costs in product cost estimates.

Tooling is the cost to design and build new durable tools or revise existing durable tools to process a specific product. Suppliers often provide the projected cost of this in product cost estimates for a lump sum reimbursement by the buying company. In this case, the buying company usually owns the tools, and they cannot be used to process similar parts for another company. Where the supplier retains ownership of the tools, the cost is usually amortized over the life of the product and is part of the product cost estimate under factory burden.

Product design is the cost of designing the product for the intended application. It could also include the cost of building and testing prototypes to verify that the design meets performance and durability requirements. Suppliers to larger companies are sometimes asked to handle the design of a product. As previously discussed in this chapter, this enhances the application of the target cost concept. Suppliers may provide the projected cost of this in product cost estimates for a lump sum reimbursement by the buying company. In other cases, the cost is allocated over the production life of the product and becomes part of the product cost estimate.

General and *administrative costs* are those costs necessary to keep the company in operation but not directly related to production in the factory. Examples are executive salaries, research costs, and public relations. Some companies are encountering an increasing amount of product warranty cost being demanded by their customers. This cost is typically charged to this category. The trend among suppliers is to recognize this added cost in product cost estimates.

Selling costs are costs directly related to selling products. Examples are the cost of salespeople who call on potential customers, and marketing studies. Some suppliers also charge a lump sum amount for preparing a product cost estimate that is paid by the customer when the quote is delivered.

Standard Versus Actual Costs

Costs may also be classified as standard or actual. A *standard cost* is an ideal cost or a predetermined cost. Working with manufacturing departments, cost accounting develops figures reflecting what a part or product should cost. When the part or product is finished, accounting determines what the actual costs were.

The variances between actual costs and standard costs provide management with a tool to evaluate the effectiveness of manufacturing departments. Variances below the standard may indicate that a department supervisor has found ways to reduce scrap, cut overtime, or decrease tool breakage and wear. Costs higher than the standard may be a sign of high scrap, poor workmanship resulting in a high part rejection rate, or excessive overtime.

On the other hand, variances above standard costs may reflect an uncontrollable cost increase. In this case, variances serve as an effective reporting system. By readily identifying costs that are out of line, management can take appropriate action. One way would be to adjust standard costs so that future estimates used for bidding are more realistic.

Costs in Relation to Product Volume

Costs are also categorized according to their behavior in relation to product volume. Fixed, variable, and step-variable cost patterns are shown in *Figure 1-2*. The definitions of fixed, variable, and step-variable costs assume the existence of upper and lower limits on production quantities. Only within this relevant range do costs behave according to their definitions. Note, the cost behavior patterns below 50 units and above 250 units in *Figure 1-2*. Fixed costs remain the same regardless of volume. Specific examples include executive salaries, secretarial services, facilities, durable tooling, and security services. Durable tooling is classified as a fixed cost because a certain level of tooling is required to produce one unit or many units. Adequate plant security probably demands at least one night watchman, regardless of production levels.

Variable costs rise in direct proportion to the number of units produced. Direct costs such as material and labor generally follow a variable curve such as the one depicted in *Figure 1-2*. Note that this curve climbs less steeply outside the

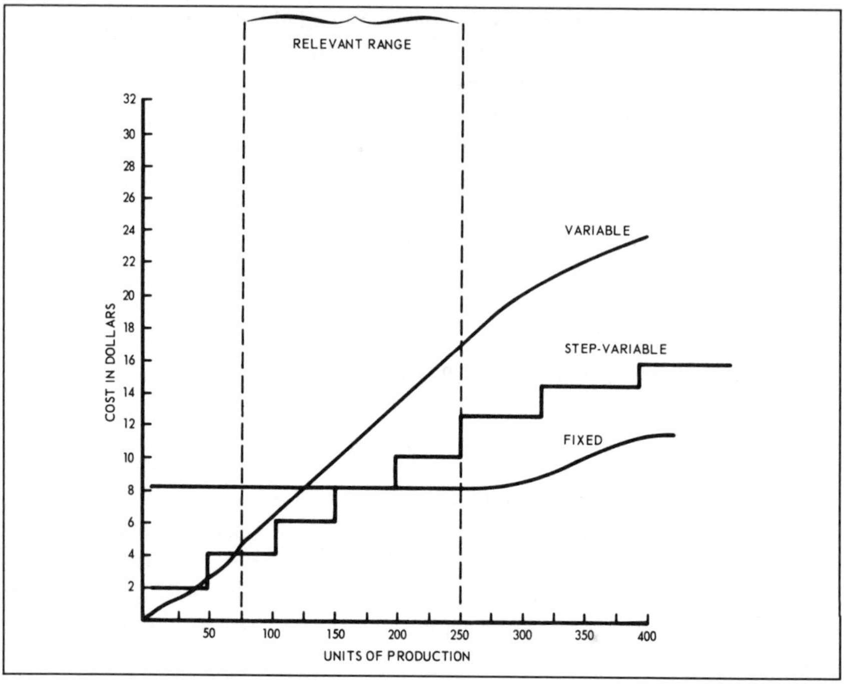

Figure 1-2. Cost volume behavior patterns.

relevant range. As larger volumes are produced, lower material costs are possible and costs per unit are lowered.

A step-variable cost is one that remains the same over a given number of production units but jumps sharply to new plateaus at certain incremental changes in volume. The cost of a machine capable of producing 50 units, for example, would be the same whether one or 50 units were actually produced. Perhaps, at 51 units, however, a new machine would need to be purchased, doubling the cost of machinery.

Costs in Relation to Length of Production Run

It is logical to most people that it will take more time to build the first unit than the last unit of a production run. This is because learning is taking place as the units are being built. The learning is by the production operator and persons in the manufacturing environment lending support to the operator. This results in each successive unit being built more efficiently. This is demonstrated dramatically in labor-intensive operations. Understanding the concept, called a *learning curve*, is critical in preparation of product cost estimates for the production of

Table 1-1. Effect of Learning on Direct Labor Required to Build One Unit.

Unit of Production	*Direct Labor Hours Required*
1	10
2	9.5
4	9.03
8	8.57
16	8.15
32	7.74
64	7.35
128	6.98
256	6.63
512	6.30

batches or relatively small quantities. It is also useful for determining launch or debugging costs for the initial units of a long production run.

Studies of labor intensive operations have shown that the direct labor hours used to make a product decreases by a fixed percentage each time that the quantity possessed doubles. If that fixed percentage is 5%, then the second unit will only need 95% of the direct labor hours taken for the first unit. The same relationship exists between the fourth unit and the second unit, the eighth unit and the fourth unit, etc, as illustrated in *Table 1-1*.For the example in *Table 1-1*, a direct labor estimate of 10 hours for each unit would be too high for a batch of 512 parts. On the other hand, a direct labor estimate of 6.30 hours for each unit is too low. A reasonable estimate is between those extremes and is determined by calculating a weighted average value.

Conceptually, the learning curve is expressed by the formula:

$$C_N = C_1 * N^{3.322*\log p}$$

Where C_N = cost of unit x
C_1 = cost of first unit produced
N = the number that unit N is in the sequence
p = fixed proportion of direct labor that each doubled quantity requires.

To calculate the cost, using this equation, of the 256th unit of the example in *Table 1-1*, use the following method:

$$\begin{aligned} C_{256} &= C_1 * 256^{3.322*\log .95} \\ &= 10*256^{-.074} \\ &= 6.63 \end{aligned}$$

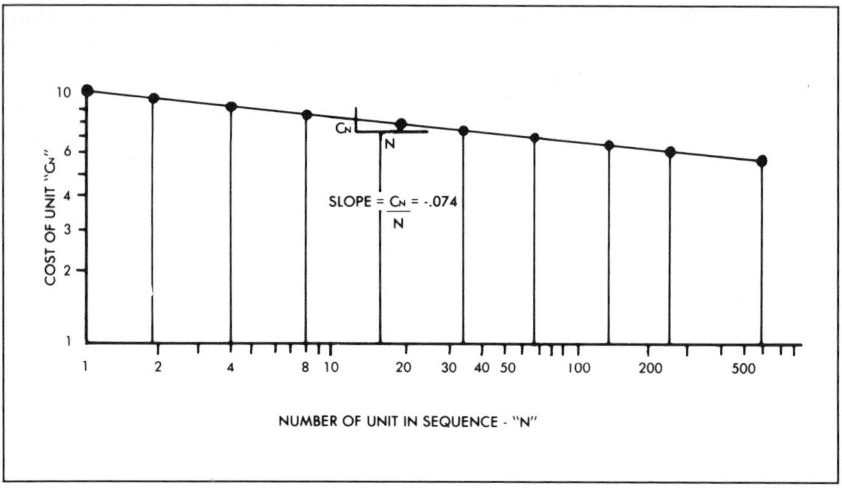

Figure 1-3. Learning curve for direct labor hours required per unit of production.

The learning curve is conventionally plotted using log-log paper. This graph paper has the log scale on both the vertical and horizontal axis. *Figure 1-3* shows the example in the table plotted on log-log paper. Note that the negative slope of the curve is the same value as the exponent in the learning curve equation.

Studies have shown that the value of p which is the fixed proportion of direct labor that each doubled quantity requires, is different for each company and product. The value of p must be determined for each individual situation through special studies of similar products. There has also been some effort at applying this concept to other costs than direct labor and in less labor intensive situations with mixed results.

Challenge of Inflation in Product Cost Estimating

With the advent of long-term contracts between suppliers and larger companies, the challenge of product cost estimating increased. This additional challenge involves predicting costs for several years in the future. The future costs are expected to be lower reflecting planned productivity and quality improvements. Complicating this planning is the effect of inflation and the necessity to determine offsetting improvements.

On a macro basis, there has always been an inflationary trend in prices of the material and wages necessary to sustain a business. This general increase can be seen in reviewing the Consumer Price Index and other indexes published by the United States Government. Many factors, yet to be fully understood, fuel this increase and the wide variation over the years in the rate of increase.

However, on a micro basis, the price performance for each of the different constituents in a product cost estimate varies widely. In fact, wide swings both up and down are seen in the price of some materials such as copper and aluminum. Items purchased from off-shore sources fluctuate in price due to changes in money exchange rates. Electronic components, like integrated circuits, now perform functions at a lower cost due to advanced technology. Energy costs have increased over the long term occasionally seeking but never reaching the prior lower price levels. Many other items are slowly increasing in price, reflecting the general inflationary increase in the cost of labor and material.

The historical levels of these prices are well documented. But, it would be naive to assume that an estimator can predict, with any accuracy, future prices of all the different constituents making up a product cost estimate using this historical information.

There may be some things that can be determined with confidence. For example, future wage increases may be in union contracts. The personnel manager may be helpful in assessing the effect of future changes in salaries and cost of benefits. Purchasing may be able to help predict price changes in purchased material through industry contacts and trade associations. There are also other organizations who specialize in predictions of future costs. Accounting may be able to identify anticipated tax increases. In fact, accounting may be the best function to coordinate packaging these predictions in a form usable for making product cost estimates. Chapter Three contains more ideas on how to handle these predictions.

Since it is difficult to predict future prices of purchased material, many companies allow suppliers to adjust their selling prices when an increase happens. They also expect decreased selling prices from suppliers if purchased material prices decrease. Many companies also allow increases in selling prices from suppliers who must pay higher wages as a result of a union contract. This is often made part of the contractual commitment between the company and the supplier.

Accuracy of a Product Cost Estimate

In preparing the estimate, time is almost always of the "essence." There is little time to get all the detailed information ideally required. Yet, this is hardly ever acceptable as an excuse for a poor estimate.

Early in the processing of an estimate, there must be a determination of what costs are readily obtained. These costs may be available because there are similar products using equivalent processes. A database summarizing relevant historical data is critical. This database must be audited periodically for accuracy, and to guarantee the accuracy of this part of the estimate.

The remaining time should be spent assessing those costs not readily obtainable. This is the portion most at risk. As much input as possible from relevant sources, especially those responsible for making the estimate, should be sought. This may also include outside suppliers of parts, tools and equipment. Often, a more detailed breakdown of the activities required to make this part of the product improves accuracy and inspires more innovative planning.

The major cause of inaccuracy of product cost estimates is misunderstandings regarding the features, performance requirements, and quality needs for the product. Often, this is because the design is not fully developed at the time costs are desired. In fact, drawings may not yet be prepared. Every effort should be made to obtain a full understanding and agreement of what parameters have been established. If this cannot be done, it should be stated in the product cost estimate and the quote. Also, the option to submit an updated quote, once these parameters are known, should be reserved.

It is critical that the product cost estimate is reviewed when a new product goes into production. Deviations from projected cost should be noted and reflected in future estimates. It is critical that this information be used to update the database summarizing relevant historical data.

Cost Responsibility

Management is responsible for a company's costing, pricing, and financial system. They usually retain close control in such areas as financing, capital investment and research. In exercising this control, management actively seeks the advice of engineers, accountants and other professionals in the firm. In other areas, management delegates control of tasks to functions within the company. Policies developed by management guide these functions in carrying out delegated tasks. For example, the accounting department may be delegating the task of controlling make-versus-buy decisions for the company.

The functions concerned with cost in a company could be categorized as:

- accounting
- productivity and quality improvement
- cost estimating.

Accounting is concerned with the recording and analysis of costs due to events that already occurred. The costs are historical in nature. In contrast, the cost estimating function is concerned with predicting what costs will be in the future. Those persons in a company concerned with productivity and quality improvement are mostly involved in analyzing present costs to devise ways to reduce future costs.

Accounting Function

The accounting function has two broad focuses concerning cost. One focus, known as *financial accounting*, provides information regarding costs and revenues to those outside the company. Those receiving this information may be banks, investors, stockholders, customers, and government tax agencies. Reports may include balance sheets, profit and loss statements, and cash flow analyses.

The second focus, called as *cost accounting*, is concerned with providing information to those inside the company. This information is used to understand internal activities and identify opportunities for improvement. Cost accounting records and monitors activities such as labor, material purchases, and scrap losses. It uses this data to prepare reports, for example, on direct labor efficiency, scrap, and material usage.

Cost accounting also develops standard costs and reports variances to these costs. A variance occurs when actual costs to do a task differs from standard costs. The efficiency of various manufacturing departments is evaluated through these variances, and productivity improvements are often identified. For example, an existing lathe may have too much downtime and should be replaced with a new one.

Cost accounting also prepares reports on inventory levels for management analysis. Depreciation values for the equipment and amortization costs for tools are also calculated by cost accounting. Much historical cost information required to make future projections for product cost estimates is furnished by this activity.

Accounting also does many other useful functions for a company. It often prepares the payroll and issues checks for the employees and suppliers. It may also maintain the computer facilities.

Productivity and Quality Improvement

The responsibility for productivity and quality improvement is shared by most, if not all, of the functions inside a company. There are many tools available to an organization to help in this effort. Some of them are value analysis, statistical quality control, design failure mode analysis, process failure mode analysis, just-in-time, and Taguchi methods. More information on these techniques can be found in the *Tool and Manufacturing Engineering Handbook*. Each recognizes that it takes team effort among the different functions in a firm to bring about continuous improvement of productivity and quality. No one entity can be delegated all of these tasks.

Many of the gains for this function are recognized in cost improvement. Future costs, through adopting new ways of doing things, will be less than existing costs. However, other gains are possible. Improved quality and more competitive selling prices, because of better designs, means more business revenue with enhanced profits. Reduced inventory levels and less scrap means existing space is available for expansion without investment in new facilities. This, too, results in more revenue and with enhanced profits.

Cost Estimating

As defined earlier, cost estimating is concerned with predicting future costs for a company. This is critical to deciding if a company should quote on a possible new product for sale to another company. It also determines whether to make an investment to provide a product for the consumer market. This function probably could not exist without accounting. To project future costs, an understanding of current costs is necessary. The cost estimating function would not be very effective without the productivity and quality improvement function. Future costs and product quality could not be predicted without understanding what improvement is being projected in productivity and quality.

PURPOSE OF ESTIMATING

Cost estimating is important to any company. A carefully prepared estimate is essential in deciding whether to submit a quote or begin manufacturing a product. In the overall planning process, the estimating phase is where product costs, tooling costs, and lead time are predicted. Managers need cost estimates for make-versus-buy decisions, bidding on contracts, and evaluating the products of competitors or suppliers.

Product cost estimates are used to make decisions about both present and future courses of action. In addition, operating departments use estimates as guides to the relative cost of equipment, tools, and services necessary to produce an item. The estimating function, for example, may supply cost data to other functions in the organization such as manufacturing engineering, tool design, materials handling, and industrial engineering for their use in planning new processes.

Estimating itself adds no value to products. It does not affect the final costs. It is, however, a valuable tool for evaluating and comparing manufacturing alternatives and materials, and developing design proposals.

A carefully executed cost estimate on a well-defined product has little risk that the activity planned, if undertaken, will not work out as anticipated. Product cost estimates may be used to:

1. Establish the bid price of a product for a quotation or contract.
2. Verify quotations submitted by suppliers.
3. Ascertain whether a proposed product can be manufactured and marketed profitably.
4. Provide data for make-versus-buy decisions.
5. Help determine the most economical method, process, or material for manufacturing a product.
6. Provide a temporary standard for production efficiency and guide operating costs at the beginning of a project.
7. Help in evaluating design proposals.

TYPES OF ESTIMATES

Product cost estimates can be classified as preliminary or final. The use of preliminary estimates is usually in the beginning phases of product planning or investment consideration. They are used to provide guidance to the planners in finalizing the concept.

Final cost estimates are prepared when the product design or investment strategy is complete. They are made just prior to a binding quote by the supplier or before a decision to proceed on an investment. It is the basis on which a decision is reached to produce products or make investments.

Preliminary Product Cost Estimates

Product designs and other plans are often not complete when preliminary product cost estimates are needed. This type of estimate is often used to compare different concepts of product designs or manufacturing processes. Suppliers may be requested to furnish preliminary information for planning purposes by larger companies. The request may also be initiated by planners inside the company.

For example, this type of estimate is used to identify ''ball-park'' cost differences for replacing a metal part with an equivalent part made from plastic. This cost difference could be coupled with assessments of performance and quality to decide whether to proceed with the plastic part. The differences in cost may include direct labor, direct material, tools, equipment, product design cost, and additional investment for facilities. If a decision is reached to proceed with the plastic part, the design and specifications are completed. Then a final product cost estimate is prepared. *Figure 1-4* illustrates a format that has been used for both preliminary and final product cost estimates.

Typically, a preliminary product cost estimate is wanted almost immediately, and there is no time for a detailed analysis. There also may be a moderate risk of inaccuracy because design information is incomplete. On the other hand, it doesn't take much time to complete the estimate. A preliminary estimate, on balance, is a cost effective way to gain information for early decision making. Where the decision is close and more accurate costs are needed for certain areas, the preliminary estimate can be modified accordingly.

Final Product Cost Estimate

The type of estimate that has the least risk of being inaccurate is a detailed analysis based upon a well defined design or investment proposal. Completion of this type of estimate is vital before preparing a quote that is binding upon a company. The *final product cost estimate* usually includes costing of every part and subassembly going into a product. This cost includes the results of detailed studies on the optimum manufacturing processes and make-versus-buy deci-

PART COST ESTIMATE

PART NAME ______ PART NO. ______
MATERIAL SPEC. ______ QUANTITY PER JOB ______ YEAR ______ MODEL ______
ROUGH MATERIAL SIZE ______ ROUGH WEIGHT ______ #.d ______ /# = ______ MATERIAL COST PER PIECE

PART NO.	PART NAME	STANDARD TIME	LABOR	VAR.	FIXED	TOTAL	TOOLS	REMARKS
								PER PIECE / PER. VEH.
								MAT'L ______
								LABOR ______
								BURDEN
								TOTAL

REQUESTED BY: ______ ESTIMATED BY: ______
FROM B/P DATED: ______ DATE ______ SHEET ______ OF ______

Figure 1-4. Preliminary and final product cost estimate form.

sions. The manufacturing process is then analyzed to determine the direct labor, direct material and tools needed and the cost of these items. Other components of cost, such as factory burden, are studied and adjusted if necessary. Intensive reviews are usually made with those responsible for achieving the projected costs prior to finalizing the estimate. When the product is released for production, information from the detailed product cost estimate is directly used in establishing standard costs and ordering necessary tools and equipment. Most, if not all, of the required planning for making the product is completed during the preparation of the final product cost estimate.

The level of detail in this type estimate varies from company to company, and product to product within a company. The size of the potential order is a major factor in how much time is spent on the estimate. Companies processing small batches cannot afford the same amount of time on each estimate as companies that usually get very large orders. Consider, for example, that it costs several hundred dollars to make a detailed estimate. If the average sales order for a company is one thousand dollars, it could not afford to perform a detail cost estimate to quote on each order. But, this type of company needs accurate cost estimating like any other company to avoid making firm quotes that are unprofitable. Obviously, one answer is that other means must be sought to get estimating done faster like, perhaps, computerizing the cost estimating function.

2

ORGANIZING AND STAFFING FOR ESTIMATING

The organization for the product cost estimating function could take several forms, depending upon the needs of the particular company. Two basic models are discussed in this chapter. Product cost estimating is a coordinated function in the first model. The actual estimating is done by those disciplines in the company responsible for the specific cost. The second model recognizes product cost estimating as a separate entity in the organization. This entity handles the estimate from start to finish without regularly consulting with the other disciplines in a company.

Both models acknowledge that pricing of products is independent of cost estimating and is handled by a pricing committee. The pricing committee is made up of the general management in a company. The managers have knowledge of competitive conditions and pricing. After reviewing costs, they decide if a quote or investment should be made. If a quote is to be made, the selling price is established by consensus of those managers on the committee.

COORDINATED PRODUCT COST ESTIMATING

Because of increasing competitive pressures, many companies see the product cost estimating function as being shared by each of the disciplines in a company. One of the disciplines acts as a coordinator to prepare the product cost estimate for the pricing committee. *Figure 2-1* illustrates this relationship.

By having all disciplines participate as a team, the product cost estimate is more likely to have the latest technology and innovative thinking. It is doubtful that one individual or one entity in a company, could possess this combined knowledge. Also, the synergism and innovativeness of groups of people working in teams is well known. By using this approach, each of the disciplines is also more committed to achieving the projected costs because they participated in determining them.

The team coordinator is responsible for pooling the talent necessary for making the best estimate. Depending on conditions, a part of the estimate may be assigned to specific disciplines. For example, where the company has a product design role, product engineering and manufacturing engineering may be asked to

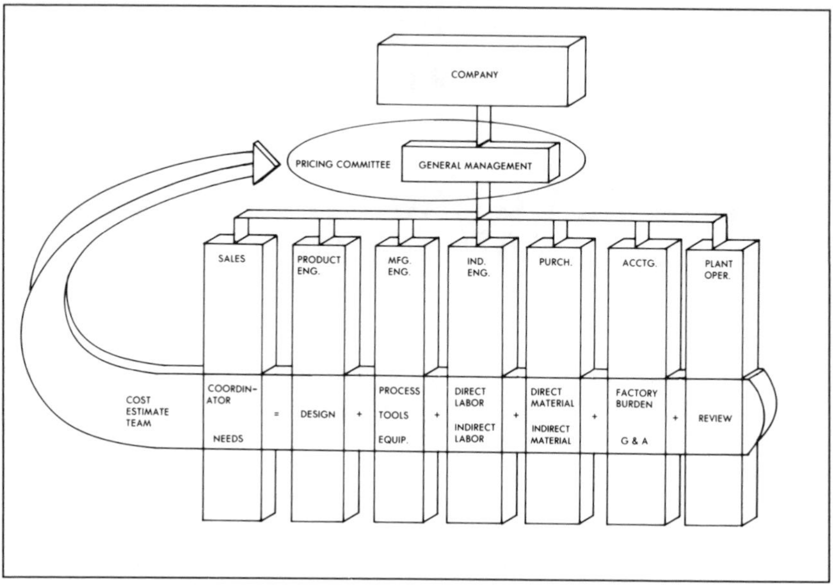

Figure 2-1. The typical approach used in coordinated product cost estimating.

work out a design that is easily manufactured before the remainder of the estimate is completed. Lacking a design role, manufacturing engineering may be asked to work directly with the company desiring the quote to improve the producibility of the product. In other cases, all disciplines may meet together to make an estimate needed quickly.

Often, where the main role for cost estimates is preparing quotes, the coordinator is someone in the sales department. The sales department is responsible for customer contact and delivering the quote. By coordinating the product cost estimate, they can assure it reaches the pricing committee in time for meeting the deadline for the quote. The sales department also has other critical roles in this process. Where the company has a product design role, the sales department is responsible for assuring that product design has a proper understanding of customer needs and quality requirements so it can be correctly translated into specific designs and specifications. If product design is handled by the company requesting the quote, the sales department must assure sufficient details are available to complete an accurate cost estimate. Sales also must assess competitive conditions in the market place so the pricing committee can make a good decision. They also identify any warranty obligations that must be included in the product cost estimate. Depending upon the company, the coordinating role may be handled by other disciplines. Sometimes the responsibility may go to the accounting department, since they have the best perspective on costs. In other cases, a member of general management may coordinate the estimate.

If the company has a role in designing the product, product engineering must translate the customer needs and quality requirements identified by the sales activity into specific designs and specifications. The design must also be within the projected capabilities of plant operations. The available details, at this point, must be sufficient to proceed on the estimate being sought. If additional design effort is required and prototypes are built for validation testing, the cost of this must be projected and included in the product cost estimate.

Manufacturing engineering develops the process by which operations in the plant make the product. They must work closely with product design or the company seeking the quote to improve the producibility of the product. Details of tools and equipment are the responsibility of this function. The cost of these must be furnished for the cost estimate. This discipline usually works closely with industrial engineering to provide other details for the estimate.

Industrial engineering usually, together with manufacturing engineering, plans the work stations and methods for the process. They determine the direct labor rates and indirect labor needed for the estimate. They also determine plant rearrangements necessary to incorporate the process in the plant. Where new facilities are needed, they develop plans for efficient operation. Costs for these items are also usually supplied for the estimate by industrial engineering.

Purchasing furnishes projected costs for material and parts that may be purchased. The cost of parts may be used in make-versus-buy decisions. They also may help in obtaining prices for anticipated tools and equipment that must be purchased for the plant operation.

Accounting usually completes the direct labor cost by supplying the hourly wage rate for the estimated direct labor hours. This wage rate includes both the hourly base wage and the adjustment for fringe benefits. Very often accounting prepares the cost analysis so that make-versus-buy decisions can be made on the parts comprising the product estimated. They also, after consulting with manufacturing engineering, adjust the factory burden cost for unusual operations and expenses. For example, heat treating may be required adding to the energy costs. Accounting also usually supplies the cost for general and administrative expenses.

The role of the people in plant operations is to review and concur with plans for manufacturing the product that was estimated. Often, this review identifies better ways of manufacturing products. A commitment to costs is also obtained from the people with the responsibility for meeting those costs when production begins.

In completing the estimate by using this approach, portions can be done simultaneously by the various disciplines involved. A well thought-out and accurate product cost estimate is obtained with a strong commitment by those who will be involved in making the product.

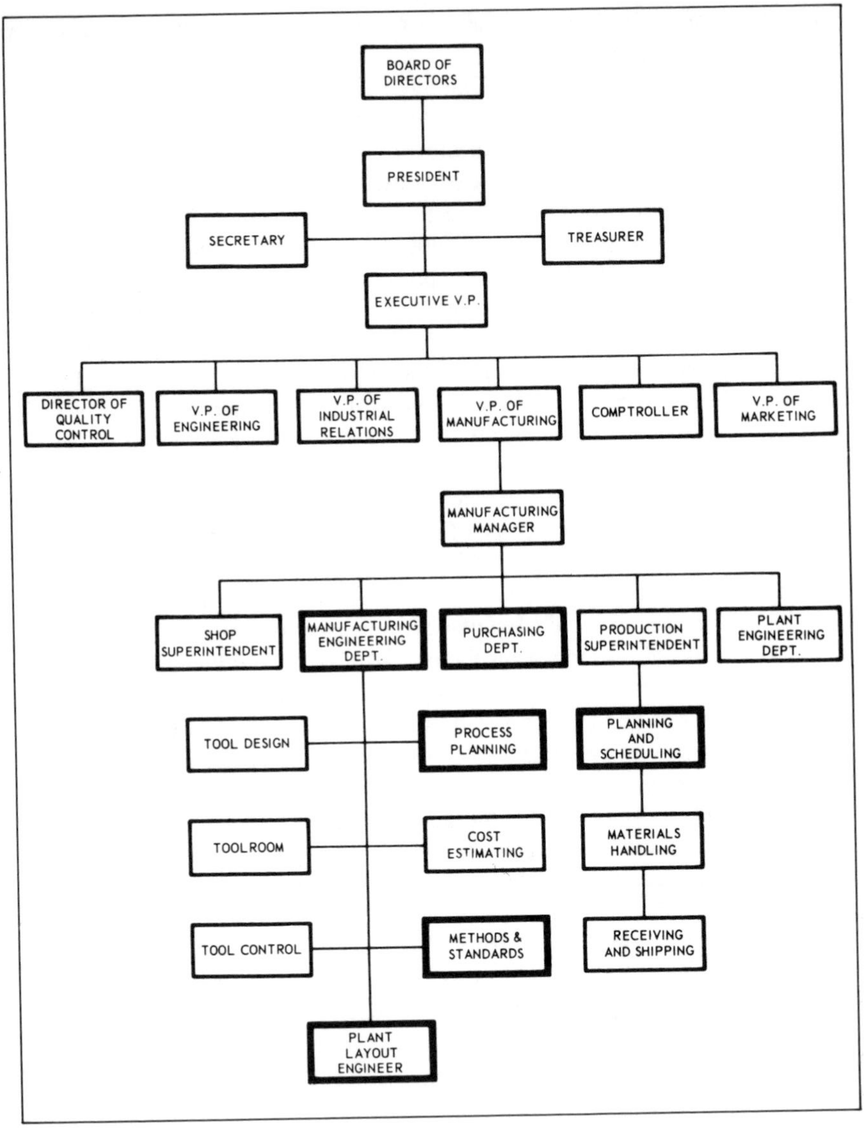

Figure 2-2. Location of the cost estimating function in one company.

COST ESTIMATING DEPARTMENT

Certain companies prefer to have a separate department handle cost estimating. Data is gathered from the other departments on a routine basis, and is used to establish a historical database of costs. The database has costs needed for estimates. Often, computer software can expedite the processing of an estimate. This approach can be adopted by a company regardless of its size.

Some of the smaller companies feel that having a cost estimating specialist, allows those in traditional functions to concentrate on day-to-day operating problems. Usually, a unique individual is in this position—one who possesses vast knowledge of the plant operation and the future plans of the company.

Larger companies may feel that their organization is too unwieldy to use a coordinated approach, and too much time would be needed to process an estimate using other disciplines. Larger organizations typically place experienced people from other disciplines in their cost estimating department.

The location of the cost estimating department within the organization of a company is not consistent. In some, it is part of sales, while in others, it may be in accounting. *Figure 2-2* illustrates when cost estimating is part of the manufacturing engineering function of a company. The heavier lines indicate the functions with which cost estimating works most closely in this company. Where the department is located seems to depend upon the personalities of those within a company.

Large, diversified manufacturers sometimes organize their estimating departments on a product basis so an estimator always works on similar items. Often, estimating departments in plants with forging, stamping, casting, and plastic capabilities may have specialists in each of these areas. In this manner, the estimator can gain specialized experience and compile a comprehensive database of costs.

An estimator may be a specialist in fuel and exhaust components or body parts, for example, but nevertheless handles a wide variety of assignments. He may develop cost data for engineering changes affecting future models, or do a competitive analysis on a competitor's part.

Estimating departments not structured by specialty usually assign requests for cost estimating on a first-come, first-served basis.

The advantage of nonspecialization is that individual estimators gain experience necessary to provide estimates on the company's entire product line. A nonspecialized department is more flexible but not necessarily more efficient.

The question of specialization versus nonspecialization is not an issue for every company. Companies manufacturing a fairly simple product may not have sufficient product variation to make specialization possible. Also, small estimating departments may have no alternative to the first-come, first-served method. Estimators for job shops that make a wide range of products in small lot sizes have little opportunity to specialize.

WHICH TYPE OF ORGANIZATION IS BEST FOR COST ESTIMATING?

The way the cost estimating function is organized best in a company depends largely upon the strengths and weaknesses of the people within that company.

Other factors are the type of product, and customers for that product. The size of the company also influences the choice of organization. Some of the issues to be considered by management in designing the role of cost estimating is having a function which allows:

- Processing of estimates in the required reaction time.
- Use of the knowledge and insight of those specialists in the company most critical in the planning process.
- Use of standard data and historical projections on similar products.
- Processing of an estimate of the accuracy and level of detail needed.
- Including in the estimate the latest technology, plans and projected capabilities of a company.
- Commitment on the part of those people who will be involved in achieving the projected costs.
- Objectivity and openness of those involved in the planning and costing.
- Biases of special interest groups to be recognized but not included if inappropriate.
- Special needs of customers to be addressed in a timely and effective manner.
- Regular feedback of results of estimates and how projected costs compare with the actual experience when production is started.
- Continuous improvement of the estimating function through such things as databases and computerization.

There is common agreement that no company can be without a cost estimating function and effectively compete in the market place. How it is organized within the company varies with the characteristics of the particular company.

The small shop may require an estimating department consisting of only one highly capable person. Often this person has extensive experience within the company and great knowledge of the products and processes. In addition, this person has the insight to know when to seek advice from others more capable in assessing needed technology and projected costs. Other small companies may use a coordinated approach where one person, who may be a member of the general management team, is responsible for allocating the necessary planning to specialists in the organization.

Larger companies making similar products in small lots for many customers may have only a few people involved in estimating because of effective use of a comprehensive computer database for projecting costs. Companies producing a single product line in large quantities may need only a few people because the number of estimates called for is relatively low. In contrast, those companies making customized products that are not very similar, may require many people in estimating because universal databases are difficult to construct. A coordinated cost estimating function may be best for such a company because of a consistent need to involve the various disciplines in the company for planning.

QUALIFICATIONS OF A COST ESTIMATOR

In general, the strengths of an estimator are much the same as those sought in any key employee in a company. Other characteristics are largely dependent upon how the cost estimating function is organized.

Many companies are using multidiscipline approaches to business. This is also true for cost estimating. Teams are used that require people with good ability in interpersonal relationships. People are also highly sought that have an analytical mind and an understanding of the scientific approach to solving problems. These people must be able to observe, generalize from the observations, and check for consistency with historical experience and standards. Other strengths useful are:

- Dedication to meeting time deadlines.
- Competence in the area that work is assigned.
- Skill to sort data into useful information.
- Ability to approach problems systematically.
- Capability to work effectively and accurately.
- Drive to investigate and keep abreast of the latest technology.
- Ability to look at situations from the general business sense, as well as, from the narrow perspective of a specialist.
- Capacity to cope with uncertainty, much responsibility and unstructured work situations.
- Potential to conceptualize details, and conform the findings with others, from under developed drawings and specifications.
- Understanding of the company structure, processes and products.
- Desire to make productivity improvements in area of specialty and also in cost estimating routines.
- Educational background to support future needs of the company.

The above characteristics are desirable for anyone concerned with cost estimating regardless of the type of organization.

For coordinated cost estimating, the person selected to integrate the various disciplines in the company should also have strong project management skills and an ability to quickly sort out those estimates that are not appropriate. This may be because the company is not interested in making such a product.

Where a separate cost estimating department is used, the persons involved may likely require a general ability in all facets of engineering and other functions of a company rather than being a specialist. Often someone with long years of experience as a manufacturing or industrial engineer in a company does well in this role.

DEVELOPMENT OF A COST ESTIMATOR

An estimator is not trained quickly but develops by exposure to many facets of manufacturing. College graduates with degrees in industrial, mechanical, or manufacturing engineering combined with manufacturing experience, are likely to be adaptable to cost estimating. Courses in mathematics, accounting, and time-and-motion study, along with a specialized course in the field in which the estimator plans to work, are beneficial. Companies must recognize the challenge of being a competent estimator and provide continuous training and support for those starting out and also those currently in such positions. This involves on-the-job training by those more experienced. Resources required to perform the job must be available such as reference books and computer software. Also, the company should encourage membership in professional societies and support attendance at seminars and conferences concerned with the area of specialty of each person involved. Local colleges are also good sources of both in-plant training and appropriate courses. The company should also reveal future plans on a regular basis helping assure that these plans are reflected in the estimates. Most importantly the company should maintain an atmosphere where those involved in estimating may prepare costs objectively and without bias.

3

COST ESTIMATING CONTROLS

Fast, economical, and accurate estimates require proper management of the estimating function. Management establishes the type of estimating function that will best serve company needs, then develops the procedures and administrative controls necessary for efficient operation.

The cost estimating function interacts with other departments. This requires control over paperwork and other forms of communications. For example, cost requests can be initiated by marketing, product engineering, or manufacturing engineering. The purchasing, industrial engineering, plant engineering, and accounting departments may then supply the estimating function with processing and cost data. All of these interactions require control.

The estimator may establish certain controls to increase the accuracy of his estimates. This can be accomplished by simplifying the estimate and by other procedures discussed later in this chapter.

ADMINISTRATIVE CONTROLS

Desirable administrative control starts with monitoring the incoming cost requests. It continues until the estimate is finalized.

Monitoring Cost Requests

Regardless of the size of a company, all cost requests should be examined before being forwarded to the estimating function. Someone should be designated to check each cost request to establish whether the desired estimate is consistent with the company's product mix, production schedule, equipment capacity, available labor skills, and company policy. Such a screening procedure reduces the cost estimating function workload by developing costs for only those jobs the company is capable of or wants to produce.

The sales department is the logical choice to carry-out this screening, since it is responsible for soliciting business for the company. The estimator is often consulted by departments requesting cost estimates before the department releases the request.

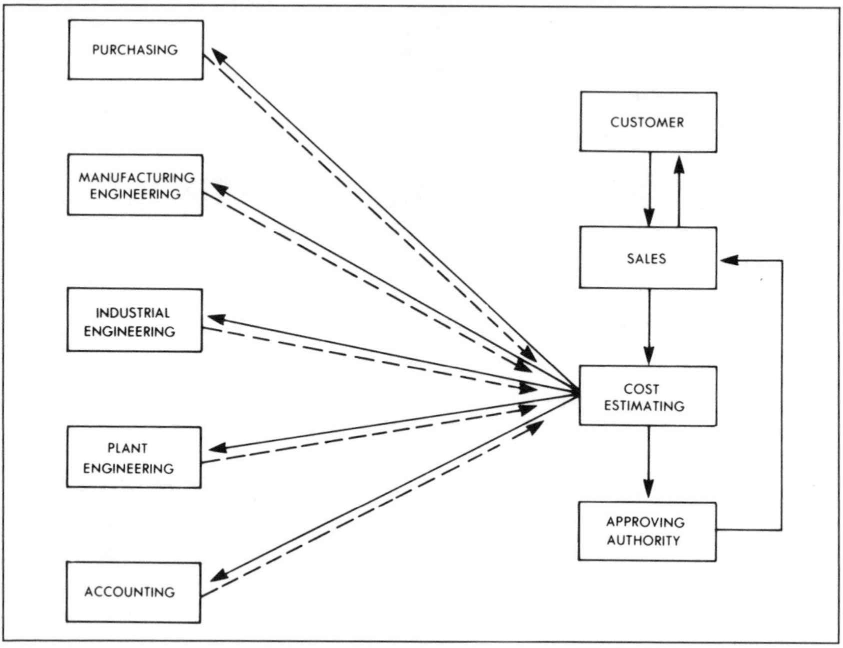

Figure 3-1. Flow diagram for cost estimate processing.

No company is capable of making every product. It may be futile to quote on a new item that can be easily underbid by a competitor. Also an unfamiliar product area should be investigated very carefully before a cost quotation is released because one unforeseen cost can quickly reduce or eliminate the profit margin.

Routing for Cost Estimates

As shown in *Figure 3-1*, the path of a cost request, in a typical company, is as follows:

1. A customer submits an order or bid request to the sales department.
2. Sales screens the request and, if approved, sends a request for an estimate to cost estimating along with all available data, e.g., drawings, specifications, and volume requirements.
3. The cost estimating function takes a different action, depending upon how it is organized. If it is a coordinated function, then appropriate parts of the estimate are given to each involved department. When each department is finished with their part, the estimate is consolidated by the cost estimating

coordinator. Where cost estimating is a separate entity, the various departments may be consulted for relevant data or concurrence with pertinent portions of the analysis.

4. Cost estimating sends the completed estimate to management for review. Adjustments are often made prior to approval.
5. The approved estimate is returned to the sales department either by routing the cost figures directly to the sales department or it may be returned to the estimating department for transmittal to sales.

The estimating department files all worksheets and summary sheets for reference. A well-planned filing system is extremely useful in processing future estimates. The sales department informs the customer whether the company can furnish the product. A selling price is quoted along with tool cost and lead time for the desired quantity.

If a request is originated by a department within the company, Steps 1, 2, and 5 are eliminated, and the originating department sends the request with all available descriptive data directly to cost estimating.

When departments other than cost estimating participate in a cost estimate, Step 3 breaks down into five sub-steps: (a) the list of purchased parts and materials is routed to purchasing for a cost, (b) the drawings and specifications go to manufacturing engineering for preparation of a manufacturing plan (c) industrial engineering estimates direct labor time, (d) facilities and material handling costs are determined by plant engineering, and (e) labor costs are entered by the accounting department. The cost estimator collects and summarizes these costs.

INITIATING COST REQUESTS

As discussed in Chapter Two, the estimator may report to any one of several places in an organization. Only rarely, does the major portion of his workload come from the department to which he reports. Although any manufacturing department may initiate cost requests, most (except in the process industries) originate in the sales department.

Next, in originating requests for costs, are manufacturing engineering and product engineering. Marketing, manufacturing engineering, and product engineering are in close contact with customers, and they rely on the estimating department to supply them with cost figures so they can decide whether to accept customer orders, make changes in manufacturing processes for existing products, or develop new products.

Cost Requests from Marketing

Marketing may request cost estimates to fulfill a specific customer's request, or to investigate the manufacturing feasibility of a new product.

REQUEST FOR ESTIMATED COST

SHEET ________ ESTIMATE NO. ________

DATE: ________

TO: FROM: ________

AN ESTIMATED COST TO SUPPLY THE GOODS AND OR SERVICES BY YARD-MAN, INC., TO THE CUSTOMER AS DESCRIBED BELOW IS HEREWITH REQUESTED

ITEM NO.	MODEL OR PART NUMBER	MODEL OR PART NAME	ENG. CHG LETTER	QUANTITY REQ. MONTH-20 DAY	QUANTITY REQ. ANNUAL TOTAL	JOB START DATE	COMMENTS

NAME OF CUSTOMER ________ ADDRESS ________ TEL. NO. ________

NAME OF CUSTOMER CONTACT MAN ________ ADDRESS ________ TEL. NO. ________

YARD-MAN, INC. TO FURNISH EVERYTHING EXCEPT: ________

YARD-MAN, INC. CONTACT MAN ________ ADDRESS ________ TEL. NO. ________

COMPLETED ESTIMATED COST DUE DATE ________

APPROVED: ________ PRESIDENT

Figure 3-2. Cost estimate request form used by marketing department.

In the first case, the marketing department receives a request for a quotation from a potential customer, screens the request to assure the company is interested in presenting a quotation, and requests a cost estimate. In the second case, marketing may also request a cost estimate for a product just developed. The marketing department would use the estimate to see whether the product could be manufactured and marketed profitably. In either case, the marketing department may request estimated costs for varying production levels, or may want to know what lot size can be manufactured at a predetermined cost.

Figure 3-2 shows a sample form used by one marketing department to request cost estimates. The sales representative fills in this form and attaches any drawings, specifications, or other data received from the customer. Any prototypes, or other physical models supplied by the customer would also accompany the form.

Cost Requests from Product Engineering

Product Engineering chooses the most economical design for a given product's function or quality by comparing estimated manufacturing and material costs for alternative designs. They also initiate cost estimates to help analyze and fix field installation and product deficiencies. Estimators use layouts, sketches,

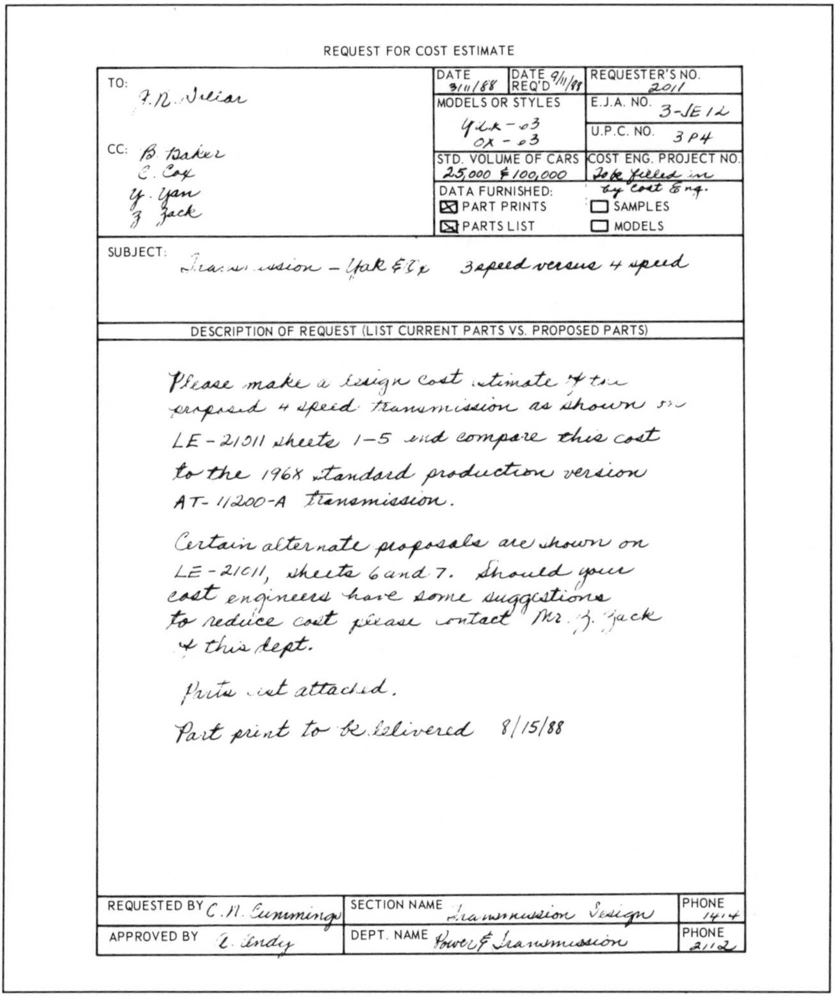
REQUEST FOR COST ESTIMATE

TO: F. N. Julian CC: B. Baker, C. Cox, Y. Yan, Z. Zack	DATE 3/11/88	DATE REQ'D 9/11/88	REQUESTER'S NO. 2011
	MODELS OR STYLES Yak-03, OX-03		E.J.A. NO. 3-JE12
			U.P.C. NO. 3P4
	STD. VOLUME OF CARS 25,000 $100,000		COST ENG. PROJECT NO. To be filled in by cost Eng.
	DATA FURNISHED: ☒ PART PRINTS ☒ PARTS LIST		☐ SAMPLES ☐ MODELS

SUBJECT: Transmission – Yak & Ox 3 speed versus 4 speed

DESCRIPTION OF REQUEST (LIST CURRENT PARTS VS. PROPOSED PARTS)

Please make a design cost estimate of the proposed 4 speed transmission as shown on LE-21011 sheets 1–5 and compare this cost to the 1968 standard production version AT-11200-A transmission.

Certain alternate proposals are shown on LE-21011, sheets 6 and 7. Should your cost engineers have some suggestions to reduce cost please contact Mr. Z. Zack of this dept.

Parts list attached.

Part print to be delivered 8/15/88

REQUESTED BY C. N. Cummings	SECTION NAME Transmission Design	PHONE 1414
APPROVED BY E. Andy	DEPT. NAME Power & Transmission	PHONE 2112

Figure 3-3. Cost estimate request form used to request a design cost estimate.

or samples of the assembled product or parts as references. Detailed layouts usually result in more accurate estimates. Material, tolerances, and surface finish specifications greatly influence costs.

Figure 3-3 illustrates a typical request for a design cost estimate.

Cost Requests from Manufacturing Engineering

Process planners from the manufacturing engineering department use cost estimates to establish costs for alternate manufacturing plans and selecting the most economical manufacturing method and tools based on a standard volume. The data also may be used to approximate the break-even points of the alternate plans for varying production quantities and rates.

Costs Requests from Other Departments

The estimating department also receives estimate requests from purchasing and productivity and quality improvement groups to assist in evaluating vendor quotations.

Departments initiate cost estimate requests to help them scrutinize production parts and discover ways to improve productivity and quality. Changes in product design or manufacturing techniques will affect cost, so cost estimating plays a vital role in establishing the soundness of a proposed change. *Figure 3-4* shows a sample form used by such a group to request a cost analysis, as well as submit such a proposal to management.

Evaluating Supplier Quotations

The purchasing department requests cost estimates on material or parts it intends to buy. For parts, a detailed estimate covering materials, tooling, and labor is needed to determine whether quoted prices are realistic. Savings may also be affected by comparing quotes on material and component costs. This allows purchasing to negotiate with suppliers for more favorable prices if a particular quote is too high. A comparison of estimates between the supplier and the purchasing company may suggest cost-saving measures as well. Tooling costs, for example, may be reduced by lending tooling to suppliers.

Figure 3-5 shows a form that can be used to analyze vendor quotations and report results to requesting departments so that a make-versus-buy decision can be made.

ESTIMATING METHODS

Estimating may be accomplished by: (1) conference, (2) comparison, or (3) detailed analysis. While the first two methods are satisfactory when a preliminary or rough estimate is needed, final cost estimates should be made only through detailed analysis. Only detailed analysis assures the accuracy needed to estimate a major manufactured product upon which the future livelihood of the company may depend.

Conference Method

In this method, representatives of various departments such as purchasing, manufacturing engineering, tool design, and industrial engineering meet and

COST REDUCTION PROPOSAL

TO: Mr. J. N. Dollar	DATE 6/17/88	ORIGINATORS FILE NO. 12010
	MODELS AFFECTED All 1988	CT NO. A-012
CC: Mr. B. Baker		UPG NO. AZA
	DATA FURNISHED: ☒ PART PRINTS ☒ SKETCHES	☐ LAYOUT ☐ SAMPLES ☐ MODELS

SUBJECT: Impeller - current production cast iron. IT-1606-A versus proposed die cast design.

DESCRIPTION OF PROPOSAL

Please prepare a manufacturing cost estimate of the proposed die cast impeller versus the production cast iron impeller IT-1606-A. Tool and facilities cost should be included in this analysis.

REQUESTED BY C. Kost	SECTION NAME Production Cost Red.	PHONE 444
APPROVED BY R. D. Pruit	DEPT NAME Administration	PHONE 445

LEAVE BLANK TO BE COMPLETED BY COMPETITIVE PRODUCT ANALYSIS DEPT

COST DATA

.65 COST PER CAR INCREASE ☐ DECREASE ☐ $.15 TOOL COST $20,000 FACILITIES None

CONTROL VOLUME 150,000 MONTHS TO AMORTIZE TOOL COST 7½

PER K Kurtz DATE 11-14-88

Figure 3-4. Form used by cost reduction group to request a cost analysis.

estimate the costs of material, labor, and tooling. A coordinator from the estimating department collects these costs and applies burden factors to develop a total manufacturing cost for the product.

The conference method may also be used within the estimating department. Estimators having specialized knowledge confer on an estimate and determine a cost figure without needing counsel from other departments.

The chief advantage of the conference method, and the main justification for its use, is its speed. It permits experts in different fields to pool their knowledge

VENDOR COST ANALYSIS

TO: Sales Dept. Jim Hill	DATE 2/29/88	DATE REQ'D 3/15/88	REQUESTOR'S NO. X-14376-Y
FROM: Cost Est. L. Backus	MODEL OR STYLE COB-X-3-RA		VOLUME 30,000/mo.
	DATA FURNISHED: ☒ PART PRINTS ☒ PARTS LIST		☐ SAMPLES ☐ MODELS

SUBJECT: Front bumper and guards

	VENDOR COST	COMPANY COST	DIFFERENTIAL	COMMENTS
MATERIALS	2.713	1.978	−.735	check to see if they are getting quantity disc.
LABOR	1.216	1.450	.234	Non-union shop
TOOLING	2.760	1.100	−1.660	They're figuring on
				new tools
TOTALS	6.689	4.528	−2.161	

SUGGESTED ACTION: Their labor is better. We can probably work out something to cut tooling costs - (We have a setup in the shop already.) They're wayoff on material - may not be figuring in the volume disc. Suggest buying part if they can get price down to 4.5 or lower.

Figure 3-5. Form used by estimating department to analyze vendor quotations.

when quick estimates are needed. The method is also useful to companies not having established estimating departments, yet still must develop product cost data.

The conference method's main disadvantage is its lack of accuracy. Resulting cost data should be treated cautiously and checked meticulously. The accuracy of any estimate depends upon the availability of specifications, drawings, and samples, and in actual practice these are seldom obtainable on short notice when quick estimates are desired.

Comparison Method

The comparison method relies on past experience and historical data. The estimator applies up-to-date costs derived from similar parts to the project and adjusts these costs to suit material, labor, and processing variations. Caution should be exercised in using data compiled from products manufactured in larger or smaller quantities and the estimate should be factored accordingly. While some of the elements will remain fairly constant, slightly lower spoilage rates sometimes result with increased production runs. Larger production lots also decrease setup costs and offer the opportunity for more efficient use of durable tooling. Labor costs similarly decline with increased efficiency developed over longer production runs.

Another way of using the comparison method is the application of a rate per unit of measure factor. The unit rate, based upon actual production data, may be hours per pound of material, dollars per cubic foot, etc. Careful judgment must be used in applying such rates because of the cost changes to which they are subject.

Like the conference method, the comparison method is used when time is short, and the two methods are often used jointly.

Detailed Analysis Method

Detailed analysis is the most reliable method of estimating. As its name implies, it includes a complete examination of all the important factors involved in the production of a manufactured item. Historical data are used, but only after validation. Estimating by detailed analysis requires strict adherence to procedure and is more time consuming than the other two methods. *Figure 3-6* is an example of an estimate prepared by the detailed analysis method.

Each of the following steps must be performed when preparing a detailed analysis estimate:

1. Calculate raw material usage, including scrap allowances and salvage material (direct material).
2. Process each individual component (write the operation sheet).
3. Compute the production time (direct labor) for each operation.
4. Determine the equipment required (new, rework, or on hand).
5. Determine the required tools, gages, and special fixtures.
6. Determine any additional equipment needed for inspection and testing.

While the conference or comparison methods are satisfactory for preliminary estimates, detailed analysis is used by almost all manufacturers despite the extra work and additional time required for its completion. This method furnishes the

PART NO. M. 40090 PART NAME Motor Mount (1) PER JOB

DATE 4/1/88 MODELS Experimental FROM B P DATED 4/14/88 PAGE 1 OF 1

PART NO	PART NAME	STD. HRS.	=	MAT'L.	LABOR	VAR. BURDEN	TOTAL VAR. COST	FIXED BURDEN	TOTAL COST	TOOLING
						200%		20%		
M-40090	Motor Mount									
Material	.089 A.I.S.I. C-1008 Cold rolled by 1000' coil by 36 x 1/4 wide									
	Length Multiple = 5" Width Multiple = 9"									
	WT/Coil = 11,200 Pcs/Coil = 9600 Wt/pcs. = 1.6600 @ $.0725/lb.			.0845					.0845	
	Total Operation	.01290			.0335	.0670	.1005	.0067	.1072	
	Cutoff and draw	.00200								$6,000.00
	Flange	.00200								3,850.00
	Trim and Pierce	.00200								5,450.00
	Wash, paint and Pack	.00500		.0155					.0155	
	Setup	.00100			Tools = 15,550 Volume = 100,000				Gauges	250.00
	Inspect	.00090			Unit Tool Cost = .1555 Value of Scrap = .0008 Equip = Available Rearrangement = None					
	Totals			$.1000	$.0335	$.0670	.1005	$.0067	$.2072	$15,550.00

Figure 3-6. Detailed analysis cost estimate for a motor mount.

most accurate prediction of anticipated costs on new products or for engineering changes on currently manufactured parts.

CONTROLLING THE COST ESTIMATE

The cost estimating function does not produce exact cost data but rather supplies cost figures having a high probability of falling within an acceptable range. As a result, product cost estimates seldom exactly coincide with actual manufacturing cost figures because preparing of precise cost figures would be time consuming, even if they were possible to predict.

Nevertheless, greater accuracy is required for some estimates than for others. Parts or products expected to be produced in large quantities over long periods of time should be estimated as closely as possible because their potential profit or loss is much higher than items of the same cost manufactured in small quantities. Similarly, expensive items, even though produced in small lots, deserve careful costing.

Deviations between estimated and actual cost figures result from several factors. Human error is a major cause. In some cases, estimators purposely do not analyze in detail every item affecting cost because to do so would waste valuable time. Unpredictable variables in the manufacturing processes and changes in material costs can also cause significant deviations.

Estimators should try to be aware of each of these factors when costing products and attempt to control them. Direct control measures include the use of machine and worker performance factors, estimate simplification, and indexes which reflect cost changes.

Deviations in Cost Estimates

An estimated cost differs from the actual cost of an item in that all the factors affecting the cost cannot be fully evaluated. The most important factors are given primary attention, but many factors of lesser important factors must be left to influence the results in a random manner. Some factors cannot be predicted with certainty at all, such as delays caused by defective material and machine breakdowns. An equipment performance factor will spread such losses over all jobs with the result that, when equipment and machinery runs smoothly, estimates will be high, but when breakdowns occur, estimates will be low.

Figure 3-7 shows how estimated costs can deviate from actual costs. The error curve resulted when the percent error of each of 157 estimates of the labor cost of making tools was calculated. Each bar represents the number of estimates within a given range of 10 percentage points of error. The deviations range from 50% low to 450% high. If an infinite number of estimates were plotted and the pattern remained approximately the same, the distribution of errors would be represented by a curve such as the one superimposed on the histogram in *Figure 3-7*.

The estimates upon which *Figure 3-7* is based were made when an abundance of orders was available and the estimator was able to estimate doubtful jobs safely. As a result, the curve is skewed to the high side. However, most of the estimates show relatively small deviations, which is a general characteristic of good estimating practice.

Average Estimates Versus Actual Costs

Although cost estimates are not expected to conform to actual manufacturing costs, the average estimates over a period of time must be reasonably close to the average manufacturing cost. Probable cost deviations, correlated with estimated costs and contingency factors, are depicted as curves in *Figure 3-8*. Such a comparison can only be made when most of the cost estimated jobs or products are manufactured in-house, establishing a verifiable actual cost. Even if identical information is available for two jobs (either similar or dissimilar) and the same method is used to estimate them, the estimates can differ from the actual costs of the jobs. Unforeseen problems may arise during one job, while no difficulties are encountered during another job.

The difficulties may include faulty tooling, machine breakdown, material shortages requiring substitution of a more expensive material, or labor problems.

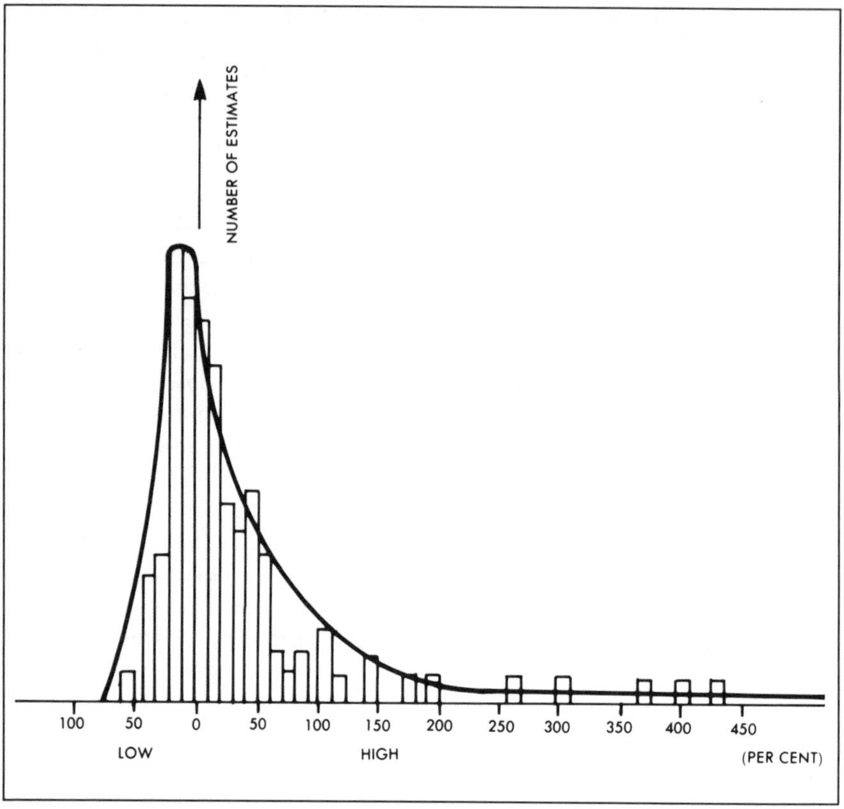

Figure 3-7. Deviation of estimated costs from actual costs.

Low Estimates

The most significant causes of low final cost estimates are:

1. Higher labor and material costs than anticipated.
2. Incorrect design information.
3. Unexpected delays resulting in premiums paid for overtime and materials.
4. Unexpected processing problems requiring deviation from the preliminary manufacturing plan.
5. Failure to rework the preliminary estimate to produce an accurate final estimate.
6. Inability to meet part print specifications using the material specified.

Every underestimated job represents a potential loss to the company. Although these losses may be balanced by gains from high estimates, this results in a break-even operation, not a profit making one.

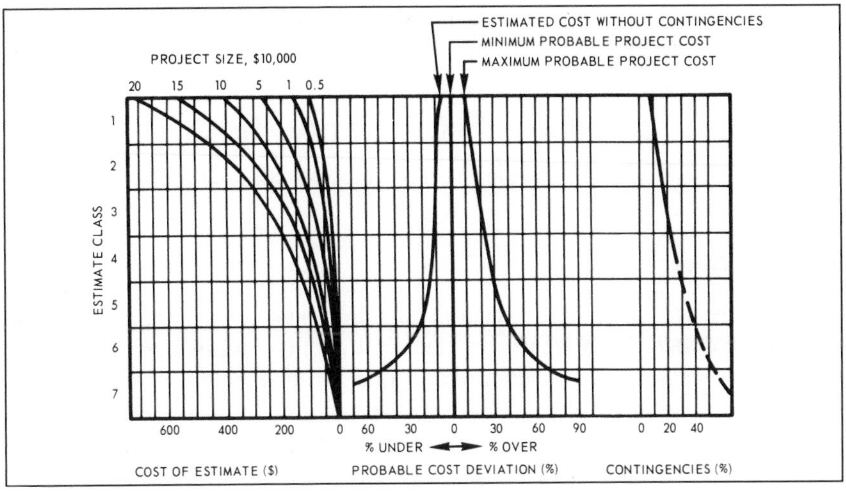

Figure 3-8. Hypothetical curves depicting cost of estimate, probable cost deviation, and a contingency factor.

High Estimates

High estimates may be caused by:

1. Overestimating bid requests that the company does not want.
2. The tendency of estimators to be overly cautious when a job requires processes that they are not familiar with.
3. Making a "guesstimate" and then increasing it to cover contingencies.
4. Planning for more processing steps or a higher level of tooling than is actually required.
5. Failure to take advantage of "price breaks" on quantity purchases of material.
6. Overestimating labor costs by failing to take into consideration tasks that can be performed by operators while machines are in cycle.

Even though a high estimate may result in greater profit than anticipated, these estimates are also undesirable because they:

1. Lead to overbidding and cause rejection of proposals that could be profitable.
2. Cause loss of customer good will if quotations are consistently high.
3. Lead to waste in design and fabrication when they become the initial standards of performance.

4. Require a larger staff of estimators because a greater number of estimates must be performed for a given volume of completed jobs.

CONTROLLING ESTIMATE DEVIATIONS

Cost estimates are characterized by two types of errors: random and biased.

Random Errors

Some cost estimating errors occur at random. Causes of error are comparable to assignable and chance causes in statistical quality control work. In quality control, the methods of correction are to find and eliminate, or minimize, the causes, and measure the probable effect of, and control the chance causes. In this manner, the true quality level and the likely quality deviation in a manufacturing operation can be determined and a warning given when conditions are out of control. The same methods can be utilized by cost estimating where sufficient historical data have been accumulated.

Biased Errors

Some errors in cost estimating are biased, they follow trends which may be due to assignable causes. Three common examples are:

1. Fluctuation in labor and material costs with economic conditions.
2. The cost of a machine, tool, or piece of equipment usually varies with size or capacity; larger sizes can be expected to cost more than smaller ones but not necessarily in direct proportion.
3. The amount of time, and, therefore, the cost of performing an operation (particularly one requiring much manual time), decreases as the number of units produced increases.

A good estimator should find that the sum of a large number of his estimates is close to the sum of the actual costs of the jobs performed. Most estimators check their performance over various periods of time to determine the percentage by which their cost estimates deviate from actual manufacturing costs. Once they are able to predict their estimating bias, they modify future estimates by means of a personal performance factor.

Project Simplification

Estimating errors are normally smaller when the elements of a project are estimated individually than when the project is estimated on an overall basis.

Likewise, the errors made in estimating for small and simple elements are fewer than those for large and complex elements.

Use of Equal Size Elements

A project must be split into elements of approximately equal size to benefit fully from estimating simplification. If a major part of a product is not closely estimated and minor details are thoroughly estimated, the sum of the two will often result in an inaccurate total estimate. Any refinement gained by thorough estimating of the minor parts is futile, since it cannot offset the effect of a cost error made when estimating the major portion.

For example, the cost of converting a regular machine tool headstock to a special headstock is to be estimated. Because the conversion requires only the replacement of a few parts in the standard headstock, a reliable estimate can be obtained from the established price of the standard headstock and a detailed study of the changes required. On the other hand, if an entirely new headstock is to be estimated, it must be broken down into elements of approximately equal size to avoid sizable cost errors.

Good estimating practice recognizes the need to build up an estimate from approximately equivalent elements, as indicated by the chart in *Figure 3-9*.

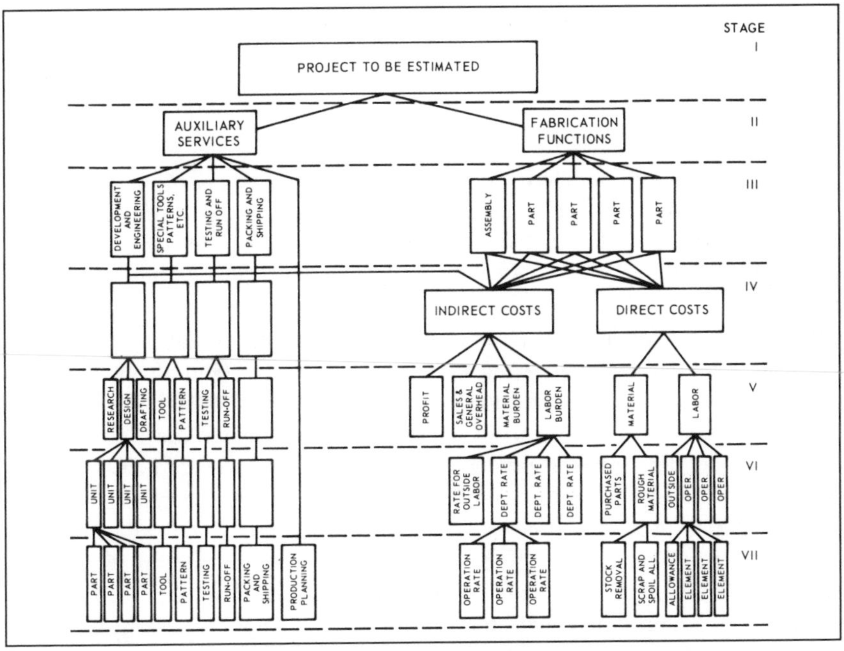

Figure 3-9. The progressive stages into which a project can be divided.

Common practice in tool estimating is to determine the operation time and material for each part (without considering possible material losses) and the overhead from one or more rates. In estimating the products manufactured in quantities, the manufacturing operations are divided into elements and all factors affecting material and labor costs are considered. Overhead is allocated according to the kinds of operations required to produce the item.

ESTIMATING IN A CHANGING COST ENVIRONMENT

Cost variations will obviously affect the estimate. If an item is to be manufactured within a few days or weeks, current costs for labor, material, and overhead are usually safe. On the other hand, using such current costs for estimating may be hazardous if actual costs are to be incurred and returns realized after a longer time lapse. If costs should increase over a period of time due to additional planning and designing, for example, a serious estimating error and consequent financial loss may result. In contrast, should prices decline, a product may not be marketable at the previously estimated profit.

Likewise, a proposed project may be similar to one already completed for which cost figures are available. During the intervening period, however, the basic labor, material, and tooling cost rates may have changed appreciably. The extent of such changes must be known in order to apply the previous project costs to the current project. Updating past costs to present cost levels requires techniques similar to those used in predicting future costs as described below.

Estimates for Future Production

Present costs and quotations must serve as starting points in preparing estimates for the future, but they may need to be modified by forecasting conditions at the expected time of manufacture. An estimator must be aware of economic trends or seek advice from a person qualified to predict price trends and market stability.

In preparing estimates for future production, not only future prices, but anticipated volume and facilities must be studied. At a lower production volume than expected, fixed and overhead costs per unit increase. A higher output may not only alleviate fixed charges, but also permit utilization of more efficient work methods. Additional lines of products may absorb plant overhead costs, or vice versa. As noted earlier, estimates for future production are generally made only for guidance or planning purposes, and are followed up by detailed estimates.

The estimator cannot recognize cost trends without an understanding of the principles behind the cost accounting system furnishing him with information. Having such an understanding, an estimator is able to appreciate why overhead rates are changing, the relationship of overhead to shop activity, labor costs, and the general production picture.

Cost Indexes

In certain circumstances, one or more of the many published price or cost indexes may be helpful in evaluating past changes in costs or forecasting future trends. A price or cost index consists of a series of index numbers, each calculated to show the price level for a particular time period in relation to the level at a reference or base period.

As an example, assume that a tool shop successfully coordinated its cost figures with one of the published indexes. If a change of one point in that index coincides with a change of .75 in tool costs, the cost of a similar tool can be easily adjusted to current prices. For instance, assume that a certain tool cost $1,000 in July, 1986, at which time the index was 169.3. The tool cost is to be adjusted to a figure for December, 1988, when the index was 180.6. The adjusted tool cost can be determined as follows:

$$1{,}000\left[1+\left([180.6-169.3]\times\frac{.75}{100}\right)\right]=\$1{,}085$$

In using a cost index for estimating, the estimator should keep a record of the index for the month or other period of time that he has used in his estimate. Periodically, the actual costs must be compared with the estimated cost to evaluate the accuracy of the estimate. Also, changes in actual costs must be compared with changes in the index so that adjustments in the factor can be made.

If published indexes do not fit the specific needs of a company, the estimator must prepare his own index based on his historical data file. Once the index has been compiled, adjustments in cost can be made to conform to it as changes warrant. Estimators concentrating in specific manufacturing areas will soon recognize the cost increase percentages of tooling and other items affecting their products and can factor the data into their indexes for reference.

DO'S AND DON'T'S OF COST ESTIMATING

The following points should be kept in mind when making a cost estimate:

1. Do use a printed form wherever possible to assure completeness in estimating. Strive to devise better printed forms, or new forms for similar estimating tasks that recur to eliminate the necessity for developing special forms for particular estimating situations as much as possible.
2. Do reduce computations to a minimum by assembling standard data in well-organized files. Supplement departmental files by adding new standard data at every opportunity.
3. Do have your computations checked by your supervisor before release. It

is difficult for an estimator to check his own work, and if not corrected the first time, the same error can perpetuate itself indefinitely.

4. Do review required tolerances on engineering specifications carefully. If tolerances are not given, query the originating department.
5. Do verify the extent of similarity between two jobs before reusing previously estimated or actual job data for a second estimating assignment. Be especially careful of material, tolerance, and quantity requirements.
6. Do keep searching for new materials, processes, machines, and techniques to improve present manufacturing procedures.
7. Do keep a properly identifiable set of notes for each estimate; include the blueprints, specifications, correspondence, and other material related to the job.
8. Do remember that much of the data and information contained in an estimate is confidential and that business is highly competitive. Try not to help a competitor by carelessly revealing the valuable information contained in an estimate.
9. Do get as many quotations for purchased parts as time permits.
10. Do make comparisons between the cost of buying a particular service and modifying company facilities to perform the operation.
11. Do not depend on "hunches" to yield a reliable estimate; analyze each step carefully.
12. Do not guess at the meaning of unfamiliar specifications or symbols. Check with the customer or a reliable source for an interpretation and get the definition in writing.
13. Do not base an estimate on the projected purchase of new equipment unless the equipment will pay for itself within a reasonable period of time.
14. Do not apply high-production manufacturing methods to low-production jobs or vice versa.
15. Do not assume that specifications are final. Unless the customer specifies no product design changes, ask for any changes that will reduce manufacturing costs and save money for the customer.
16. Do not accept verbal engineering changes or similar directives; insist on written documents and file them in the appropriate folder with all other relevant data.

4

ESTIMATING PROCEDURES

The best estimating methods for a company are those that effectively meet the needs of its organization and customers. The methods differ widely among companies and are influenced by complexity of the organization, sophistication of products, and variety of product mix.

Small plants manufacturing basic products usually rely on simple techniques. For example, the owner of a small shop, may scan a part print and make cost calculations directly on the drawing. The size of the organization mandates simple estimating methods in this case, and the owner's memory serves as the source of historical cost information.

At the other end of the spectrum is the manufacturer with many employees producing a wide variety of items. Formal procedures are used to cope with complicated situations. In many instances, a computer provides accurate cost data for quotes as well as cost data for decision making. Extensive records of cost information are maintained in a computer database. While there are wide differences between the two estimating methods described above, assuring an adequate profit for the company is the objective of each. Steps to make accurate cost estimates are:

1. Analyze the request to ensure all essential information is included.
2. Analyze the part or product and list all purchased parts and the parts to be fabricated in-house.
3. Develop the manufacturing process for each appropriate part or assembly.
4. Compute the material costs for the purchased and fabricated parts.
5. Determine the costs of new durable and perishable tools.
6. Estimate the manufacturing time for each operation listed in the manufacturing process plan.
7. Apply labor and burden rates to each operation.

It is difficult to generalize about the time required to produce a good estimate. Although accuracy and speed are largely a function of a person's skill, there is no doubt that an estimate improves as more time is allowed for completion. However, the principal expressed by Parkinson's Law—which states that work expands to fill the time allocated for it—applies to estimating as to any other function. As a result, a balance must be struck between the need for accurate estimates and the need for timely completion.

If up-to-date cost data is not on file for material, tooling, equipment, and purchased parts, additional time is required to obtain this from the responsible departments. A database of historical costs helps reduce reliance upon suppliers and other departments speeding up the estimating process.

ESTIMATE ANALYSIS

After a request for an estimate has been made, it should be analyzed for completeness by carefully inspecting all accompanying material. The request should be checked for:

1. Estimate due date—if overdue, check to see if an extension can be granted.
2. General design specifications—a brief description of the product, its function, performance, and purpose, e.g., a pump to lift a highly corrosive fluid 20 ft. at a rate of 10 gpm.
3. Total quantity and volume requirements.
4. Assembly or layout drawings—these usually have only general dimensions. Often processes, raw materials for the parts, dimensions, and tolerances may not be specified.
5. List of the proposed subassemblies of the product.
6. Detail drawings and a bill of materials for the product.
7. Surface finish or protective coating requirements for the part or product.
8. Test and inspection requirements.

The more complete the information is, the more accurate the estimate is likely to be. However, a more accurate cost estimate, usually requires more effort. As shown in *Table 4-1*, *all* pertinent information must be available to do a Class 1 estimate. For a Class 7 estimate, *only general design specifications and quantities* are necessary. A Class 7 estimate is based on intuitive judgement regarding product details or comparisons with a similar product.

Classes of estimates differ, according to the amount of information needed, the method by which the estimating is done, and the effort required. Class 1 and 2 estimates, depend on firm quotations of machine tools, equipment, tools, and materials, and a detailed analysis of all processes. For the Class 2 estimate, note that all the information is necessary for estimating the product except the area and building requirements.

PART ANALYSIS

Cost estimate requests should include a complete bill of materials. When one is not provided, it must be compiled from the available drawings. A bill of

Table 4-1. Cost Estimating Data.

Description of Data	*Class of Estimate*						
	1	*2*	*3*	*4*	*5*	*6*	*7*
PROVIDED BY CUSTOMER OR REQUESTOR:							
General design specification, quantity, and prodiction rate	x	x	x	x	x	x	x
Assembly or layout drawings	x	x	x	x	x	x	
Proposed subassemlies	x	x	x	x	x		
Detail drawings and bill of material	x	x	x	x			
Test and inspection requirements	x	x	x	x			
Packaging and/or transportation requirements	x	x	x	x			
OBTAINED INTERNALLY:							
Manufacturing routings	x	x	x	x			
Machine tool and equipment requirements	x	x	x	x			
Detailed tool, machine tool, gage and equipment lists	x	x	x				
Operation analysis and workplace studies	x	x					
Standard time data	x	x					
Material release data	x	x					
Subcontractor cost and delivery data	x	x					
Area and building requirements	x						

materials is a detailed list of the components of the product, serving several purposes:

1. It prevents omission of details acting as a checklist.
2. Separates purchased parts from those to be fabricated.
3. Lists all parts to be estimated.

Make-or-buy decisions start with examining the bill of material. Small items such as bolts or screws are generally purchased, as are parts too large, too small, or otherwise unsuitable for existing plant operations.

Subcontracting

Even if a part can be processed in-house, it is sometimes advisable to subcontract it because:

1. A heavy shop load may prevent it from being made internally in time to meet a customer's requirements.
2. The profit margin for a particular component, when subcontracted, may be greater than if it had been made internally.
3. The profit margin for a particular component that has been subcontracted may be greater, particularly when sufficient other work is anticipated to keep the in-house equipment running.

The latter reason usually requires a decision from top management and may require additional effort and time. Where possible top management should be made aware of any subcontracting advantages.

Comparison Method

In reviewing the detailed bill of materials, previous estimates should be checked for similar parts in order to expedite the procedure. In making comparisons, a good filing system or computer database for past estimates is very helpful.

Suggesting Changes

While processing an estimate, changes in specifications to make the product easier to produce and reduce cost should be addressed. In reviewing the engineering drawing, obvious errors should be noted and corrections suggested. By this time, the designer will have already worked out the best possible solution.

Implementing changes depends on the amount of time left to complete the estimate and how critical it is to the quote. When the change is critical, it must be submitted to the designer for review.

PRELIMINARY MANUFACTURING PLAN

Determining the cost of the various steps involved in fabricating a part or assembly is one of the most demanding estimating tasks. Each part must have a processing plan which is drawn up by the manufacturing engineering deparment. This must include the tooling, equipment, and time necessary to produce the product. Tool and equipment costs must be estimated.

In a small shop, the processing plan may be developed by the owner and may involve little documentation. In larger companies, manufacturing engineering must assure that the plan is based on the latest and best manufacturing techniques. Often, as little as 10% of the work estimated will return as orders. Because of this, the preliminary process plan should be brief yet sufficient to maintain estimating accuracy.

FACILITIES

Sometimes, new products require the rearrangement of machines, relocation of sources of utilities and alterations to the building structure. New material handling equipment, such as overhead conveyors, may have to be provided. Estimates of the cost of this must be provided in the estimate for top management review in pricing the product to the customer. In many companies, the facilities planning group provides this cost data.

Table 4-2. Machinery Installation Costs.

Machine Weight (lb.)	*Costs by Trade or Operation*				
	Rigging	*Assembly*	*Setting*	*Leveling*	*Electrical*
1,000 to 2,000	....	....	$150	$ 60	$375
2,000 to 4,000	....	....	$300	$150	$750 with disconnect and S. jack
4,000 to 8,000	$150	$ 600	450	300	$900 with starter; $1500 without starater disconnect and swing
8,000 to 12,000	300	200 to 300	600	450	$600 to $1500; $1800 with MG set
Over 12,000	$600	$1200	$900	$200	$2100; $2700 with MG set

Foundations:

$90 per cu. yd. with reinforcing steel and anchor bolts
$180 per cu. yd. with forms, reinforcing steel, and anchor bolts
$30 per cu. yd. to excavate and haul away
$7.50 per sq. ft. for saw cutting existing slab, break out, and haul away

The analysis should include (1) the areas where the equipment is to be placed, (2) the existing facilities, (3) the required facilities, and (4) the new product flow pattern. From this analysis, a preliminary plant layout can be made and used as a basis for the estimate. The completeness of the layout is determined by the size and complexity of the facility changes, the required accuracy of the estimate, and the estimate lead time.

When the layout is complete, each piece of equipment is analyzed to determine what is required for its installation. This step is similar to preparing manufacturing processing or operations sheets for a part or product.

After determining the effort required, the costs are found by using the labor rates for all trades and skills involved and the cost of materials to be used for the installation. For example, to install a resistance welder, a millwright is needed to move the machine into position and fasten it to the floor. An electrician is also required to make electrical connections. A laborer may be needed to clean up the area before and after the machine is installed. For other installations, it may be necessary to consider ventilation, which would require the services of a sheet metal worker. Changes made to building foundations or the addition of water storage tanks would require carpenters and cement finishers.

Estimating the cost of installing a large number of machines sometimes is done by classifying the machine according to weight. *Table 4-2* lists typical costs, by trade or operation, used by one company in estimating machine costs. These costs differ depending upon the company and its geographical location.

As an example, the costs of installing a machine weighing 10,000 lbs. which is completely assembled upon arrival at the plant can be determined from this table. The required operations include rigging, setting, leveling, and electrical installation. For an 8,000 to 12,000 lb. machine, these costs are $300, $600, $450, and $900, respectively. The total cost is $2250. The actual cost may be slightly higher or lower than this but the cost should average out in the long run.

Depending on company policy, the costs may be prorated into the overall manufacturing cost estimate of the particular product being estimated. Major facility changes or improvements frequently affect more than one product and are prorated accordingly. In any case, it will be a factor for top management to consider in pricing the product to the customer.

DIRECT MATERIAL COST

All materials on the bill of materials can be divided into two basic categories: (1) purchased parts, and (2) material for in-house fabricated parts.

Often the cost of these parts is obtained directly from the purchasing deparment. In order to proceed properly, the purchasing department needs to know the configuration and quantity of each part. Also, special requirements such as heat treatment or surface finish should be noted.

To save time, cost tables are sometimes prepared for frequently used parts. *But, such tables must be used cautiously*. Prices change frequently, and a wrong price can distort the entire estimate. In addition, the purchasing department is generally more aware of applicable price breaks at various purchasing volumes.

The purchasing department should keep the estimating department informed of the latest cost figures on purchased parts. For companies using an integrated electronic data processing (EDP) system, such reports are easily obtainable.

A list is usually made of every part to be made in-house. Details required include the quantity, size, weight, configuration, and type of raw materials required for each part.

Raw Material Quantity

Each item is analyzed to determine the exact amount of raw material or stock that must be purchased. The cost of raw material for a part is determined by multiplying the unit cost of the material by the weight of the rough stock used per piece. If a piece is machined, the amount of stock removed by machining must be added to the finished dimensions. The volume is computed from the dimensions prior to machining. If the piece is irregularly shaped, it is divided into simple geometric shapes and the volumes of the shapes found separately. The volume is multiplied by the density of the material to obtain the weight. Sometimes, experienced people are able to judge the weights of intricate pieces, such as castings, surprisingly close by comparing them with similar pieces.

Depending upon the type of stock used, various formulas are used to determine material requirements and costs. In the case of a stamping made from steel coil stock, the following four-step procedure can be used:

1) Weight of coil = gage × width × density × length

2) $\text{Parts per coil} = \dfrac{\text{length of coil}}{\text{length required for one part}}$

3) $\text{Weight per part} = \dfrac{\text{weight of coil}}{\text{parts per coil}}$

4) Parts material cost = weight per part × steel price per lb.

For bar stock, handbook tables are often referenced. The length of the part, plus an allowance facing and cutoff, is multiplied by the weight or price per inch of the diameter of stock as given in the tables.

The material lost in processing through scrapped pieces, butt ends, chips, etc., must be included in an estimate. Losses vary from 1% to 12% depending on the process, material, and practice. An average allowance of 5% is often added to material estimates to account for these losses.

Some of the material loss is recovered through selling to scrap dealers. Note the allowance in the final cost estimate illustrated in *Figure 4-1*.

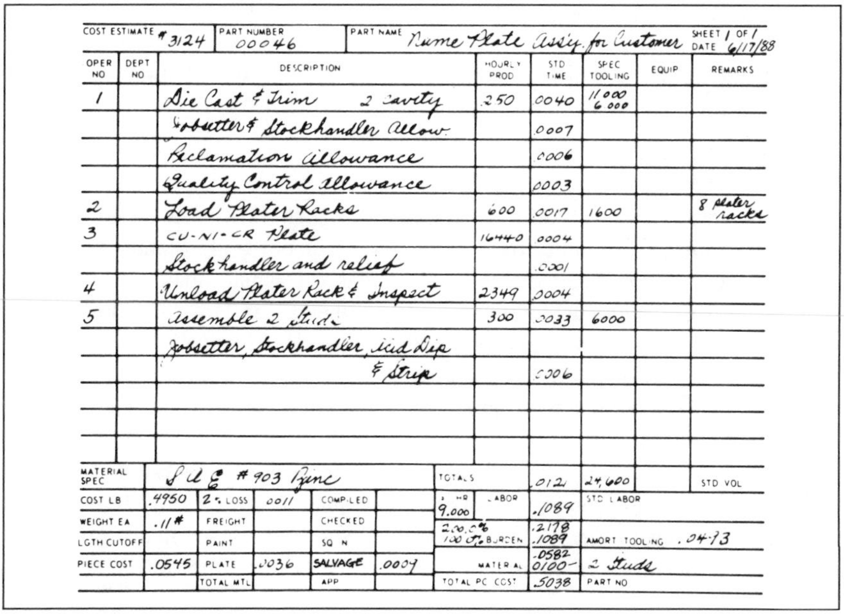

COST ESTIMATE # 3124 | PART NUMBER 00046 | PART NAME Name Plate Assy. for Customer | SHEET 1 OF 1 | DATE 6/17/88

OPER NO	DEPT NO	DESCRIPTION	HOURLY PROD	STD TIME	SPEC TOOLING	EQUIP	REMARKS
1		Die Cast & Trim 2 cavity	250	0040	11 000 6 000		
		Jobsetter & Stockhandler Allow.		0007			
		Reclamation Allowance		0006			
		Quality Control Allowance		0003			
2		Load Plater Racks	600	0017	1600		8 plater racks
3		CU-NI-CR Plate	16440	0004			
		Stockhandler and relief		.0001			
4		Unload Plater Rack & Inspect	2349	0004			
5		Assemble 2 Studs	300	0033	6000		
		Jobsetter, Stockhandler, Acid Dip & Strip		0006			

MATERIAL SPEC	S A E #903 Zinc					TOTALS	.0121	24,600	STD VOL
COST LB	.4950	2% LOSS	0011	COMPILED		HR 9.000 / LABOR	.1089	STD LABOR	
WEIGHT EA	.11#	FREIGHT		CHECKED		200.0% / 100.0% BURDEN	.2178 .1089	AMORT TOOLING	.0473
LGTH CUTOFF		PAINT		SQ IN					
PIECE COST	.0545	PLATE	.0036	SALVAGE	.0007	MATERIAL	.0582 0100–	2 Studs	
		TOTAL MTL		APP		TOTAL PC COST	.5038	PART NO	

Figure 4-1. Final cost estimate on a name plate assembly.

Price Breaks

Usually, there are price breaks for quantity purchases of material. Some companies include in the estimate the price break applicable to the quantity of material that must be purchased for the part or product being estimated. Most, however, prefer to use the price break applicable to the company's actual purchase of raw material for all products. This is especially true for companies manufacturing a wide range of products fabricated from the same basic material.

Companies often have slitting and shearing equipment so they can mill stock and slit it to required sizes. This permits them to purchase in greater quantity and reduces material costs.

Material Cost Data

In general, someone in a company knows the current cost of raw materials normally used for fabricating parts within the plant. Maintaining a file of current material cost reduces the time involved in contacting suppliers each time an estimate is processed.

Estimating Forms

To assist in computing material costs, an estimating form is sometimes used that incorporates the most commonly manufactured items. Estimating forms should provide sufficient description of the part so any person familiar with that kind of manufacture will obtain a quick, clear picture of the situation. (*Figure 4-2*.)

Standard Costs

If standard costs are used for materials, raw material cost is found by multiplying the number of units by the standard cost per unit. Standard costs are generally not established for materials purchased in small quantities.

Standard costs are useful to provide estimates for large job-shops which manufacture many items in low production quantities. Typically, the accounting department annually establishes the average cost per unit of each type of material purchased by the company. Appropriate allowances for price changes that may occur serve as the standard cost.

The form shown in *Figure 4-2* was designed for use in a general machine shop which specializes in producing gears in small quantities. Space is allowed at the bottom of the sheet to indicate the operations required and estimated production time. The material calculations are shown at the bottom right of the form.

ESTIMATE SHEET

QUOTATION NO 2350 CUSTOMER INQUIRY NO. C 823 DATE 7/13/88

CUSTOMER Columbia Geneva Steel Div U S Steel Corp.

DRAWING NO. 22947 REV. 13 MK. D

PRICE EACH $631.61 & $120.80 DELIVERY 8 Weeks

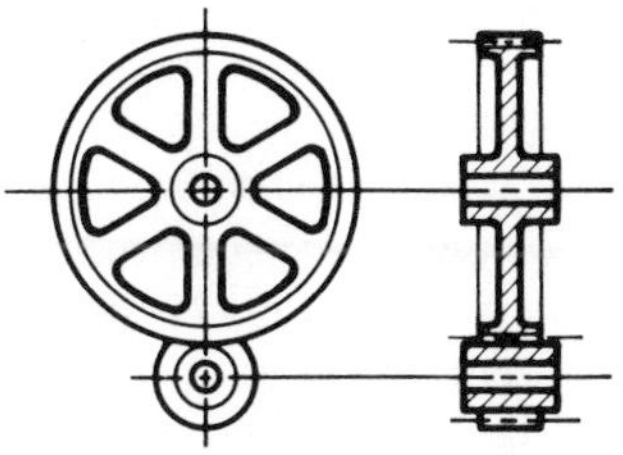

SPUR GEAR		SPUR PINION	
	FURNISH ✓		FURNISH ✓
QUAN. 12	C.T.O.	QUAN. 2	C.T.O.
TEETH 96	FACE 6"	TEETH 13	FACE 6 7/8"
PITCH 4 DP	P.A. 20° Stub	PITCH 4 DP	P.A. 20° Stub
PITCH DIA. 24.000"	O.D. 24.400"	PITCH DIA. 3.250"	O.D. 3.650"
BORE 5.125 +.0015 −.000	K.W. 1" x 1/2"	BORE 1.250	K.W. 3/8 x 3/16 tapered
THRU BORE 6"	S.S. None	THRU BORE 6 7/8"	S.S. Two 1/4" @ 90°
HUB DIA. 8"		HUB DIA. 2 5/8"	
MATERIAL 1040 Stl.	H.T. 245-265 Bhn	MATERIAL 4140 leaded	H.T. 290-320 Bhn
FORG___ CASTING* ✓	BAR STK.	FORG___ CASTING___	BAR STK.
EST. WT. GROSS 334 lbs.	NET 270 lbs	EST. WT. GROSS 21.5 lbs.	NET 12.3 lbs.

*IF CASTING: I.D. UNDER RIM 22"
TYPE: WEB___ SPOKE ✓

REMARKS: Pattern on hand

Casting 334# @ 0.69 230.46
H T 334# @ 0.105 35.07
265.53
Plus 15% 39.83
11.45 hrs @ 28.50 326.25
631.61

Total wt 21.5 x 12 = 258#
21.5 lbs @ 61.50 /cwt
3.15 extra
64.20 = 13.80
Cutting = 2.94
H.T. 18.7 @ 0.15 2.80
19.54
Plus 15% 2.93
22.47
3.45 hrs @ $28.50 98.32
120.79

H. T. –
Turn 3.25
Cut Kway 0.70
Hob teeth 7.50
11.45 hrs.

Saw to 6 7/8" –
H.T. –
Turn 1.25
Grind bore 0.35
Cut Kway 0.60
Hob teeth 1.25
3.45 hrs.

Figure 4-2. Cost estimating form for job lots of mating gear and pinion.

TOOLING COSTS

Tooling is an integral part of the manufacturing process. New tooling, both durable and perishable, are likely to be required to make new products. A tooling cost estimate can provide the costs of alternative methods of tooling. Manufacturing engineers know their company's tooling capabilities, and can determine tooling requirements for new products.

In addition to its role in the product cost estimate, tooling estimates are frequently requested by engineers to determine the cost differentials in proposed process changes on current production.

Tooling is a significant cost item in a product cost estimate. It usually is a distinct part of the product cost estimate, rather than being included as part of factory burden.

Purchased Tooling

The tooling for most products is likely to be purchased from outside suppliers. Few manufacturing companies possess the specialized knowledge and equipment required to design and build their own tools. Therefore, tool cost is generally determined in much the same manner as the costs for other purchased items. The purchase price of the tooling includes any applicable transportation and handling charges.

Estimating the costs involved when the company develops its own tools is more complicated. One large stamping plant has found the following percentages to be typical for tooling costs for metal stamping dies:

3%	Models and templates
12%	Designs
3%	Patterns, castings, and labor
50%	Build
22%	Material
10%	Tryout and testing
100%	Total tool cost

Estimating the cost of in-house tooling requires knowledge of previous tooling development costs. A database of previous cost data is very helpful in this circumstance.

Tool Cost Assignment

Information from previous production runs and data from suppliers are useful in determining the life of perishable tools. In computing the number of perishable tools for a production run, allowance must be made for rework and scrapped parts.

When durable tooling is usable only on the product being estimated, its entire cost (less any salvage value) must be assigned to the product. If the tooling can be used on similar products, it should be prorated accordingly. Knowledge of future production plans may help in assigning a reasonable percentage of the tool cost to the product being estimated. Because of the difficulty in assigning costs accurately for durable tooling, some companies include this in factory overhead.

Data for Estimating Tooling Costs

Tooling costs change frequently and a database on tooling costs may need frequent revisions.

Tool suppliers are the best source of cost information on tools. Past estimates may supply some guidance but require adjustments to reflect to present cost levels.

In purchasing tooling from suppliers, two or three bids should be requested for the same tooling to obtain a realistic idea of actual tooling costs.

By studying past cost figures for similar items of tooling, the annual rate of cost increase for tools used by the plant can be determined. When a new product requires tools similar to those used on a previous job, the rate of cost increase may be applied to the old tooling cost to arrive at a new figure.

MANUFACTURING TIME

Labor costs and factory burden require determining the time necessary to accomplish each manufacturing step. Operations can be viewed as machine operations, machine setups, and process treatments.

Machine Operations

A machine operation is comprised of all the steps needed for a worker to complete a discrete task such as boring, cutting, or grinding a specific part.

The time is estimated for each operation outlined in the manufacturing processing plan. This is done either by referring to standard data developed from previous products or by breaking each operation into its elemental motions.

When standard data on previous operations is not available, operation times are determined by the use of predetermined time and motion elements such as MTM Handbook formulas which can be used along with standard processing data tables giving operating information such as speeds, and feeds.

Standard data compiled from actual plant processes usually includes traditional allowances for such factors as machine downtime, operator fatigue, and maintenance. The use of standard data requires less time than predetermined elemental motions, but may not be as accurate. In many companies this information is provided by industrial engineers.

Machine Setups

Setup time is estimated separately from machine operation time. It can be determined from standard data gathered from earlier products. It also may be built up through a study of the elements or steps required to make the setup.

In job-shop operations it is difficult to develop a formula for setup costs. Generally, the owner of a small shop will rely upon past experience to establish the setup time for each batch of products.

For high-volume runs, setup costs are calculated on a unit basis by dividing total setup cost by the number of units in the production run.

Example:

$$\frac{\text{Number of Setups} \times \text{hrs/Setup}}{\text{Number of Units}} = \text{hrs/Unit}$$

Where:

Quantity = 100,000 Units
Number of Setups To Produce 100,000 Units = 2 Setups
Time Required To Perform One Setup = 10 hrs.

$$\frac{2 \times 10 \text{ hrs.}}{100{,}000 \text{ units}} = .00020 \text{ hrs.}$$

Therefore, .00020 hours per each unit is required for setups.

This formula is useful and reasonably accurate even if the production lots following individual setups vary in quantity. When lot sizes are equal in quantity, setup costs assignable to each unit would be the same whether the costs were assigned on a total production run basis or on the basis of separate production lots.

Process Treatments

Often, time estimates are not made for process treatments such as plating, painting, and dipping. Instead of time, material usage serves as the basis for labor and factory burden costs.

Additional material is not added to the product with process treatments such as cleaning, curing, sand blasting, and drying. For these processes, time is usually computed as it is for machine operations.

DIRECT LABOR COSTS

Labor costs are found by multiplying the times for component manufacturing operations, by appropriate labor rates.

The accounting department furnishes these in many companies. The rates generally include fringe benefits such as contributions to social security, group insurance, and retirement plans, in addition to hourly wages.

FACTORY BURDEN

The accounting department normally determines burden rates.

Fixed and Variable Burden

Burden consists of both fixed and variable costs. Separate rates are often established for each. Fixed burden includes all continuing costs regardless of the production volume for a given item, such as salaries, building rent or mortgage payments, and insurance. Variable burden costs, on the other hand, increase or decrease as the volume of production rises or falls. Indirect material, indirect labor, electricity used to operate equipment, and certain tooling are classified as variable burden items.

Cost Centers

Often the variable burden rate is different for various cost centers within the plant.

For example, cleaning and plating, may be set up as a cost center. For a chromium plated automobile bumper, the direct material cost of the chromium plating material would be determined first. Then the burden cost would be found by using the cost center burden rate.

Assume that the cleaning and plating cost center burden rate was 170% of direct material. If the direct material cost was $.69, the cleaning and plating burden would be $1.17. Total costs (the sum of direct material and cost center burden) would be $1.86.

When cost centers have different burden rates the product cost is found without variable burden. Fixed burden costs are calculated based upon this product cost. The estimate for the automobile bumper is shown in *Table 4-3*.

Table 4-3. Cost Estimate for Automobile Bumper.

Cost Element	*Cost per Part*	*Burden Rates (%)*		*Burden*
		Fixed	*Variable**	
Direct material				
steel (8 lbs. @ $7.25/hwt.)	$1.740	....	....	....
Chrome plate				
1.2 lbs. @ $59.28/hwt	.690	....	170	$ 1.173
Direct labor				
stamping				
.16 hrs. @ $21.45	3.432	....	310	10.640
Tooling	2.34	....	210	4.914
Total direct costs	$8.202	73	....	5.987
Total burden				$22.714

*Note that different factors are used to compute variable burden. Direct labor is used for the stamping operation, while direct material is used for cleaning and plating. Total cost for the bumper would be $30.916, the sum of total direct costs and total burden.

Burden Assignment Methods

The method of assigning factory burden to individual products differs widely among companies. Any quantifiable factor may be used to assign burden costs as long as there is a full and equitable burden distribution. The factors most frequently used are:

1. Direct labor cost
2. Direct material cost
3. Number of parts produced.

One large manufacturer assigns both fixed and variable burden on the basis of direct labor cost. Fixed burden is assigned at 100% of direct labor, and variable burden at 340%. Thus, the burden cost on an item requiring $.120 in direct labor is $.528–$.120 for fixed burden and $.408 for variable burden.

Depending upon a company's product line, direct material cost or number of parts produced may be more accurate in distributing burden costs. Direct material cost is favored by process type industries and other companies manufacturing products in which direct material is the major cost element. A company that makes a stable line of products selling for approximately the same price can use the number of items produced to assign burden.

It is critical to understand what costs are covered by burden rates and which must be computed separately.

TOTAL MANUFACTURING COST

The total product manufacturing cost or "cost of goods produced" is the sum of the cost of direct labor, direct material and burden cost. Selling prices are sensitive to market conditions and often not directly related to costs. Tool costs, product design cost, general and administrative costs and selling costs must be added to the "Cost of Goods Produced" to determine the company's total cost for each product.

The difference between the selling price and the total cost is the profit for the company. A negative value for this difference means the company is losing money on the product. Profits are used to pay taxes to the government, dividends to the stockholders and in many cases profit sharing to the employes. They are also used for reinvesting in the business.

5

COMPUTER APPLICATIONS

Author Glenn Graham, in his SME book entitled *Automation Encyclopedia: A to Z in Advanced Manufacturing*, discusses briefly the development of the personal computer. The following 12 paragraphs are taken from his book.

Personal computers are completely self-contained computer systems which were originally designed to be used by single users for tasks which usually support activities that are normally performed by an individual.

Personal computers are usually micro-based which include all five of the key parts of a computer which are: the processor, the memory, the input/output (I/O), disk storage, and the programs. Personal computers are usually designed to be a size which can easily fit on top of a desk to be used by a single person, although a popular alternate arrangement is to place the system unit on the floor, with only the monitor and keyboard on the desktop. Personal computers do not require special environmental conditions to function properly, but can easily operate in most environments which are comfortable to the human operator.

Personal computers are usually physically arranged into three major parts. There is the main box or system unit, which contains the motherboard and any expansion cards, the diskette drives and the hard disk (Winchester disk) drive(s). Other options, such as cartridge tape drives or micro-Bernoulli drives may also be installed in the system unit. The keyboard is the second part of the personal computer system, and usually is included as standard with purchase of a system unit. The monitor is the third part of the basic system. Several options exist such as monochrome or color or enhanced graphics displays, with several choices within each category. The monitor is frequently treated as a required option when purchasing a personal computer. Usually a printer is needed to produce hard copy output, and a modem may be needed for communication with other computers at remote locations. A vast array of additional optional peripherals, such as pen-plotters, mice, digitizing tablets, etc., can also be used with a personal computer.

HISTORY

Personal computers first came on the scene through Radio Shack and Apple in the mid-1970s. In August of 1981, IBM announced the IBM PC. By the spring of 1982 the PC was an astounding success with shipments much greater than predicted. The first ''clone'' to a PC was the Compaq computer, which was intended to be a portable device, although the difficulty in carrying the heavy machine coined the term ''luggable.'' In the spring of 1983, IBM introduced the XT model (XT for extended technology) which contained a high capacity hard disk in addition to the floppy diskette drive. Compaq matched the XT with another portable called the Compaq Plus.

In 1983, IBM stumbled with the introduction of of the PCjr, which was not a sales success. The PCjr, also known as the ''Peanut'', which was its internal development name, was discontinued in 1985.

In 1984, Compaq introduced the Compaq DeskPro, which was the first machine to have more computing power than the original IBM PC. Shortly thereafter, IBM introduced the AT model (AT for advanced technology) which had much greater computing speed than either the original PCs or the Compaq offerings. Most recently, IBM has introduced a new series of personal computers called the Personal System/2 or PS/2, which uses a new ''microchannel'' bus. The high end models incorporate the 80386, which is the latest in the Intel 8086 family series of CPUs.

From 1985 to the present, many manufacturers, including Asian and European companies have developed ''clones'' that are personal computers which are sometimes more or less compatible with the IBM products, but usually offer something greater in terms of features and almost always a lesser price. The success of clones has become so great that many institutions including Fortune 500 companies, universities and the U.S. Government who need large quantities of personal computers have made decisions to purchase clones instead of machines made by IBM. The competition in the marketplace continues to drive the retail price of personal computers lower.

Another scenario which was occurring during the era of the development of the IBM PC and its clones was the development of the Macintosh or ''Mac'' as it is affectionately called, using the Motorola 6800 family series of CPUs instead of the Intel 8086 family. The current Mac Plus and the ''Fat'' Mac uses the 68020 processor chip which is equivalent to the Intel 80386 in terms of general computing capabilities.

FUNCTION AND PROGRAMMING

The functions of the five parts of a basic computer system can be described by the following: the processor is the brains of the machine, which in a personal computer will usually be a variation of the Intel 8086 family. The CPU may sometimes be assisted by a numerical coprocessor chip such as the 8087 or 80287. The memory is the ''workspace'' of the computer and has several constraints in a PC. The design of the Intel 8086/8088 in the PC and PC XT limits the physical memory to 1024K bytes. An IBM PC AT (or compatible) has a physical addressing limit of 16 megabytes (16,000K) of memory but the DOS operating system can only address 640K of the user memory, with 384K, reserved for the BIOS and display adapter. Schemes such as expanded memory exist to allow user programs to address more than 640K of memory. When an operating system is available to operate the 80286 in protected mode, programs will be able to be much larger while running multiple applications simultaneously.

The input/output or I/O section of a personal computer is the portion which can take in or put out data, such as the keyboard and communications ports for data input and the video display and the same communications ports for data output. Some machines have a parallel printer port, which is usually unidirectional in the output direction only. The parallel port is normally capable of two way data communications, and can be used as a higher speed data channel than the serial ports. The larger Macintosh computers provide an SCSI (Small Computer Systems Interface) port for daisy chaining devices such as printers and disk drives.

While disk storage devices are also I/O devices, they have such an important role in the functioning of the personal computer that they are described and considered separately. Disk storage is typically the only mass storage for the computer. Disks provide the only permanent storage for when the power is interrupted to the computer and the diskettes provide quick and inexpensive means of transferring data between machines. Diskettes are still the primary form of providing software to customers for personal computers. Hard disks also provide access to large quantities of data in a sufficiently fast access mode for many applications such that the 640K memory limit of DOS doesn't cause much problem for the user.

Programs are the last of the five key parts of a computer and that is definitely true with a personal computer. Without programs and the other related application software and the operating systems, personal computers wouldn't perform any useful functions. Some operating environments have been developed for personal computers which run under DOS and are intended to provide a more uniform interface for the development of applications software and more familiar and consistent user interface. Microsoft Windows is probably the most familiar, with Deskview and GEM desktop being two others. Some of the applications programs in use were first perfected for use on PCs before mainframe and minicomputers. The most noticeable is spreadsheet software. Lotus 1-2-3 has set the standard for PC based spreadsheet software, and now products with similar capabilities are being developed and are available for minicomputers and mainframes. The reason the spreadsheet was enhanced for the personal computer first is because the concept of a personal computer provides dedicated and available computing resources for a user to constantly perform the interactive calculations required for most normal spreadsheet applications. The former mentality of time sharing and batch computer systems of mainframes is inconsistent with the present thinking of PCs providing available dedicated computing resources.

COMPUTER APPLICATIONS

In the past decade, the use of computers by industry has increased dramatically. Much of this growth has been in the area of personal computers. Interestingly enough, many personal computers are more powerful than some mainframe computers in use today. The wide availability of personal computers, at reasonable prices, has encouraged many business applications previously requiring a mainframe. Cost estimating is one of those applications.

Software for cost estimating is currently available that can be run on a personal computer. Many companies, regardless of size, can utilize this software to prepare accurate and consistent estimates. No longer does the advantage of a computer to prepare estimates belong only to those companies that can afford a custom program for their mainframe computer.

CHARACTERISTICS

There are certain characteristics common among almost all cost estimating software, whether for mainframe or personal computer. The first is that the software has a knowledge base. This is a database that calculations can be based upon. It may consist of formulas or information on existing production or prior estimates. Usually, it can be updated with new or revised information.

A second characteristic is that the software has provisions for calculating the costs by using information in the knowledge base combined with other data that may be input as the program is run. The third feature of cost estimating software is that it sums the costs in desirable classifications such as direct labor, direct material and factory burden. Lastly, the output from the software is formatted to make information useful to those who need it.

ADVANTAGES

There are substantial advantages to using the computer for cost estimating. For one thing, the effort required to do most estimates is reduced. Since the knowledge base contains much of the information, manual searching of files for data is virtually eliminated. The calculation, summation and preparation of output reports is automated, eliminating laborious and lengthy effort. Accuracy is also improved, and the number of mistakes associated with manual effort is minimized. The improvement in accuracy, in turn, eliminates the need for extensive checking and correction. Reducing effort means estimates can be done quicker, shortening time needed to furnish information to customers.

The knowledge base is a feature that enables more consistent estimates to be prepared. For similar parts, it is also likely that the same information or formulas can be found in this database. Traditional methods of cost estimating often do not result in identical references being found because of the awkwardness involved in manually searching files.

Information that is much more comprehensive can be stored in a knowledge base also. There is a practical limit to accessibility of information stored in files for traditional cost estimating, a characteristic that does not appear to exist in a properly designed computer based system.

The knowledge base makes it easier to add information that is new or revised. In a traditional cost estimating system, this may be a major problem. In many cases, files that are manually accessed may require restructuring. In others, the new information is cross-referenced making accessibility difficult.

Another advantage of computer based estimating systems is that similar estimates can be grouped for detailed analysis. Ways to improve bid results may be identified through this analysis. For example, adjustments to the knowledge base may be necessary. Also, specific improvements required in plant operations to sharpen competitiveness may become obvious.

PRECAUTIONS

A considerable problem presented by using computer based cost estimating programs involves keeping the knowledge base up-to-date on plant operations at the time the product will be made. Often, this is due to the people controlling the knowledge base being unfamiliar with its contents. When that happens, it is difficult to judge when updates are necessary. It may also occur because of apathy over maintaining the knowledge base. Because the cost estimating function is a vital part of doing business for most manufacturers, it is essential that the knowledge base be regularly updated without exception.

Another cause for concern regarding commercially available cost estimating software is that the knowledge base provided with the software is provided to all purchasers. A competitor using the same software may arrive at the same costs under identical conditions. To prevent such an occurrence, the knowledge base must be changed to fit the conditions of use. This type software is usually easily changed by revising formulas or other data in the knowledge base.

CUSTOM COST ESTIMATING SOFTWARE

The use of custom cost estimating software started soon after the widespread availability of the mainframe computer in the 1960s. Originally, programs were designed by the data processing department and only economically justifiable in relatively large companies. Data was entered on a computer form and subsequently keypunched on cards for processing on a card reader. The programs performed calculations and printed out a summary sheet. Data entry by terminals networked to the mainframe started in the 1970s. This was a vast improvement over the previous method of data entry.

Knowledge bases, unique to cost estimating, were added on some applications minimizing the data that had to be entered. The development of a single database which can be used for the company operation as well as for the cost estimating program is still in the future. Work is also underway in adapting the cost estimating function as the initial step in computerized process planning for some large companies.

Industry witnessed the widespread use of the personal computer in the 1980s. Computer literacy was no longer confined to those in the data processing function. Professionals concerned with cost estimating programmed the personal computer to meet their particular needs. The availability of the hard drive allowed the use of a knowledge base on the personal computer for cost estimating. Also, personal computer users could readily access the mainframe databases through data lines or a modem. A customized cost estimating program fitting the unique needs of any company is now possible for the personal computer.

COST ESTIMATING SOFTWARE IN THE CONCEPT PHASE

It is commonly agreed that there is a strong relationship among product design, material, and the manufacturing process. Often, the product engineer needs help from the materials engineer and the manufacturing engineer as how to proceed with the concept for a new product. A significant factor is the identification of the cost of the various alternatives. Estimating the "ball-park" cost of various alternatives for a product at this stage proceeds without much knowledge of the details.

Recently, cost estimating software has become commercially available on injection molding and machining processes that appears to be of help in this situation. Other similar software for sheet metal parts, forgings, powdered metal applications, die cast parts and others may also be available.

A "summary screen" is shown in *Figure 5-1* for a preliminary estimate of the cost of producing a thermoplastic part. It includes the mold cost, the processing cost and the material cost. Data required to make this estimate, not in the knowledge base, is minimal and includes such things as batch size, general configuration, overall dimensions, tolerance, color, and alternate materials.

The knowledge base can be revised to reflect, for example, current equipment availability, wage rates and material purchased cost. The machine required is selected automatically. If it is not in the knowledge base, the specification for the required machine is provided.

The mold cost is calculated based upon the part size, tolerance, appearance factors and geometric complexity. Cost sensitivity to many variables such as production volume and number of mold cavities can be readily seen using the software.

Estimated Injection Molding Costs For: COVER
Thermoplastic: polycarbonate

Total prod'n volume (thousands)	No. of cavities	Total mold base costs ($)	Cavity/core manuf. costs ($)	Total mold cost ($)	Mold cost per part (cents)
600	4	5205	10504	15709	2.6

Machine size (kN)	Machine rate ($/hr)	Cycle time (s)	Manuf. cost per part (cents)
800	32	19.8	5.1
Part volume (cu.cm)	**Part weight (gms)**	**Polymer cost ($/kg)**	**Polymer cost/part (cents)**
9.60	11.52	4.60	5.30

Select required option: 1

1. Screen edit
2. Show mold cost/cycle elements
3. Print results and responses
4. Change basic cost date
5. Change responses/polymer
6. Exit

Total part cost (cents) = 13.0

Figure 5-1. Result summary screen. (*From Boothroyd Dewhurst, Material Selection and Cost Estimating for Injection Molding, Wakefield, R.I., 1988*)

Software allowing preliminary cost estimates to be made using only minimal information has great promise in helping guide developing products and processes from concepts to detailed designs.

TYPICAL COMMERCIAL COST ESTIMATING SOFTWARE

Specific Application For Part Cost

The main menu from a commercially available part cost estimating software designed for a machine shop is shown in *Figure 5-2*. The program is menu driven and first prompts the user for information regarding the part to be machined and production volumes. Next, the user can select the first operation that needs to be estimated. This may be, for example, turning or milling. This process continues until all inside operations are complete. Costs can also be entered for supplier costs such as plating or heat treating.

The machine desired for each operation is selected by the user from over 80 specific machines in the knowledge base. For example, a milling operation can use eleven different types of vertical and horizontal milling configurations.

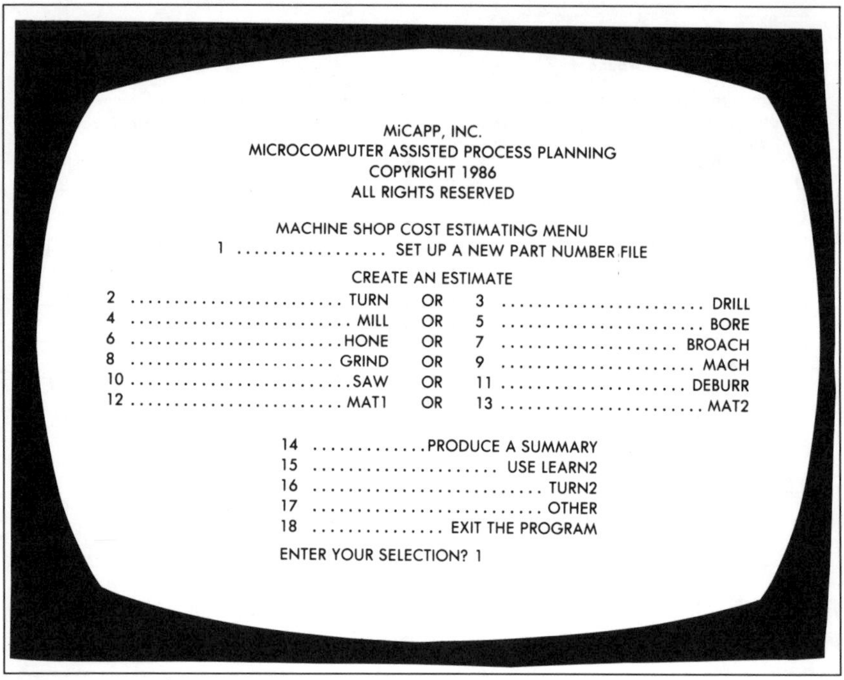

Figure 5-2. Main menu from part costing software for a machine shop. (*Courtesy of MiCAPP, Inc.*)

There are 34 major material groups and over 900 sizes of stock that can be selected from the knowledge base. Costs for other material, such as forgings and castings, can be directly entered in the program.

Tooling can be specified as either HSS or Carbide. The speeds and feeds are calculated from algorithms and adjusted as necessary for differences in material hardness.

This particular software also considers the learning curve in calculating costs. The program can be easily customized to reflect specific conditions in the company. Once the estimate is complete, a summary can be produced as shown in *Figure 5-3*.

General Application for Part Cost

Another commercially available cost estimating package can make part cost estimates on many metalworking and plastic manufacturing operations. Initially, the user must prepare a detailed list of operation elements to be used in manufacturing the part. *Figure 5-4* illustrates the worksheet appearing on the computer monitor. The user enters information via the keyboard to proceed with

* *

SUMMARY OF THE ESTIMATE

CUSTOMER NAME B & W MACHINE
PART NAME SAMPLE PART NUMBER 123
DATE 7/21/87

MACHINE	TIME/PC.	PC./CYCLE	S/U TIME	OFF STD.	W.C. RATE
S.S. N/C LATHE	7.341626	1	35	.2	$35
MILL	1.25	1	60	.25	$30
HEAT TR	.85	1	25	.15	$30
TOTAL	9.441626		120		

ODD LOT PRODUCTION OPERATION AND SETUP COSTS

LOT NO.	LOT SIZE	TOTAL COST PER PIECE
1	100	$7.172889
2	200	$6.791014
3	300	$6.663722

ESTIMATE WITH MATERIAL COST - PRICES ARE PER PIECE

LOT NO.	LOT SIZE	OPER COST	MAT COST	TOTAL
1	100	$7.172889	$3.5	$10.67289
2	200	$6.791014	$3.45	$10.24101
3	300	$6.663722	$3.25	$ 9.913721

GRAND TOTAL ESTIMATE WITH MATERIAL AND OSS COST

LOT SIZE	OPER COST	OSS COST	MAT COST	G TOTAL
100	$ 717.2888	$ 0	$350	$1067.289
200	$1358.203	$ 0	$690	$2048.203
300	$1999.117	$ 0	$975	$2974.117

TOOLING COSTS

MACHINE	S.S. N/C LATHE	TOOLING COSTS	$200
MACHINE	MILL	TOOLING COSTS	$100
MACHINE	HEAT TR	TOOLING COSTS	$ 0
OTHER TOOLING COSTS			$ 0
ENGINEERING COSTS			$ 0
TOTAL TOOLING			$300

GRAND TOTAL UNIT COSTS FOR OPERATIONS, OSS AND MATERIAL

LOT NO	LOT SIZE	G TOTAL COST / PC.
1	100	$10.67289
2	200	$10.24101
3	300	$ 9.913721

Figure 5-3. Summary of the estimate. (*Courtesy of MiCAPP, Inc.*)

the estimate. To complete the information on the worksheet, the user must access the appropriate table in the knowledge base.

The knowledge base contains tables of relationships between, for example, the part configuration and the time required. This database is an accumulation of thousands of "real" time elements drawn from actual observations of manufacturing operations. It includes over 24 major manufacturing operations and considers about 150 types of equipment. The tables include different time values for different cutting tools, such as HSS or carbide, and for various workpiece materials. The tables in the database can also be revised to reflect the conditions in the company using the software.

Lot Quantity 87 | Material Aluminum | Unit Material Cost 0 00

Process Opn No	Table Number	Process Description	Table Time	Adjustment Factor	Cycle Minutes	Setup Hours
10	7 4	Ram Milling				
	7 1 S1	Basic	1 45			1 45
	7 1 S2	Make piece	0 02	2		0 04
	7 1 S3	Tolerance	0 13			0 13
	7 4 1	Pick up, move	0 20		0 20	
	7 4 2	Clamp, unclamp	0 09	2	0 18	
	7 4 4	Mach operation	0 06		0 06	
	8 2 1	Traverse element	0 08	2	0 16	
	7 4 5	Clean, lubricate	0 05		0 05	
	1134	End milling	0 01	2	0 02	
	7 4 5	Clean, lubricate	0 15		0 15	
	1142A	Mill tool life	0 00		0 00	
	2213	Inspection	0 29		0 29	
	7 4 1	Pick up, move	0 06		0 06	
Total Lot Hours		3 32			1 17	
20	18 5	Hand Deburring				1 52
	18 5 S	Setup	0 05			0 05
	18 5 1	Handling repos	0 15		0 15	
	18 5 2	Tool handling	0 04	2	0 08	
	18 5 3B	Holes over ½ in	0 08		0 08	
	18 5 1	Handling repos	0 05		0 05	
	18 5 4A	Break edges	0 11		0 11	
Total Lot Hours		0 73			0 47	0 05
30	24 1	Pack				
	24 1 S	Setup	0 15			0 15
	24 1 1	Order paperwork	2 00	4	0 50	
	24 1 2	Get and position	0 09		0 09	
	24 1 10	Paper carton	1 51	4	0 38	
	24 1 10	Paper carton	0 22	4	0 05	
	24 1 15	Miscellaneous	0 26	4	0 06	
Total Lot Hours		1 73			1 09	0 15

Figure 5-4. Estimating worksheet. (*Courtesy of Penton Publishing*)

COST SUMMARY

Lot Quantity 87 | Material Aluminum | Unit Material Cost: 0 00

Operation Number	Cost Estimator Table No	Machine Process or Bench Description	Lot Hours	Productive Hour Cost ($)	Total Operation Cost ($)
10	7.4	Vertical-Spindle	3.32	43.50	144.27
20	18.5	Hand Deburring	0.732	21.35	15.62
30	24.1	Bench, Machines	1.73	27.75	47.92

Total Lot Hours	5.77	
Total Operational Productive Hour Cost	($)	207.81
Unit Operational Productive Hour Cost	($)	2.39
Unit Material Cost	($)	0.00
Total Direct Cost Per Unit	($)	2.39
Total Job Cost	($)	207.81

Lot Quantity 87 | Material Aluminum | Unit Material Cost: 0.00

Operation Number	Cost Estimator Table No	Machine Process or Bench Description	Lot Hours	Productive Hour Cost ($)	Total Operation Cost ($)
0	7.4	Vertical-Spindle	3.32	43.50	144.27
0	18.5	Hand Deburring	0.73	21.35	15.62
0	24.1	Bench Machines	1.73	27.75	47.92

	Total Lot Hours	5.77		
Operational PHC Unit	($)	2.39	Total ($)	207.81
Total Unit Cost	($)	2.39	Total Job Cost ($)	207.81

Figure 5-5. Cost summary. (*Courtesy of Penton Publishing*)

Other information can be entered in the program such as the burden rate and costing rate for the company using the software. By combining the information in the worksheet with the data in the knowledge base, a cost summary is prepared as shown in *Figure 5-5. Application to Costing Tools and Dies* There is also commercially available software for estimating jigs, fixtures, gages, and dies. A key feature of this software is a knowledge base for including prior estimates in various levels of detail. The knowledge base is custom, in that the data used is from the company using the software. A classification system is used for ease of retrieval. Where the tool or die was produced, the actual effort and material used is substituted for the estimated values improving accuracy. A search routine can retrieve the entire estimate or various levels of detail. This information can be used for a reference in preparing a new estimate on the software.

SUMMARY

In the beginning, personal computers were limited mostly to basic applications. As a greater variety of quality software was developed and became available on a wide scale, the role of the personal computer expanded to include more sophisticated programs like shop floor applications. Commercially available software for cost estimating may be very useful to a company. In many cases, demonstration software can be obtained at low cost. This will allow the company to evaluate the usefulness prior to purchase.

6

ESTIMATING DIE CASTING MACHINING COSTS

This chapter, and those following, have examples of cost estimates that illustrate the principles and procedures of estimating described in Chapter Four.

The estimating forms used are examples of those utilized by industry, and their format can be employed as shown, or adapted to fit individual circumstances. The cost figures applied in individual examples are approximations only and should not be used as actual cost data.

Assume that the cost estimating coordinator has been requested to prepare an estimate for a cam drive bracket. Detailed process sheets and tool design drawings (not shown) accompanied the cost request, and all necessary fixtures, gages, and other tools have been designed and are listed on the manufacturing process plan. *Figure 6-1* shows the assembly drawing, with machining dimensions of the part being estimated.

Each manufacturing operation listed on the manufacturing process plan will be analyzed, and the material, labor, burden, and tool costs per unit summarized on the cost estimate form (*Figure 6-2*).

Purchased Parts

The bracket (Detail 1 in *Figure 6-1*), an aluminum die casting ASTM B 85-49 alloy SC-6, is to be purchased without any machining. The purchasing department requested cost quotations for the die casting from several companies. The lowest quoted cost was \$66 per 100 pieces (\$.66 each) plus a die cost of \$5,430. The bushings (Detail 2), are standard sintered metal powder parts purchased at a cost of \$.114 each. The stud, Detail 3, will be purchased at a cost of \$.111 each.

These material and tool costs are entered on the cost estimate form shown in *Figure 6-2*. In Operation 001, the \$.66 bracket is entered in the "Material Cost" column, and the \$5,430 (die cost) is entered under the "New Tool Description." The cost of the stud (\$.111) is entered as the material cost for Operation 100, and the bushings (\$.114 each) as material cost for Operations 110 and 120.

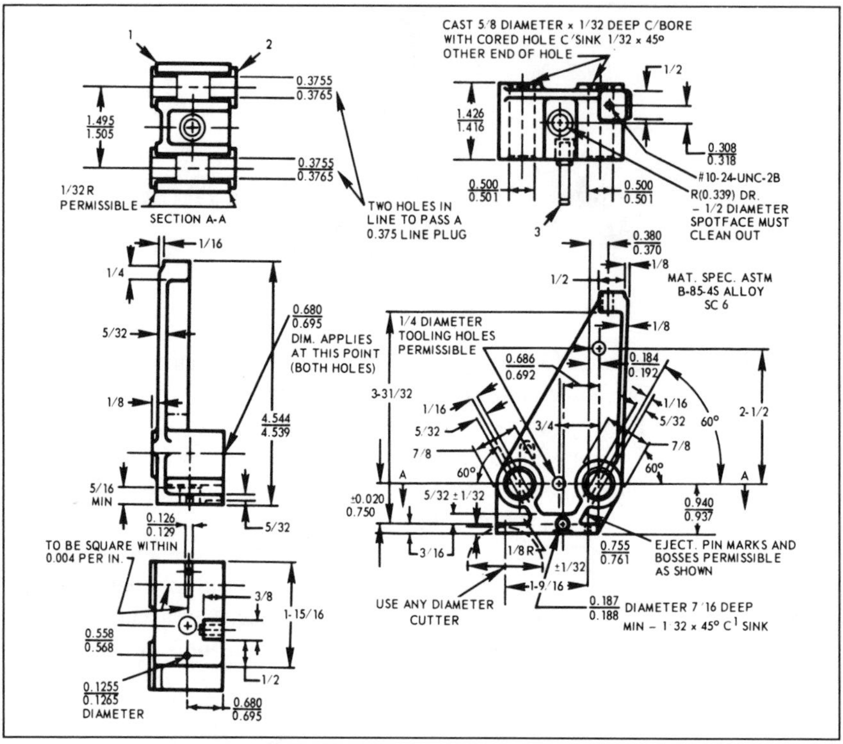

Figure 6-1. Assembly drawing of a cam drive bracket.

HANDLING AND MACHINE TIMES

The time required for each separate manufacturing operation must be computed before the appropriate labor, burden, and tooling costs can be summarized on the estimate form (*Figure 6-2*).

Standard data compiled from time studies of previous plant operations were used for estimating the handling and machine times in this estimate. *Table 6-1* gives examples of these data.

Hole *Y* is the 1/4 in. diameter tooling hole on the centerline of the two bushing holes (see *Figure 6-1*). Operation 010 calls for this hole to be reamed on machine 07-015. This machine number code indicates that the operation is to be performed on a single-spindle drilling machine in the drilling department (No. 07).

The time study operation sheet for Operation 010 is shown in *Figure 6-3*. The data entered on this sheet were taken from *Table 6-1* and *Table 6-2*. Assuming that the chips are brushed from the machine table every third piece, the time required for Work Act No. 4 (see *Figure 6-3*) is divided by 3; thus a time of .010

PART NAME Bracket, cam drive PART NO 790-3X
ENG MEMO NO ______ SHEET 1 OF 1 LOT SIZE ______ DATE 6/17/88
LABOR $ 1.608 MAT'L $ 1.227 TOTAL L&M $ 2.835
TOOL DESIGN $ 1641 TOOLROOM $ 7806 DIES $ 5430 TOTAL TOOLS $ 14877

OPER	DEPT	LC	OPER OR MAT'L DESCRIPTION	MAT'L QUAN	MAT'L COST	P C	LABOR STD	L G C	L&B COST	NEW TOOL DESCRIPTION	TOOL COST
001	30	R	Purchase complete								
			to B/P except machining								
			& Assy. (1) BL-790-3	1.000	$.660					Die Cost ($5430)	
010	07	05	Ream "Y"			E	.149	6	$.036	No new tools	
020	06	10	Straddle Mill H & E 125			E	.550	6	.149	Milling fixture	825.00
										(2) Side milling Cutters	375.00
										Flush Pin GA	384.00
										Snap Gage	60.00
030	18	51	Burr H & E			E	.430	7	.090	Standard Tools	
040	14	08	Bore G & U & chmf.			E	1.584	5	.474	Boring Fixture	1260.00
										Set Master	135.00
										(2) Boring Bars }	243.00
										(4) Nibs	
050	07		Drill-C'Bore-Drill etc.			E	2.091	6	.501	Drill Jig	1074.00
										.339 C'Bore	39.00
										½ C'Bore	39.00
										C'Bore Fixture	84.00
060	06	09	Mill-M-L-S 125			E	.299	6	.081	Fixture	642.00
										Cutter	60.00
										Flush Pin Gage	153.00
										Centrality Ga. & Feeler	1143.00
070	01	19	Wash				—		—		
080	09	07	Burr Complete			E	.201	9	.042	No new tools	
090	32	N	Inspect			—	—	—		—	
100	21	A05	Assemble -AK-				.195		.042		
			790-125	1.000	.111					Fixture	138.00
110	21A	03	Assemble AE & AF				.460		.096	Fixture & Studs	1050.00
			BU-675	2000	.228						
120	21A	02	Assemble AA & AD				.460		.096	Studs	81.00
			BU-675	2000	.228						
130	21	AN	Inspect Final								
					$1.227				$1.608		$7806.00
										Die Cost	5430.00
										Tool Design	1641.00
										Total tools	$ 14877

Figure 6-2. Cost estimate for the bracket assembly.

min. per piece is entered on the sheet. The total floor-to-floor time is estimated as .149 min.

The labor and burden rate per minute for department No. 07 is $.24. The cost per piece is .149 min. x .24/min = $.036 which is entered in the "L & B (labor and burden) Cost" column of the estimate form (*Figure 6-2*) for Operation 010.

Operation 020 calls for straddle milling surfaces H and E. The process sheets stipulate that the part is to be milled in a fixture by 8-in.-diameter side milling cutters on a milling machine. The spindle speeds and table feeds for this machine are given in *Table 6-3*. The estimator notes that a small duplex mill would be a better machine to use. However, this machine is loaded to capacity and is not available.

For this operation, standard data are used to estimate the handling time only.

Table 6-1. Standard Data for Time Study.

Work Act Description	*Weight (lbs.)*	*Standard Time (min.)*
Tote box to machine—counting	.00– 1.00	.030
	1.01– 2.00	.035
	2.01– 3.00	.045
	3.01– 4.50	.050
Piece in and out of jig—place	.00– .50	.099
	.50– 3.00	.126
	3.00– 5.00	.157
Piece in and out of jig—locate	.00– .50	.132
	.51– 3.00	.168
	3.01– 5.00	.193
Piece on and off block or nest	.00– 1.00	.045
	1.01– 2.00	.079
	2.01– 3.00	.103
Tighten and loosen handwheel—all types spin on and off	....	.079
Open and close hinged jig leaf:		
one	....	.043
two	....	.064
Tighten and loosen—T wrench:		
one nut	....	.189
two nuts	....	.285
Tighten and loosen thumbscrew	....	.096
Open and close sliding clamp	....	.040
Up and down spindle:		
full travel	....	.067
normal travel	....	.041
less than ½ in. travel	....	.020
Change tool—quick change chuck	....	.103
Oil tap with brush or up can	....	.049
Place and remove bushing—each	....	.069
Wash jig with soda water	....	.070
Wash jig with nozzle	....	.070
Brush off table	....	.189
Gaging:		
threaded gage go—no go	.00– .37	.250
	.38– .74	.380
scale	....	.110
feeler gage	....	.110
snap gage	....	.110
gage—counter sink with screw	....	.125
Jig handling elements:		
up to first spindle and position	.00– 4.00	.040
	4.01–25.00	.066
	26.00–40.00	.086
Shift—hole to hole	.00– 4.00	.020
	4.01–25.00	.030
	26.00–40.00	.050
Away from last spindle	.00– 4.00	.030
	4.01–25.00	.046
	26.00–40.00	.058

TIME STUDY OPERATION SHEET

DEPT. 07-015 DATE 6/17/88 MAT'L DES Alum. Die Casting

PART NO. 790-3X NAME Bracket cam-drive

OPER. NO. 010 TYPE Ream

MACHINE NO. TYPE Delta Drill Press

TOOLS Standard holding block SPEED FEED Hand

NO.	DESCRIPTION OF WORK ACT.	OCCURRENCE	STD. TIME, MIN.	TIME ALLOWED, MIN.
1	Piece from tote box to	1:1	0.030	0.030
	machine and count			
	(0 to 1 lb.)			
2	Piece on and off block	1:1	0.045	0.045
	or rest			
3	Up & down spindle	1:1	0.020	0.020
	(less than 1/2" travel)			
4	Clean block, 3 places	1:3	0.030	0.010
5	Plug gage	1:2	0.010	0.005
		Total handling time		0.110
	Machining time			
6	Ream (0.2505)	0.140 in. @	0.105 in./min.	0.015
		overtravel	0.015	0.015
				0.030
	From Table 6-2 min.	time allowance is		0.039
			Total time	0.149

Figure 6-3. Time study operation sheet for Operation 010.

The work acts are defined in a manner similar to that used for Operation 010. The estimated handling time is .275 min.

The machine time is estimated as follows. Using a recommended 800 sfpm., the required rpm. of the spindle is determined by sfpm/cutter perimeter. Thus, $800/\pi \times 8/12 = 384$ rpm. From *Table 6-3*, the nearest spindle speed for the machine is 380 rpm. A feed of .005 in. per tooth is selected for the operation. A cutting tool catalog reveals that an 8-in.-diameter HSS side milling cutter has 26 teeth. With these data, the appropriate formula is used to determine the optimum feed in inches per minute for the operation:

$$\text{rpm.} \times \text{Number of Teeth} \times \text{Feed per Tooth} = \text{Feed (in/min)}$$
$$380 \times 26 \times .005 = 49.4 \text{ in/min}$$

Table 6-2. Standard Data for Drilling, Reaming, and Tapping Aluminum.

	Drilling		*Tapping*	
Diameter of Tool (in.)	*Approach of Drill Point (min.)*	*Standard Time (min/in)**	*Tap Size*	*Standard Time (min/in)*‡*
3/32	.028	.080	2–56	.09
1/8	.037	.090	3–48 and 4–48	.08
5/32	.047	.100	4–40	.07
3/16	.056	.115	5–44	.08
7/32	.066	.125	5–40	.07
1/4	.075	.130	6–40	.08
9/32	.084	.135	6–32	.06
5/16	.094	.140	8–36	.08
11/32	.103	.145	8–32	.07
3/8	.113	.150	10–32	.09
13/32	.122	.155	10–24	.07
7/16	.131	.160	12–28	.09
15/32	.141	.165	12–24	.08
1/2	.150	.170	1/4–28	.10
17/32	.160	.175	1/4–20	.07
9/16	.169	.180	5/16–24	.11
5/8	.188	.185	5/16–18	.08
			3/8–24	.14
			3/8–16	.09
			7/16–20	.13
	***Reaming**†**			
3/32– 9/64	. . . .	.075	7/16–14	.09
5/32–13/64	. . . .	.090	1/2–20	.15
7/32–17/64	. . . .	.105	1/2–13	.10
9/32– 3/8	. . . .	.120		
13/32– 1/2	. . . .	.135		

*Use .039 standard minute as a minimum time.
†Add a constant of .015 standard minute to the reaming times for overtravel of the reamer.
‡Add the tap diameter to the length of the tapped hole to obtain total tool travel.

Referring to *Table 6-3*, the maximum feed rate is 30 in/min. The length of cut is 2 3/8 in. plus 1/8 in. overtravel, giving a total of 2 1/2 in.

Next, an allowance must be made for cutter approach (the distance the work must travel into the cutter before the cutter is at the full depth of cut):

$$\text{Approach} = \sqrt{r^2-(r-c)^2}$$

Where: c = depth of cut (in.)
r = cutter radius (in.)

Table 6-3. Data for Milling Machine.*

Spindle Speeds (rpm.)				*Table Feeds (ipr.)*			
50	126	302	760	$^3/_4$	2	$5^3/_8$	14
63	159	380	955	1	$2^1/_2$	7	18
79	200	475	1200	$1^1/_4$	$3^1/_4$	$8^7/_8$	23
100	250	600	1500	$1^5/_8$	$4^1/_4$	11	30

*Machine and tool manufacturers differ regarding optimum speeds and feeds; the ones shown here are illustrative only and are not recommendations.

Using a depth of cut of 1.4 in., the approach is calculated to be 3.04 in. With an approximate length of cut of 2.50 in. plus a 3.04 in. approach, the table travel is 5.54 in. The machine time is calculated by dividing the table travel by the feed per inches. Thus 5.54 in. ÷ 30 in/min = .185 min.

An allowance must also be made for rapid machine table traverse. In this case .030 min. is needed for rapid approach and .060 min. for rapid return. Adding the cutting time of .185 min. and the rapid traverse time of .090 min. gives a total time of .275 min.

The total man machine time for Operation 020 is .275 min. handling time plus .275 min. machine time, or .550 min. per piece.

The labor and burden rate for the milling department is $.27 per minute. Thus, the cost per piece is .550 min. x $.27 per min. = $.149. These costs are entered on the estimate form (*Figure 6-2*).

The remaining operations, because of their number, will be summarized in *Table 6-4* rather than presented in detail. The cost for each operation is entered on the estimating form (*Figure 6-2*).

TOTAL MANUFACTURING COST

When all the manufacturing operations are entered on the estimate form (*Figure 6-2*) with their corresponding cost, these costs are added to arrive at a material cost per unit, a labor and burden cost per unit, and a total tooling cost.

The total cost of manufacturing the cam drive bracket in *Figure 6-1* can be summarized as follows:

Material, cost/unit	$1.227
Labor and burden cost/unit	1.608
Total material and L & B/unit	2.835

Table 6-4. Summary of In-Plant Manufacturing Operations and Their Costs.

Operation Number	*Description*	*Time (min.)*	*Multiplied by L & B ($)*	*Estimated Cost*
001	purchased item	....	....	....
030	burr *H* and *E*	.430	.27	.0301
040	bore *G* and *U*, chamfer *AG* and *B*	1.584	.30	.1584
050	drill, counter bore, etc.	2.091	.24	.16728
060	mill M-L-S	.299	.27	.02691
070	wash*	....	....	no charge*
080	burr complete	.201	.21	.01407
090	inspect*	....	....	no charge*
100	assemble *AK*	.195	.21	.01365
110	assemble *AE* and *AF*	.460	.21	.03220
120	assemble *AA* and *AC*	.460	.21	.03220
130	final inspection*	....	....	no charge*

*In this company wash department, inspection, trucking, receiving, and shipping costs are considered as overhead. This practice is not universal and varies greatly from company to company.

Tooling:	
Die cast die	$5,430
Fixtures, cutting tool, and gages	7,806
Tool design	1,641
Total tooling cost	$14,877

In order to assign the tooling cost to individual units, the production quantity must be known. Assuming a lot size of 2,000 units, the tooling cost per unit is calculated as follows:

Material, labor, and burden per unit	$2.835
Lot size	x 2000
Total material, labor, and burden	$5,670
Total tooling cost	+ 14,877
Total costs	$20,547

When the total cost of $20,547 is divided by the number of units produced (2,000) the total cost per unit is $10.27. The total cost per unit declines as the production quantity increases and tooling cost is absorbed by more units. Total cost per unit for a production quantity of 3,000, for example, would be $7.80 for 5,000 units, the unit cost decreases to $5.82.

Overhead and Profit

Allowances are made for general and administrative expenses (overhead) and profit before a price is quoted to the customer. The estimating department may make these calculations based on predetermined rates, but in most companies the estimating department forwards the cost estimate to the pricing committee to determine the final price.

7

ESTIMATING MACHINING COSTS FOR AN ALUMINUM FORGING

Assume that a customer has requested a price quotation on the manufacture and delivery of 2,000 completed forged aluminum housings. An engineering drawing (*Figure 7-1*) and complete blueprint (not shown) accompanied the request. The customer's schedule specifies initial delivery of 500 parts within eight months, with delivery of the remaining 1,500 parts in three lots at three-month intervals. Because the company receiving the cost request does not have forging capabilities, it purchases rough forgings on orders of this type and machines them to specifications.

Preparing the Estimate

In order to give an accurate price quotation, the company prepares a complete cost estimate. The steps followed are:

1. preliminary screening,
2. gathering information,
3. compiling the data,
4. extending the data by adding costs, and
5. establishing the selling price.

Preliminary Screening

The sales department studies the request in terms of profitability, plant capabilities, and scheduling to determine whether to submit a quotation. The request meets these criteria, and the sales department sends a cost estimate request to the estimating coordinator, specifying an estimate deadline.

Gathering Information

Upon receiving the request, the estimating coordinator analyzes it for necessary information, and requests certain data from other departments. These departments are:

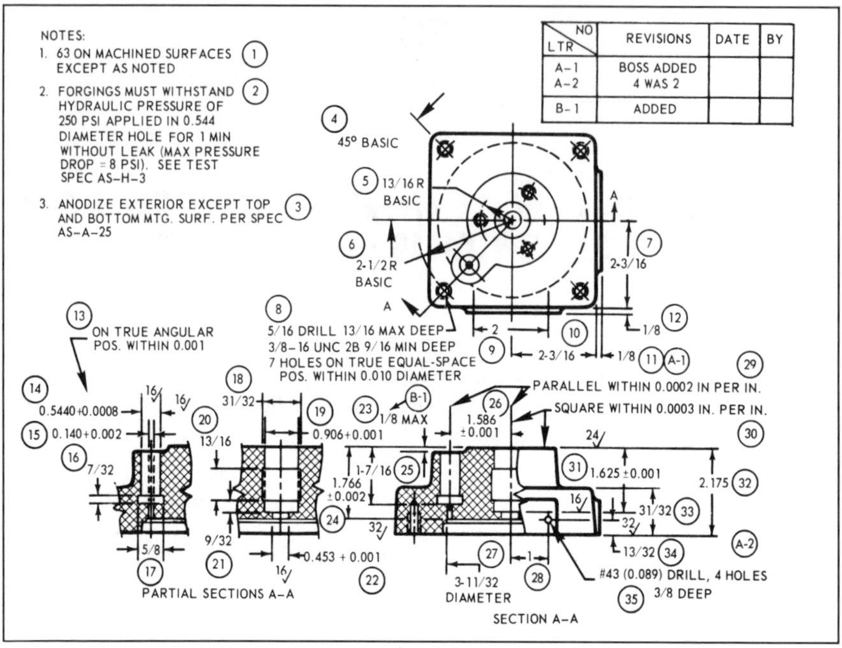

Figure 7-1. Forged aluminum housing.

1. The manufacturing engineering department, which has knowledge of practical methods, proven equipment, and realistic machine times. This department determines the manufacturing processes and tooling necessary to produce the part.
2. The purchasing department which obtains prices on forgings and other items listed for outside purchase.
3. The production control department which advises the estimating department whether the customer's specified delivery dates can be met without upsetting existing production schedules. This information can be furnished only after the manufacturing plan has been established and machine times calculated.

COMPILING THE DATA

As the groups listed above forward information, the estimating coordinator enters the data on a cost estimate form.

The estimate is prepared in duplicate; a "reference" copy containing all information except costs, and an "action" copy on which cost data are entered.

The reference copy is available to any interested personnel, but the action copy is distributed on a "need-to-know" basis only.

Figure 7-2 shows the first page of the cost estimate. At this point in the preparation of the estimate, only the operation number, description, machine name, list of tools, and the notation of standard tools would be entered on the form.

The labor grades and machine times, based on standard data collected and maintained by the estimating department, are entered in their respective columns. *Figure 7-3* shows a typical form for applying standard data to a turret lathe for Operation 60. On the front side of the form (*Figure 7-3* top) the estimator lists all the machine manipulations normally encountered in the appropriate columns. The circled items are those relating to the component affected by this operation.

The reverse side, *Figure 7-3* bottom, contains space for calculating the time for variables, plus applicable standard data. This side is completed first, starting with the entries for tool station number, machine operation, and tool material. Diameters of cuts are entered in column A. Values shown in surface feet per minute (sfpm.) in column B are based on standard data for the pertinent material available from handbooks. In column C, the left hand figures are derived from the formula at the head of the column, and those to the right are machine speeds for the applicable machine. Similarly, the left-hand figures in column D represent standard suggested feeds, while those to the right are actual machine feeds.

The values for "length of cut" include an arbitrary amount for "approach," since the operator cannot be expected to advance the tool by hand and engage the automatic feed exactly at the point of contact with the work. In the "Machine Time" column, internal (concurrent) cuts are circled to indicate that they are not to be included in the total machine time for the piece.

Percentage allowances for tool sharpening and in-process gaging are found in the standard data table at the top of the sheet and are entered in their respective columns. These figures are based on AISI B1113 material and, like all other standard data used in this estimate, have been found by the company through its studies to represent a norm for its particular operations.

After totals for the last three columns are entered, the allowance figures are adjusted to suit the material being cut. The forging's free-machining aluminum material wears cutting edges 55% less than AISI B1113, with a proportionate reduction in the need for tool inspection, resulting in the reduced allowances shown. These are added to constant personal and machine adjustment values to obtain a percentage value for all allowances.

On the front side of the form, all applicable units of the tabulated elements are encircled, the number of their occurrences are entered, and the two are multiplied. The results, representing the actual accountable time for these elements, are entered in the last column and added. To this sum is added the total machine time, entered from the reverse side, giving a value for total machine manipulation and machining time. Multiplying this by the total allowance percentage

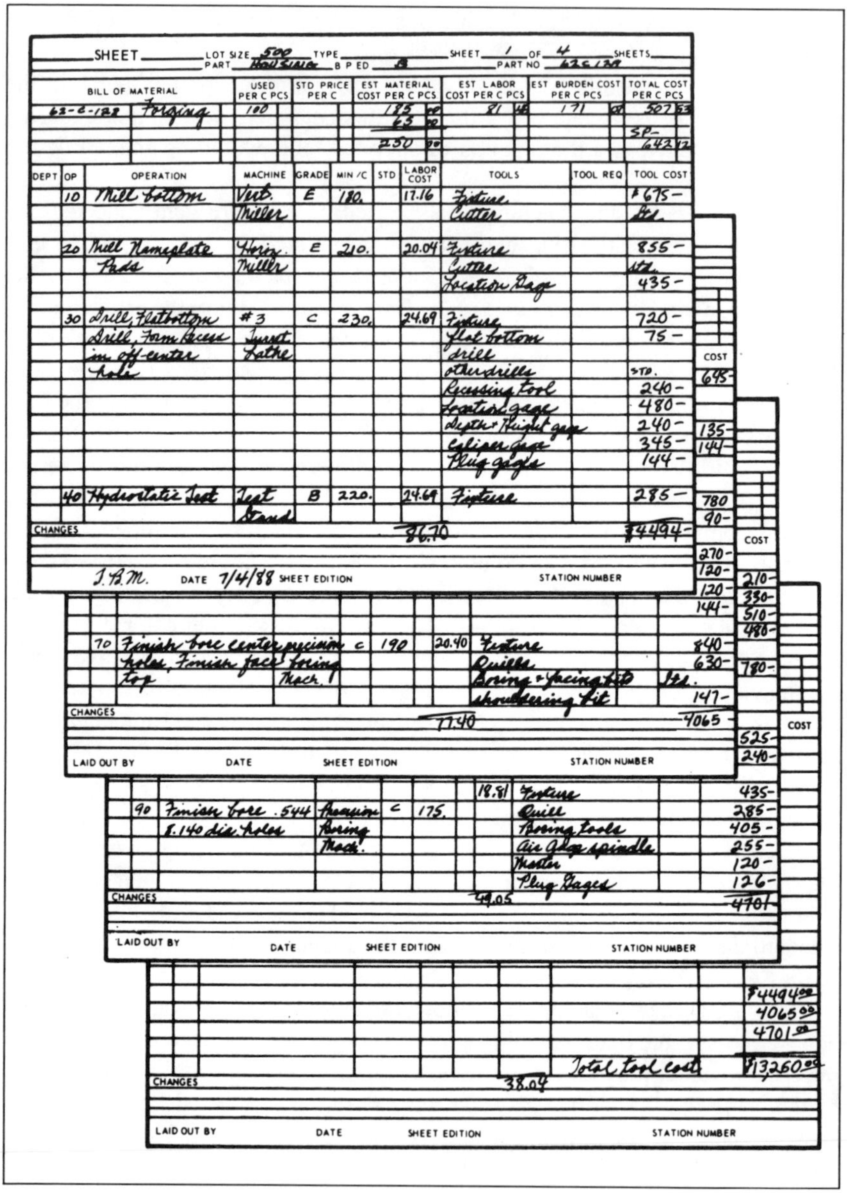

Figure 7-2. Estimate sheets for forged aluminum housing.

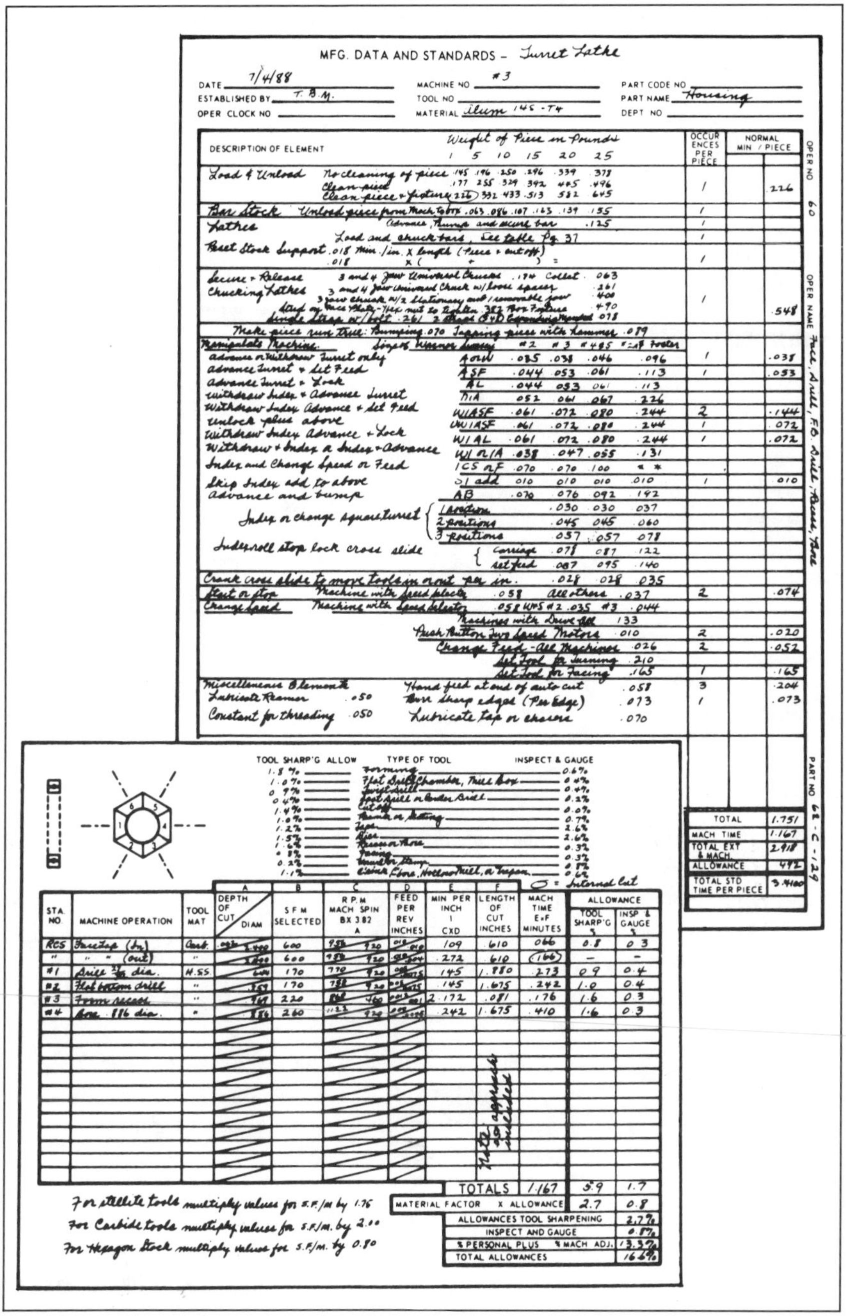

MFG. DATA AND STANDARDS – Turret Lathe

DATE 7/4/88 | MACHINE NO #3 | PART CODE NO
ESTABLISHED BY T. B. M. | TOOL NO | PART NAME Housing
OPER CLOCK NO | MATERIAL Alum 145-T4 | DEPT NO

OPER NO 60 | OPER NAME Face, Drill, F.B. Drill, Recess, Bore | PART NO 68-C-129

DESCRIPTION OF ELEMENT — Weight of Piece in Pounds: 1, 5, 10, 15, 20, 25	OCCURENCES PER PIECE	NORMAL MIN / PIECE
Load & Unload — No cleaning of piece .145 .196 .250 .296 .339 .378; Clean piece .177 .255 .329 .392 .445 .496; Clean piece + fixture .226 .332 .433 .513 .582 .645	1	.226
Bar Stock — Unload piece from Mach to box .063 .086 .107 .123 .139 .155	1	
Lathes — Advance, Bump and secure bar .125	1	
Load and chuck bars, See table Pg. 37	1	
Reset Stock Support .018 Min./in. X length (Piece + cut off) .018 X (+) =	1	
Secure + Release Chucking Lathes — 3 and 4 Jaw Universal Chucks .174 Collet .063; 3 and 4 Jaw Universal Chuck w/loose spacer .261; 3 jaw chuck w/2 stationary and 1 removable jaw .400; Stud on Face Plate – Hex nut to tighten .382 Box Fixture .490; Single Strap w/bolt .261 2 Straps (S4D) Expanding Mandrel .078	1	.548
Make piece run true: Bumping .070 Tapping piece with hammer .089		
Manipulate Machine. Sizes of Warner Swasey #2 #3 #4&5 #2-1A Foster		
advance or Withdraw Turret only — A or W .035 .038 .046 .096	1	.038
advance Turret + Set Feed — ASF .044 .053 .061 .113	1	.053
advance Turret + Lock — AL .044 .053 .061 .113		
withdraw Index + Advance Turret — WIA .052 .061 .067 .226		
Withdraw Index Advance + Set Feed — W/ASF .061 .072 .080 .244	2	.144
Unlock plus above — UW/ASF .061 .072 .080 .244	1	.072
Withdraw Index Advance + Lock — W/AL .061 .072 .080 .244	1	.072
Withdraw + Index or Index + Advance — WI or IA .038 .047 .055 .131		
Index and Change Speed or Feed — ICS or F .070 .070 .100 * *		
Skip Index add to above — SI add .010 .010 .010 .010	1	.010
advance and bump — AB .070 .076 .092 .192		
Index or change square turret — 1 position .030 .030 .037; 2 positions .045 .045 .060; 3 positions .057 .057 .078		
Index roll stop lock cross slide — Carriage .078 .087 .122; set feed .087 .095 .140		
Crank cross slide to move tools in or out per in. .028 .028 .035		
Start or stop — Machine with speed selector .058 All others .037	2	.074
Change Speed — Machine with Speed Selector .058 W&S #2 .035 #3 .044		
Machines with Drive All .133		
Push Button Two Speed Motors .010	2	.020
Change Feed – All Machines .026	2	.052
Set Tool for Turning .210		
Set Tool for Facing .165	1	.165
Miscellaneous Elements — Hand feed at end of auto cut .058	3	.204
Lubricate Reamer .050 — Burr sharp edges (Per Edge) .073	1	.073
Constant for threading .050 — Lubricate tap or chasers .070		

TOTAL	1.751
MACH TIME	1.167
TOTAL EXT & MACH.	2.918
ALLOWANCE	.492
TOTAL STD TIME PER PIECE	3.4100

TOOL SHARP'G ALLOW	TYPE OF TOOL	INSPECT & GAUGE
1.8%	Forming	0.6%
1.0%	Flat Drill Chamber, Mill Box	0.4%
0.9%	Twist Drill	0.4%
0.4%	Spot Drill or Center Drill	0.2%
1.4%	Cut off	0.0%
1.0%	Turn or Sizing	0.7%
1.2%	Taps	2.6%
1.5%	Dies	2.6%
1.6%	Ream or Bore	0.3%
.8%	Facing	0.3%
0.2%	Knurl or Stamp	0.8%
1.1%	C'sink, C'bore, Hollow Mill, or Trepan	0.6%

◯ = Internal Cut

STA. NO.	MACHINE OPERATION	TOOL MAT	A DEPTH OF CUT / DIAM	B SFM SELECTED	C RPM MACH SPIN BX 382 A	D FEED PER REV INCHES	E MIN PER INCH 1 CXD	F LENGTH OF CUT INCHES	MACH TIME E×F MINUTES	ALLOWANCE TOOL SHARP'G %	ALLOWANCE INSP & GAUGE %
RCS	Face Top (In)	Carb.	.032 / 3.400	600	955 / 920	.010 / .010	109	.610	066	0.8	0.3
"	" " (out)	"	3.400	600	955 / 920	.010 / .004	.272	.610	(.166)	–	–
#1	Drill 37/64 dia.	H.S.S.	.604	170	770 / 920	.008 / .0075	.145	1.880	.273	0.9	0.4
#2	Flat bottom drill	"	.757	170	758 / 920	.008 / .0075	.145	1.675	.242	1.0	0.4
#3	Form recess	"	.967	220	868 / 460	.0012 / .001	2.172	.081	.176	1.6	0.3
#4	Bore .886 dia.	"	.886	260	1122 / 920	.005 / .0045	.242	1.675	.410	1.6	0.3

TOTALS	1.167	5.9	1.7
MATERIAL FACTOR X ALLOWANCE		2.7	0.8
ALLOWANCES TOOL SHARPENING			2.7%
INSPECT AND GAUGE			0.8%
% PERSONAL PLUS % MACH ADJ.			13.3%
TOTAL ALLOWANCES			16.6%

For stellite tools multiply values for S.F./M by 1.76
For Carbide tools multiply values for S.F./M. by 2.00
For Hexagon Stock multiply values for S.F./M. by 0.80

Figure 7-3. Standard data for turret lathe.

Table 7-1. Derivation of Selling Price for Aluminum Forgings in Lots of 100.

Materials			
Blank forgings @ $5.55 × 100 =	$555		
Anodizing = $195/100 pieces +	195		
Total Material Cost	$750		$ 750.00
Labor			
Direct labor for all machining and ancillary operations		$ 244.38	244.38
Standard burden rate		×210%	
Burden Cost		$ 513.21	513.21
MLB (Sum of Materials, Labor and Burden)			$1507.59
General and Administrative Factor (15%)			
	MLB $1507.59		
	×. 15		226.14
	$226.14	Total Cost	$1733.73
Profit Percentage (Selling Price = Total Cost / 90% (100% − 10% profit))			
		$1733.73 / .90	= $1926.37

gives the allowance value in minutes, which is added to the last previous value to arrive at the total time per piece for the operation.

COST EXTENSIONS

When all job grades and machine times have been entered, the reference copy of the estimate is retained by the estimator and the action copy is forwarded to the accounting department (separate from the estimating department in this company). The cost department enters cost extensions, computing them on the basis of job grades and machine times established by the estimating department. A summary of the extensions, detailed in the following sections, is given in *Table 7-1*.

Typical rates used for eight classes of labor are shown in *Table 7-2*. To facilitate calculation, these rates are for 100 min. rather than per hour. Thus, the direct labor cost for Operation 10, for example, is found by multiplying the minutes of machine time (180) by the Class E rate ($9.54) to arrive at a cost of $17.16 per 100 pieces.

A factory burden rate is used to cover such miscellaneous operations as handling, inspection, engineering time, machine setup time, production starting costs, standard cutting tools, etc., when these are not itemized in the estimate. Since unproductive costs vary by department, the use of separate burden percentages is advisable, although some companies prefer to apply a standard over-

Table 7-2. Typical Labor Rates per 100 Minutes.

Job Grade	*Rate*
A	$11.82
B	11.28
C	10.74
D	10.23
E	9.54
F	9.45
G	9.12
H	$ 8.82

all figure. Using the latter approach, the sum of the direct labor costs for all machining and ancillary operations performed on the aluminum forging within the plant ($244.38) is multiplied by a standard burden rate of 210%, resulting in a burden cost of ($513.21).

The purchasing department furnishes information to the cost department showing that blank forgings will cost $5.55 each, and that the charge for anodizing by an outside supplier will be $195 per 100 pieces. As an expedient, these two items are grouped under "Materials" for a total of $750 per 100. Thus the material, labor, and burden (MLB) sum will be $1,507.59 per 100.

Selling Price

Next the estimate goes to the accounting department which establishes final selling price. Percentages are added for general and administrative costs (G and A) and for profit. These vary from one company to another, but the normal factors are 15 and 10%, respectively.

First, the G and A allowance is applied by multiplying the MLB sum by this company's figure of 15%, resulting in a G and A cost of $226.14. Adding this to the MLB amount gives a total cost of $1,733.73.

Profit

To apply profit (10%) for the selling price, this formula is used:

$$\text{Selling Price} = \frac{\text{Total cost}}{.90}$$

The resulting selling price for the aluminum housing is $1,926.36 per 100 pieces, or $19.26 per piece.

Customer Quotation

After the selling price and applicable discount allowances are entered on the action copy of the estimate, the action copy goes to the sales department, and sales prepares a formal proposal for the customer. The proposal indicates the company's intent to meet requested quantity and delivery specifications, or may suggest alternatives deemed necessary, or to the customer's advantage. It also shows the price of the article (usually per 100 pieces) with applicable discounts, the cost of tooling if quoted separately, and a payment schedule. Prices are usually quoted f.o.b. the manufacturer's address but, if not, cost and type of transportation are also specified.

8

SCREW MACHINE COST ESTIMATING

Parts made on automatic screw machines require complicated calculations to compute machine time. This example explains the steps necessary to derive proper machine times and determine other necessary manufacturing costs for the two parts shown in *Figure 8-1*.

PARTS ANALYSIS

At first glance, the two parts in *Figure 8-1* seem identical except for shank length. However, closer analysis shows the short pin, view *a* has a tolerance of $\pm.002$ in. on the .312-in.-diameter, whereas the long pin, view *b*, has a tolerance of $^{+.000}_{-.001}$ -in. on the same diameter.

Raw Stock

The $\pm.002$-in. tolerance on the short pin will permit the use of mill run cold-drawn steel. To maintain the $^{+.000}_{-.001}$-in. tolerance of the longer pin, it will be necessary to use 21/64-in.-diameter stock and box turn or cross-slide form the .312-in.-diameter. Larger-diameter stock also should be used on parts with high concentricity and straightness requirements. However, the larger-diameter stock may necessitate using a larger machine.

Processing Requirements

Further study of the part in view *b* indicates a slenderness or shank length-to-diameter ratio of 6.25:1. When forming a diameter using cross slide tools, this ratio should not normally exceed 3:1. As a result, the shank on part *b* of *Figure 8-1* must be turned with a turret tool instead of forming with a cross slide tool. To produce a required tolerance of $\pm.001$ in. and the surface finish of 40 microin., a rough and finish cut will be required.

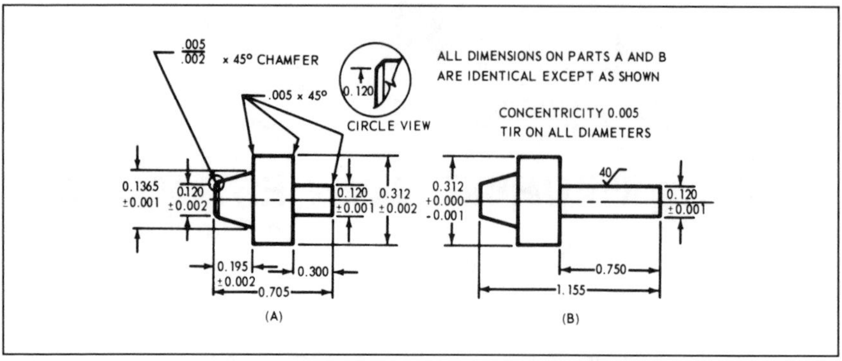

Figure 8-1. Two pins made on an automatic screw machine.

Short Pin

The manufacturing costs associated with producing the short pin are estimated and summarized on the "Machining Estimate" form in *Figure 8-2*. The top portion develops labor and burden costs, while the bottom lists material, tooling, general and administrative costs.

Tool Layout

The complete list of tools required for this part and their hypothetical costs are:

5/16-in.-diameter collet	$ 45.00
5/16-in.-diameter feed finger	24.00
Stock stop for turret	10.50
Front cross-slide circular form tool holder	45.00
Rear cross-slide circular form tool holder	45.00
Front cross-slide circular form tool	60.00
Rear cross-slide circular form tool	48.00
Set of cams consisting of front cross-slide cam, rear cross-slide cal and turret slide cam	180.00
	$457.50

This is a complete tool estimate. All items except the circular form tools and cams, however, are usually purchased with the machine. Only the cost of these latter tools ($288) is included in the estimate in *Figure 8-2*.

A sketch of the short pin and an outline of the tools used to machine it are shown in *Figure 8-3*. The front slide tool *A* forms the tapered portion, the

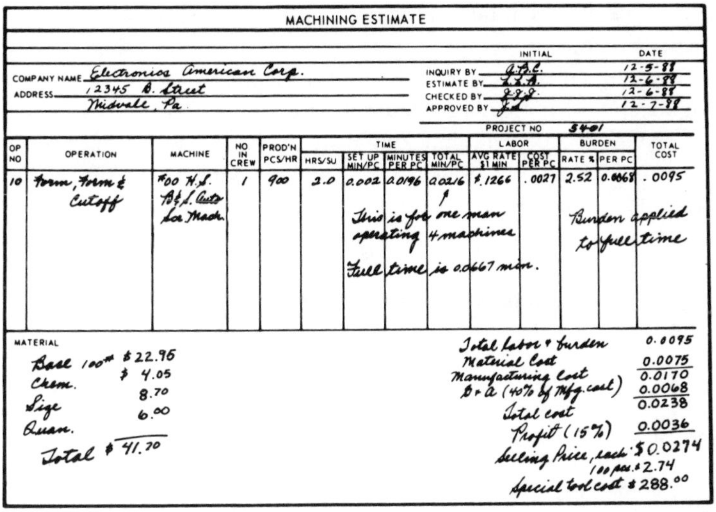

MACHINING ESTIMATE

COMPANY NAME Electronics American Corp.
ADDRESS 12345 B. Street
Midvale, Pa.

	INITIAL	DATE
INQUIRY BY	A.B.C.	12-5-88
ESTIMATE BY	L.L.A.	12-6-88
CHECKED BY	J.J.J.	12-6-88
APPROVED BY	[illegible]	12-7-88

PROJECT NO 5401

OP NO	OPERATION	MACHINE	NO IN CREW	PROD'N PCS/HR	TIME HRS/SU	TIME SET UP MIN/PC	TIME MINUTES PER PC	TIME TOTAL MIN/PC	LABOR AVG RATE $1 MIN	LABOR COST PER PC	BURDEN RATE %	BURDEN PER PC	TOTAL COST
10	Form, Form & Cutoff	#00 H.S. B&S Auto Scr Mach.	1	900	2.0	0.002	0.0196	0.0216	$.1266	.0027	2.52	0.0068	.0095

This is for one man operating 4 machines
Full time is 0.0667 min.
Burden applied to full time

MATERIAL
Base 100# $22.95
Chem. $ 4.05
Size 8.70
Quan. 6.00
Total $ 41.70

Total labor + burden	0.0095
Material Cost	0.0075
Manufacturing Cost	0.0170
G + A (40% of Mfg. cost)	0.0068
Total cost	0.0238
Profit (15%)	0.0036
Selling Price, each	$0.0274
100 pcs.	$2.74
Special tool cost	$288.00

Figure 8-2. Machining estimate for short pin.

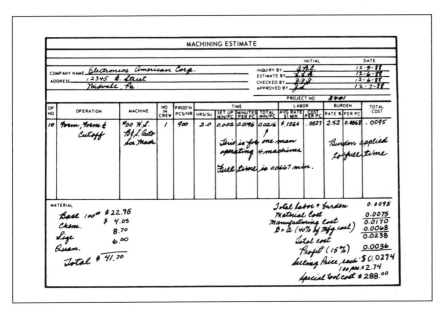

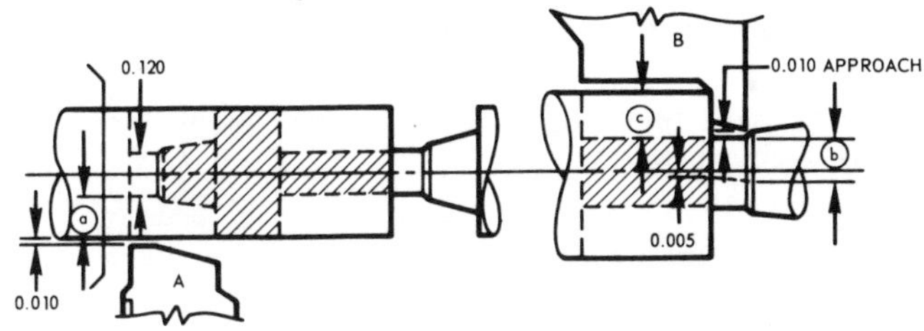

Figure 8-3. Tool layout for workpiece A in *Figure 8-1.*

chamfer on the left-hand side of the large diameter, and necks the cutoff area to a .120-in.-diameter. The rear slide tool *B* forms the .120-in.-diameter shank and cuts off the previously formed part.

Machine Time

Determining the machine time necessary to fabricate this part requires the following steps:

1. Determine the proper spindle speed to machine the specified material.
2. Figure the throws of the cam lobes and the spindle revolutions required for the cutting operations.
3. Determine which operations can be overlapped.
4. Figure spindle revolutions required for the nonproductive operations such as feeding of stock and indexing of the turret.
5. Determine operation sequence by the following procedure: (a) provide clearance for cross-slide and turret tools, (b) find total estimated spindle revolutions required to finish the piece and select actual revolutions available with regular change gears that are nearest to the estimated number, and (c) adjust estimated spindle revolutions for each operation so that the total will equal the actual number available on the machine.

Speeds and Feeds

The recommended speeds for machining steels are given in *Table 8-1*. From this table the cutting speed for AISI C1213 or B1113 steels is found to be 225 sfpm. From a table of standard data listing rpm.'s for cutting speeds and diameters, it can be surmised that a 5/16-in.-diameter workpiece rotating at 225 sfpm. has an approximate rpm. of 2,750. Referring to the production table for the No. 00 automatic screw machine (*Table 8-2*), the selected speed would be 3,085 rpm. as the nearest speed available to the suggested speed of 2,750 rpm.

The suggested speeds for standard tools on single-spindle screw machines are given in *Table 8-3*. Under Column E, a form tool 1/4 to 3/8 in. wide has a suggested feed of .0009 ipr. A circular cutoff tool has a feed of .0013 ipr. Since a forming operation is performed with the cutoff operation, the forming tool feed of .0009 ipr. will apply.

The number of spindle revolutions for each cutting tool is estimated as follows:

For tool *A*, the dimension *a* must be calculated.

Stock diameter	.312 in.
Formed diameter	−.120 in.
Difference is 2*a*	.192 in.
Dimension *a* is	−.096 in.
	.096 in.
Approach	+.010 in.
Total tool travel	.106 in.

Spindle revolutions for tool *A* is .106 in. ÷ .0009 ipr. = 117.7 or 118 revolutions.

Table 8-1. Cutting Speed and Machinability Rating for Steels.

AISI No.	*SAE No.*	*Speed (sfpm.)*	*Relative Speed (per cent)**
C1145 annealed	1145	130	78
C1146	1146	115	70
C1151	1151	115	70
C1151 annealed	1151	135	81
C1211	....	155	94
C1212	....	165	100
C1213 (RSC 1213)	....	225	136
Carbon Steels			
C1008	1008	110	66
C1010 (light feeds)	1010	120	....
C1011 (light feeds)	....	120	....
C1012 (light feeds)	....	120	....
C1013 (light feeds)	....	120	....
C1015	1015	120	72
C1016	1016	130	78
C1017	1017	120	72
C1018	1018	130	78
C1019	1019	130	78
C1020	1020	120	72
C1021	1021	130	78
C1022	1022	130	78
C1023	....	125	76
C1024	....	110	66
C1025	1025	120	72
C1026	1026	130	78
C1027	1027	110	66
C1029	....	115	70
C1030	1030	115	70
C1031	....	115	70
C1033	1033	115	70
C1034	....	115	70
C1035	1035	115	70
C1036	1036	105	64
C1037	1037	115	70
C1038	1038	105	64
C1039	1039	105	64
C1040	1040	105	64
C1041	1041	95	57
C1042	1042	105	64
C1043	1043	95	57
C1045	1045	95	57
C1045 annealed	1045	120	72
C1046	1046	95	57
C1049	1049	90	54
C1050	1050	90	54
C1050 annealed	1050	115	70
C1051	....	90	54
C1052	1052	80	49
C1053	....	90	54
C1054	....	90	54
C1055 annealed	1055	85	51
C1059 annealed	....	85	51
C1060 annealed	1060	85	51
C1061 annealed	....	85	51
C1064 annealed	....	80	49
C1065 annealed	1065	80	49
C1066 annealed	....	80	49
C1069 annealed	....	80	49
C1070 annealed	1070	80	49
C1071 annealed	....	80	49
C1074 annealed	....	75	45
C1075 annealed	....	75	45
C1078 annealed	1078	75	45
C1080 annealed	1080	70	42
C1084 annealed	1084	70	42
C1085 annealed	1085	70	42
C1086 annealed	1086	70	42
C1090 annealed	1090	70	42
C1095 annealed	1095	70	42
B1010	....	130	78
Alloy Steels			
1330 annealed	1330	100	60
1335 annealed	1335	100	60
1340 annealed	1340	95	57
3140	3140	70	42
3140 annealed	3140	110	66
E3310 annealed	3310	85	51
4012	4012	130	78
4023	4023	130	78
4024	4024	130	78
4027	4027	110	66
4028	4028	120	72
4037 annealed	4037	120	72
4042 annealed	4042	115	70
4047 annealed	4047	110	66
4063 annealed	4063	85	51
4118	4118	130	78
4130 annealed	4130	120	72

Table 8-1. Cutting Speed and Machinability Rating for Steel *(Continued)*.

AISI No.	*SAE No.*	*Speed (sfpm.)*	*Relative Speed (per cent)**	*AISI No.*	*SAE No.*	*Speed (sfpm.)*	*Relative Speed (per cent)**
			Alloy Steels				
4135 annealed	....	115	70	8115	8115	115	70
4137 annealed	4137	115	70	8615	8615	115	70
4140 annealed	4140	110	66	8617	8617	110	66
4142 annealed	....	110	66	8620	8620	110	66
4145 annealed	4145	105	64	8622	8622	110	66
4147 annealed	....	105	64	8625	8625	105	64
4150 annealed	4150	100	60	8627	8627	105	64
4320 annealed	4320	100	60	8630 annealed	8630	120	72
4337 annealed	....	90	54	8637 annealed	8637	115	70
4340 annealed	4340	95	57	8640 annealed	8640	110	66
4422	4422	120	72	8642 annealed	8642	110	66
4427	4427	115	70	8645 annealed	8645	105	64
4520	4520	115	70	8650 annealed	8650	100	60
4615	4615	110	66	8655 annealed	8655	95	57
4617	....	110	66	8660 annealed	8660	90	54
4620	4620	110	66	8720	8720	110	66
4621	....	110	66	8735 annealed	8735	115	70
4718	4718	100	60	8740 annealed	8740	110	66
4720	4720	100	60	8742 annealed	....	110	66
4815 annealed	4815	85	51	8822	8822	105	64
4817 annealed	4817	80	49	9255 annealed	9255	90	54
4820 annealed	4820	80	49	9260 annealed	9260	85	51
5015	5015	130	78	9262 annealed	9262	80	49
5046 annealed	5046	115	70	E9310 annealed	9310	85	51
5115	5115	125	76	9840 annealed	9840	85	51
5120	5120	125	76	9850 annealed	9850	75	45
5130	5130	95	57	TS4150 annealed	....	100	60
5132 annealed	5132	120	72	TS14B35 annealed	....	120	72
5135 annealed	5135	120	72				
5140 annealed	5140	115	70	50B40 annealed	50B40	115	70
5145 annealed	5145	110	66	50B44 annealed	50B44	115	70
5147 annealed	5147	110	66	50B46 annealed	50B46	115	70
5150 annealed	5150	105	64	50B50 annealed	50B50	115	70
5155 annealed	5155	100	60	50B60 annealed	50B60	105	64
5160 annealed	5160	100	60	51B60 annealed	51B60	100	60
E50100 annealed	50100	70	42	81B45 annealed	81B45	110	66
E51100 annealed	51100	65	40	86B45 annealed	86B45	105	64
E52100 annealed	52100	65	40	94B15	94B15	115	70
6118	6118	110	66	94B17	94B17	110	66
6120	....	95	57	94B30 annealed	94B30	120	72
6150 annealed	6150	100	60	94B40 annealed	94B40	110	66

**Based on AISI B1112 as 100%.*

Table 8-2. Spindle Speeds and Revolutions per Piece for Laying Out Cams. *Production table, 240 rpm, driving shaft, No.00 automatic Screw Machine.*

High spindle speeds in combination with low speeds

200	5970	5035	4305	3715	3085	2580	2270	1915	1690	1425	1255	1050	870	750	640	540	450	*Ratio*
130*	2600	2190	1875	1615		1125	990	835	735	620	545		380	325	280	235	195	2.3
625*	2175	1835	1570	1355	1125		825	700	615	520		380	320	275	235	200	165	2.7
305*	1910	1615	1380	1190	990	825		615	540		400	335	280	240	205	175	145	3
945*	1615	1360	1165	1005	835	700	615			385	340	285	235	205	175	145	120	3.7
715*	1425	1200	1025	885	735	615	540			340	300	250	210	180	155	130	105	4.2
450	1200	1015	865	745	620	520		385	340		250	210	175	150	130	110	90	5
270	1055	890	760	655	545		400	340	300	250		185	155	135	115	96	80	5.6
065	885	745	635	550		385	335	285	250	210	185		130	110	95	80	67	6.7
885	735	620	530		380	320	280	235	210	175	155	130		92	79	67	55	8
765	635	535		395	325	275	240	205	180	150	135	110	92		68	58	48	9.3
650	540		390	335	280	235	205	175	155	130	115	95	79	68		49	41	11
550		385	330	285	235	200	175	145	130	110	96	80	67	58	49		34	13
	380	320	275	235	195	165	145	120	105	90	80	67	55	48	41	34		16

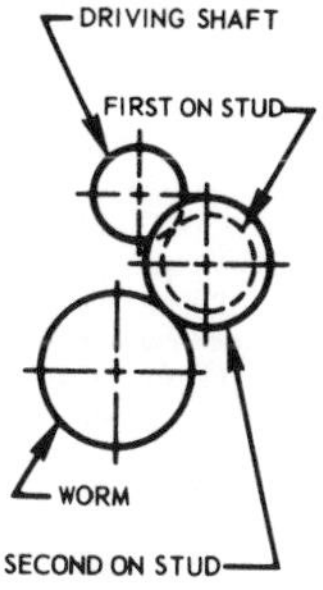

Revolutions at max speed to feed stock or index turret ¼ sec.

Revolutions of spindle at max speed to make one piece

30	25	21	18	15	13	11	9	8	7	6	5	4.4	3.6	3.1	2.7	2.3	1.9	*Time, sec.*	*Gross product per hr†*	*Gear on driving shaft*	*1st gear on stud*	*2d gear on stud*	*Gear on worm shaft*	*Hundredths of cam surface to feed stock*
90	75	63	54	46	39	32	28	24	21	18	16	13	11	9	8	7	6	$\frac{3}{4}$	4800	100	20	80	60	34
105	87	73	63	54	45	38	33	28	25	21	18	15	13	11	9	8	6.5	$\frac{7}{8}$	4114	100	20	40	35	29
120	100	84	72	62	51	43	38	32	28	24	21	18	15	13	11	9	8	1	3600	80	20	50	40	25
150	124	105	90	77	64	54	47	40	35	30	26	22	18	16	13	11	9	$1\frac{1}{4}$	2880	100	20	40	50	20
180	149	126	108	93	77	65	57	48	42	36	31	26	22	19	16	14	11	$1\frac{1}{2}$	2400	100	25	50	60	17
210	174	147	126	108	90	75	66	56	49	42	37	31	25	22	19	16	13	$1\frac{3}{4}$	2057	80	35	50	40	15
240	199	168	144	124	103	86	76	64	56	48	42	35	29	25	21	18	15	2	1800	100	25	50	80	13
270	224	189	161	139	116	97	85	72	63	53	47	39	33	28	24	20	17	$2\frac{1}{4}$	1600	80	20	25	45	12
300	249	210	179	155	129	108	95	80	70	59	52	44	36	31	27	23	19	$2\frac{1}{2}$	1440	80	20	25	50	10
330	274	231	197	170	141	118	104	88	77	65	58	48	40	34	29	25	21	$2\frac{3}{4}$	1309	80	20	25	55	10
360	299	252	215	186	154	129	113	96	85	71	63	53	44	38	32	27	23	3	1200	80	20	25	60	9
390	323	273	233	201	167	140	123	104	92	77	68	57	47	41	35	29	24	$3\frac{1}{4}$	1107	80	20	25	65	8
420	348	294	251	217	180	151	132	112	99	83	73	61	51	44	37	32	26	$3\frac{1}{2}$	1028	100	35	40	80	8
450	373	315	269	232	193	161	142	120	106	89	78	66	54	47	40	34	28	$3\frac{3}{4}$	960	50	25	40	60	7
480	398	336	287	248	206	172	151	128	113	95	84	70	58	50	43	36	30	4	900	50	20	40	80	7
504	418	352	301	260	216	181	159	134	118	100	88	74	61	53	45	38	32	$4\frac{1}{5}$	857	100	35	25	60	6
540	448	378	323	279	231	194	170	144	127	107	94	79	65	56	48	41	34	$4\frac{1}{2}$	800	80	40	25	45	6
576	478	403	344	297	247	206	182	153	135	114	100	84	70	60	51	43	36	$4\frac{4}{5}$	750	100	40	25	60	5
600	498	420	359	310	257	215	189	160	141	119	105	88	73	63	53	45	38	5	720	80	40	25	50	5
660	547	462	395	341	283	237	208	176	155	131	115	96	80	69	59	50	41	$5\frac{1}{2}$	654	80	40	25	55	5
719	597	503	431	371	308	258	227	191	169	143	125	105	87	75	64	54	45	6	600	80	40	25	60	5
779	647	545	466	402	334	280	246	207	183	154	136	114	94	81	69	59	49	$6\frac{1}{2}$	553	80	40	25	65	4
839	697	587	502	433	360	301	265	223	197	166	146	123	102	88	75	63	53	7	514	50	35	40	80	4
899	746	629	538	464	386	323	284	239	211	178	157	131	109	94	80	68	56	$7\frac{1}{2}$	480	80	50	25	60	4
959	796	671	574	495	411	344	303	255	225	190	167	140	116	100	85	72	60	8	450	100	40	20	80	4
989	821	692	592	511	424	355	312	263	232	196	173	144	120	103	88	74	62	$8\frac{1}{4}$	436	50	55	40	60	3
079	896	755	646	557	463	387	340	287	254	214	188	158	131	113	96	81	68	9	400	50	45	40	80	3
124	933	787	673	580	482	403	355	299	264	223	196	164	136	117	100	84	70	$9\frac{3}{8}$	384	80	60	40	100	3
199	995	839	718	619	514	430	378	319	282	238	209	175	145	125	107	90	75	10	360	80	40	25	100	3
259	1045	881	753	650	540	452	397	335	296	249	220	184	152	131	112	95	79	$10\frac{1}{2}$	342	50	35	20	60	3

*These combinations not to be used in opposite directions.
†Net will vary with factory conditions and the character of the work.

Table 8-3. Approximate Cutting Speeds and Feeds for Standard Tools on a Single Spindle Automatic Screw Machine.

	Cut		*Feed (ipr.) for Material Type*								
Type of Tool	*Width or Depth (in.)*	*Diameter of Hole (in.)*	*A*	*B*	*C*	*D*	*E*	*F*	*G*	*H*	*I*
Boring Tools	.005	....	....	.0062	.0055	.005	.005	.0048	.0045	.0042	.004
Box Tools	1/32	....	.012	.0105	.0093	.0085	.0085	.0077	.0068	.0059	.005
One-chip finishing	1/16	....	.010	.0085	.0075	.0068	.0068	.0061	.0054	.0047	.004
V back rest – brass	1/8	....	.008	.0075	.0066	.006	.006	.0053	.0045	.0038	.003
Roller rest – steel	3/16	....	.008	.0063	.0056	.0051	.0051	.0044	.0036	.0028	.002
	1/4	....	.006	.0052	.0046	.0042	.0042	.0036	.0029	.0022	.0015
Finish cut – V rest	.005	....	.010	.010	.0093	.0085	.0085	.0079	.0073	.0066	.006
Center Drills	....	Under 1/8	.003	.0018	.0016	.0015	.0013	.0013	.0012	.0011	.001
		Over 1/8	.006	.0044	.0038	.0035	.003	.0031	.0027	.0024	.002
Cutoff Tools:											
Angular	....	....	.0015	.0008	.0007	.0006	.0005	.0005	.0005	.0004	.0004
Circular, over 1/8 diameter	3/64 to 1/8	....	.0035	.0018	.0016	.0015	.0013	.0013	.0012	.0011	.001
Straight, under 1/8 diameter	.020 to .040	....	.002	.001	.0009	.0008	.0007	.0007	.0006	.0006	.0005
Drills, Twist	....	.020	.0017	.0012	.0011	.001	.0009	.0009	.0008	.0007	.0006
		.040	.0024	.0017	.0015	.0014	.0012	.0012	.0011	.0009	.0008
		1/16	.0048	.0025	.0022	.002	.0017	.0018	.0016	.0014	.0012
		3/32	.0072	.0031	.0027	.0025	.0021	.0022	.002	.0018	.0016
		1/8	.011	.0044	.0038	.0035	.003	.0031	.0027	.0024	.002
		3/16	.014	.005	.0044	.004	.0034	.0038	.0035	.0032	.003
		1/4	.016	.0062	.0055	.005	.0043	.0045	.004	.0035	.003
		5/16	.016	.0069	.006	.0055	.0047	.005	.0045	.004	.0035
		3/8	.014	.0075	.0066	.006	.0051	.0055	.005	.0045	.004
		1/2	.012	.0075	.0066	.006	.0051	.0055	.005	.0045	.004
		5/8	.010	.0075	.0066	.006	.0051	.0055	.005	.0045	.004
Form Tool	1/8 and 1/4	....	.002	.0012	.0011	.001	.001	.0009	.0008	.0008	.0007
	3/8	....	.0018	.0011	.001	.0009	.0009	.0008	.0007	.0007	.0006
	1/2	....	.0015	.001	.0009	.0008	.0008	.0007	.0007	.0006	.0005
	5/8 and 3/4	....	.0012	.0009	.0008	.0007	.0007	.0006	.0006	.0005	.0004
	1 in. and up	....	.001	.0007	.0007	.0006	.0006	.0005	.0005	.0004	.0004
Balance Turning:											
Turned diameter under 5/32	1/32	....	.012	.012	.011	.010	.0085	.0095	.009	.0085	.008
	1/16	....	.010	.010	.0095	.009	.0077	.0082	.0075	.0066	.006
Turned diameter over 5/32	1/16	....	.012	.012	.0115	.011	.010	.0102	.0095	.0087	.008
	1/8	....	.012	.012	.011	.010	.0085	.0095	.009	.0085	.008
	3/16	....	.010	.010	.009	.008	.0068	.0075	.007	.0065	.006
	1/4	....	.009	.0087	.0077	.007	.006	.0063	.0057	.0051	.0045
Knee Tool	1/64	....	.015	.015	.013	.012	.0105	.0115	.011	.0105	.010
	1/32	....	.012	.012	.011	.010	.0085	.0095	.009	.0085	.008
Knurl Tool	....	....	.020	.018	.0165	.015	.0127	.0137	.0125	.0122	.010
Turret on	....	....	.040	.037	.033	.030	.0255	.0287	.0275	.0262	.025
Turret off	....	....	.004	.0025	.0022	.002	.002	.002	.002	.002	.002
Side or swing	....	....	.006	.005	.0044	.004	.0034	.0037	.0035	.0032	.003
Top	....	....	.005	.0037	.0033	.003	.0026	.0027	.0025	.0022	.002
		....	.008	.0075	.0066	.006	.0051	.0055	.0005	.0045	.004
Pointing and Facing	....	....	.001	.001	.0009	.0008	.0007	.0007	.0006	.0006	.0005
		....	.0025	.0025	.0022	.002	.0017	.0017	.0014	.0011	.0008
Reamers and Bits	....	Under 1/8	.007	.007	.0065	.006	.0051	.0055	.005	.0045	.004
	.003 to .004	....	.010	.010	.0088	.008	.0068	.0075	.007	.0065	.006
		Over 1/8	.010	.010	.010	.010	.0085	.009	.008	.007	.006
	.004 to .008	....	....	....	....	....	....	.0095	.009	.0085	.008
Recessing Tool, end cut	....	....	.001	.0008	.0007	.0006	.0005	.0005	.0005	.0004	.0004
		....	.005	.0037	.0033	.003	.0025	.0027	.0025	.0022	.002
Inside cut	1/16	....	.0025	.0025	.0022	.002	.0017	.0018	.0017	.0016	.0015
	1/8	....	.0008	.0008	.0007	.0006	.0005	.0005	.0005	.0004	.0004
Swing Tool, forming	1/8	....	.002	.0009	.0008	.0007	.0006	.0006	.0006	.0005	.0005
	1/4	....	.0012	.0006	.0006	.0005	.0004	.0004	.0004	.0003	.0003
	3/8	....	.001	.0005	.0004	.0004	.0003	.0003	.0003	.0002	.0002
	1/2	....	.0008	.0004	.0003	.0003	.0002	.0002	.0002	.0002	.0002
Turning Straight†	1/32	....	.008	.0075	.0066	.006	.0051	.0053	.0047	.0041	.0035
	1/16	....	.006	.005	.0044	.004	.0034	.0038	.0035	.0032	.003
	1/8	....	.005	.0037	.0033	.003	.0025	.0027	.0025	.0022	.002
	3/16	....	.004	.0031	.0027	.0025	.0021	.0022	.002	.0017	.0015

Note: Figures in this table are only approximate, to be used as a basis from which proper figures for the job in hand may be calculated. They are averages; if the work has any features out of the ordinary, take these into consideration and alter the figures accordingly. *(Footnotes continued on bottom of p. 95)*

Table 8-4. Angles and Thicknesses for Circular Cutoff Tools.*

A is 23 deg. when cutting brass, aluminum, copper, silver, and zinc.
A is 15 deg. when cutting steel, iron, bronze, and nickel.
Least thickness used when cutting off into tapped holes is the lead of two and one-half threads plus .010 in.
Least thickness used when cutting off into reamed holes smaller than 1/8 in. diam. is .040 in.
Thickness used when cutting off tubing is two-thirds *T* as given below for corresponding diameters of stock.
Thickness used when angles or radii start from outside diameter of tool is governed by varying conditions and determined accordingly.

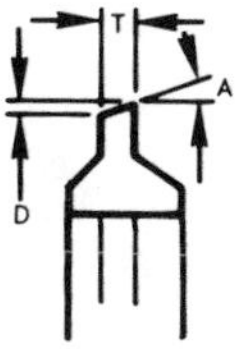

Diameter of Stock	***Thickness T***	***Depth of Angle D***	
		For Brass	*For Steel*
1/16	.020	.0085	.0055
3/32	.030	.013	.008
1/8	.040	.017	.011
3/16	.050	.0215	.0135
1/4	.060	.0255	.016
5/16	.070	.030	.019
3/8	.080	.034	.021
7/16	.090	.038	.024
1/2 to 9/16	.100	.042	.027
5/8 to 3/4	.120	.051	.032
13/16 to 1	.140	.059	.038
1 1/16 to 1 5/16	.160	.068	.043
1 3/8 to 1 7/8	.190	.081	.051
2 to 2 1/2	.220	.093	.059

* All dimensions are in inches.

For tool *B*, dimensions *b* and *c* must be calculated and the larger used to determine the number of spindle revolutions.

Dimension *b*		Dimension *c*	
Formed diameter	.120 in.	Stock diameter	.312 in.
1/2 formed diameter	.060 in.	Formed diameter	+.120 in.
Dimension *D* from *Table 8-4*	.011 in.	Difference is 2c	.192 in.
Tool travel past center	.005 in.	Dimension *c*	.096 in.
Approach	+.010 in.	Approach	+.010 in.
Total tool travel	.086 in.	Total tool travel	.106 in.

* A. Free-cutting brass. Use maximum spindle speed available on machine.
B. 2011-T aluminum, 800 spfm.
C. 2017-T and 5052-T aluminum, 550 sfpm.
D. 2024-T aluminum, 400 sfpm.; copper, 300 sfpm.; naval brass and Tobin bronze, 200 sfpm.
E. High-sulfur steel B-1113, X-1112, and B & S 12A, 225 sfpm.; C-1113, 196 sfpm.; B-1112, 165 sfpm.
F. Type 416 stainless steels and steels machined at 130 sfpm.
G. Steels machined at 112 sfpm.
H. Steels machined at 95 sfpm.
J. All other stainless steels; tool steels, 75 sfpm.; monel, 60 sfpm.; phosphor bronze, high-speed steel, 65 sfpm.
† Feeds for swing tools when turning a taper are the same as straight turning for the greatest depth of cut.

Table 8-5. Machine Spindle Revolutions for Part A in *Figure 8-3*.

Operation	*Revolutions*		
	Estimated	*Adjusted*	*Actual*
Feed Stock	12	14.4	16
Form (Tool *A*)	118	118.0	118
Form and Cut Off (Tool *B*) (118 − 46 overlap)	72	72.0	72
Total revolutions	202	204.4	206

The number of spindle revolutions for tool *B* is .106 in. ÷ .0009 ipr. = 117.7 or 118.

The cutting operations should be performed at the same time for the greatest production economy. Since tool *A* is cutting closer to the spindle than tool *B*, tool *A* should not generate a diameter (in this case, less than 1/4 in.) before tool *B* has finished forming the .120±.001 in. diameter. This 1/4 in. dimension is based on the 3:1 slenderness ratio previously established.

The tool travel for the overlapping operations is one-half the difference in diameters cut, plus the approach. Thus the tool overlap is:

$$\left(\frac{.312-.250}{2} + .010\right) \div .009 = 45.5 \text{ or } 46 \text{ revolutions}$$

Since the part is machined completely from the cross-slides, the only non-productive operation requiring consideration is stock feeding. From the past experience, stock feeding is estimated at 12 revolutions. A more accurate estimate will be made in the next step.

From the above calculations three operations for making this part have been established: feed stock, form with tool *A*, and cut off with tool *B*. These operations and number of spindle revolutions required are tabulated in *Table 8-5*.

The estimated number of spindle revolutions to complete the part is 202. In the production table for the No. 00 high-speed automatic screw machine (*Table 8-2*) under the column headed 3085, the closest number is 206 revolutions; the same line of the right-hand column shows that .07 of the cam surface is required to feed the stock. For cam design calculations and estimating purposes, the 206 revolutions represent a complete cam surface having 100 divisions; or one division equals 2.06 revolutions. Multiplying .07 by 2.06 shows that 14.42 spindle revolutions are required to feed the stock. This is entered in the adjusted column of *Table 8-5* and gives a total of 204.4 spindle revolutions in the adjusted column, which is 1.6 less than the required 206 given in *Table 8-2*. Since the stock must be fed in not less than 14.4 spindle revolutions, the 1.6 revolutions can be added to this item rather than to the machining operations.

From *Table 8-2*, the time required to make one piece is 4 sec., or 900 pieces per hour at 100% efficiency. This is equivalent to .0667 min. per piece.

ESTIMATE FORM

At this time, the estimator enters the accumulated data on the "Machining Estimate" (*Figure 8-2*). This form provides space for a full description of each machining operation.

The labor cost per piece is determined by multiplying total time per piece by the labor rate ($.1266).

Total time per piece must be determined. On simple screw machine parts, operators will frequently tend three of four automatic screw machines. It is safe to estimate that an operator can tend at least two machines making more complex parts. In this example, one operator will be considered as tending four machines, with an allowance of 5% for personal, fatigue, and tool trouble delays, or an efficiency of 85%.

The number of minutes required per piece is .0667 ÷ .85 = .0785 min. Labor time required per piece per machine is .0785 ÷ 4 = .0196 min. This value is used as the direct labor time in the estimate. Setup time per piece of .002 is added to the direct labor time per piece (.0196) to give a total labor time per piece of .0216 min. Total labor time is multiplied by the labor standard ($.1266) to give a labor cost per piece of $.0027.

Burden is determined by multiplying the burden rate (252%) by the labor cost per piece. Burden per piece is $.0068 and total labor and burden is $.0095. This cost is centered on the "Machining Estimate" (*Figure 8-2*).

The material costs for both the short and the long pin are based on the following prices:

Base per 100 lbs.	$22.95
Chemistry	4.05
Size	8.70
Quantity	6.00
Total for 100 lbs.	$41.70

Assuming 12-ft. bar stock and a 2-in. stub for the short pin, the number of pieces per bar is calculated as follows:

$$(144-2) \div (.750 + .040) = 179 \text{ pieces/bar}$$
$$144 \div 179 = .804 \text{ in. of stock per piece}$$

The weight of the 5/16-in.-diameter steel is .022 lb/in. The rough weight is then .804 × .022 = .0177 lb/piece. Material cost is .0177 × $.417 = $.00738 per piece.

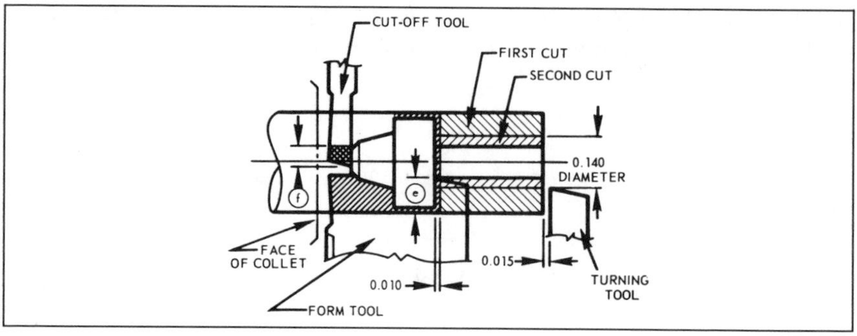

Figure 8-4. Tool layout for workpiece B in *Figure 8-1*.

This material cost (rounded to \$.0075) is added to total labor and burden on the "Machining Estimate" form (*Figure 8-2*) to arrive at the manufacturing cost for the part.

Overhead and Profit

General and administrative costs (overhead) and profit are taken as percentages of the manufacturing cost (excluding the "special tool" cost). General and administrative costs are obtained by multiplying the G and A factor (40%) by the manufacturing cost of \$.0170 per part. Next, G and A costs (\$.0068) are added to the manufacturing cost (\$.0170) to obtain total cost (\$.0238). Profit is next computed by taking 15% of total cost (\$.0238) and adding the result to the total cost to obtain the selling price (\$.0274).

When a quotation is made to the customer, the selling price is given as \$2.74 per hundred, plus a special tool cost of \$288.00.

Long Pin

Estimating machining time and the various costs associated with manufacturing the long pin shown in Part B, *Figure 8-1* requires the same steps described in the previous section. Although a "Machining Estimate" form is not included for this part, manufacturing data and costs should be recorded as in the previous section.

A tool layout for this part is shown in *Figure 8-4*. In turning the shank for this part, a rough cut to .140-in.-diameter and a finish cut are taken with box tools mounted in the hexagon turret. Since the turning tool cannot satisfactorily finish to a square shoulder, .010 in. is left to be machined by a cross-slide form tool. An allowance of .015-in. is made for the approach of the turning tool. To

Table 8-6. Machine Spindle Revolutions for Part B in *Figure 8-1*.

Operation	Revolutions		
	Estimated	*Adjusted*	*Actual*
Feed stock	15	15	15
Rough turn	111	111	110
Double index turret	23	24	24
Finish turn	89	89	88
Tool clearance for front slide	36	39	39
Form	143	143	141
Cutoff	66	66	65
Total revolutions	483	487	482

maintain the required tolerance on the .312-in.-diameter, 21/64-in. diameter stock is used.

The length of cut for the turning tools is .750 + .015 – .010 = .755 in. The depth of cut is (.328—.140) ÷ 2 = .094 in. From *Table 8-3*, the rough turning feed is .0068 ipr.; for finish turning, the feed is .0085 ipr. The spindle revolutions required for the rough cut are .755 ÷ .0068 = 111 revolutions; for the finish cut, .755 ÷ .0085 = 89 revolutions. To obtain a favorable hill-to-valley relationship between the rough and finish cuts, the feed rate for finish turning was increased over that for rough turning. This was done because it would not be possible to increase the spindle speed satisfactorily for the finish turning operation.

Calculations for the front slide form tool and cutoff tool are:

Form Tool		Cutoff Tool	
Stock diameter	.328	Formed diameter	.120
Formed diameter	–.120	1/2 formed diameter	.060
Difference (2*e*)	.208	Dimension *D*' from Table 8-4	.011
Dimension *e*	.104	Tool travel past center	.005
Approach	+.010	Approach	.010
Total tool travel	.114 in.	Total tool travel	.086 in.

Spindle revolutions for form tool: .114 ÷ .0008 = 142.5 or 143
Spindle revolutions for cutoff tool: .086 ÷ .0013 = 66.1 or 66

Operation Sequence

The sequence of operations and number of spindle revolutions for each operation are shown in *Table 8-6*.

The four machining operations have a subtotal of 409 revolutions. From *Table*

Table 8-7. Hundredths Required to Index for Throws from Full-Height Cam.* (Cut down plus cam throw).

4 to 5 1/2 sec.		*6 to 33 sec.*		*36 sec. and over*	
Drop (in.)	*Hundredths*	*Drop (in.)*	*Hundredths*	*Drop (in.)*	*Hundredths*
11/32	2 1/2	0 – 15/32	2 1/2	0 – 5/8	2 1/2
11/32 – 1/2	3	15/32 – 11/16	3	5/8 – 7/8	3
1/2 – 5/8	3 1/2	11/16 – 13/16	3 1/2	7/8 – 1 1/16	3 1/2
5/8 – 3/4	4	13/16 – 31/32	4	1 1/16 – 1 7/32	4
3/4 – 27/32	4 1/2	31/32 – 1 3/32	4 1/2	1 7/32 – 1 3/8	4 1/2
27/32 – 15/16	5	1 3/32 – 1 3/16	5	1 3/8 – 1 1/2	5
15/16 – 1/16	5 1/2	1 3/16 – 1 5/16	5 1/2		
1 1/16 – 1 1/8	6	1 5/16 – 1 3/8	6		
1 1/8 – 1 1/4	6 1/2	1 3/8 – 1 7/16	6 1/2		

*5 1/2-in. cam on No. 00 machine.

8-7, .025 (2 1/2 hundredths) is required to index the turret. Using 4.5 revolutions per .01 of the cam surface, the number of revolutions to double index the turret is 2 × 2.5 × 4.5 = 22.5 or 23 revolutions. The required clearance, for turret and cross-slide tools, is .08 (see *Table 8-8*). The number of revolutions is 8 × 4.5 = 36. The subtotal is now 468 revolutions. From *Table 8-2* under the 3085 rpm. column, across from 463, .03 is required to feed the stock, or about 15 revolutions. The total estimated revolutions is 483. Referring to *Table 8-2*, the nearest number of revolutions is 482. The estimated revolutions must now be adjusted to this new value:

Feed stock:	4.82 × 3 = 14.46 or 15 revolutions
Double index turret:	2 × 2.5 × 4.82 = 24.1 or 24
Tool clearance:	8 × 4.82 = 38.56 or 39

The total of the adjusted column is 487 or 5 revolutions above the required 482. The revolutions for the nonproductive operations are fixed; therefore the 5 revolutions must be deducted from the machining operations as shown in the right-hand column of *Table 8-6*. The time required to make the piece is 9 3/8 sec., or 384 per hour at 100% efficiency. At 85% efficiency, the time is .1254 min. The direct labor time when one worker is operating four machines is .0314 min.

The direct labor time (.0314) is multiplied by the labor rate to arrive at labor cost per piece, and the burden rate is applied to the resulting cost figure to give a total labor and burden cost.

The cost per cwt. of bar stock is the same as for the short pin, $41.70. Material cost is calculated on the following page.

Table 8-8. Clearance in Hundredths between Turret Tools and Cross-Slide Circular Tools (2).

Tool No.	*Turret Tools*	*Clearance*									
		Front Cross-Slide Tool					*Back Cross-Slide Tool*				
		No. 00	*No. 0*	*No. 2*	*4*	*6*	*No. 00*	*No. 0*	*No. 2*	*4*	*6*
BA-00C	Balance turning tool	6	....	....	....	....	6				
BA	Balance turning tool	....	6	....	....	....	....	6			
C-20D-22B-22G	Balance turning tool	....	7	7	....	....	....	7	7		
A-24L-26	Balance turning tool	....	....	....	6	6	....	....	....	6	6
K-20K-22D	Box tool	8	7	7	....	....	6	7	6		
A-24L-2G	Box tool	....	....	....	7	7	....	....	....	6	6
L-20L-22G	Box tool	6	6	6	....	....	7	7	7		
BM-20BA-22BA	Box tool	8	7	7	....	....	5	5	4		
CA-20CM-22AA	Box tool	8	7	7	....	....	6	6	6		
DA-20H-22G	Box tool	5	7	7	....	....	7	6	6		
EB-00FB	Box tool	8	....	....	....	....	6				
EB-20FB	Box tool	....	7	....	....	....	....	6			
EB-22FB	Box tool	....	....	7	....	....	....	....	6		
D-00CA	Centering and face tool	8	....	....	....	....	4				
D-11BA	Centering and face tool	....	7	....	....	....	....	3			
D-22CA	Centering and face tool	....	....	7	....	....	....	....	3		
	Self-opening die head	8	7	7	7	7	8	7	7	7	7
AB-20AB-22AB	Combination right- and left-hand knee tool	6	5	5	....	....	4	4	4		
D-20D-22DA	Knurl holder	7	6	6	....	....	7	6	6		
A-26	Knurl holder	....	....	....	6	6	....	....	....	5	5
BA-20C-20DA-22BA-22DA	Pointing tool	7	7	7	....	....	5	6	6		
CA	Pointing tool	8	....	....	....	....	6				
DA	Pointing tool	5	....	....	....	....	7				
A-24L-26	Pointing tool	....	....	....	6	6	....	....	....	6	6
BA-26B	Turret tool post	....	....	....	3	3					

NOTE: For No. 00 size machines, double the time given in table for No. 00 size machine, if a 3-sec. job or faster. On a 4-sec. job add undredths, and on a 5-sec. job add 4 hundredths of cam surface to figures given in table for these machines.
*Not given.

$$(144-2) \div (1.155 + .040) = 110 \text{ pieces/bar}$$
$$144 \div 110 = 1.309 \text{ in. of stock per piece}$$

The weight of the 21/64-in.-diameter steel is .024 lb/in. The rough weight is 1.309 × .024 = .0314 lb/piece. The material cost is .1032 × .417 = .0429 per piece.

9

ESTIMATING SAND CASTING COSTS

To estimate castings, the estimator should be acquainted with material specifications, heat treatment specifications, final inspection requirements, and the casting design as specified in the cost estimate request. Material and heat treatment specifications add cost to castings, and are often called out in notes on engineering drawings without being mentioned in the estimate request. Some companies establish their own code numbers for material specifications, heat treatment and inspection operations with which the estimator should be familiar. Estimators should also understand the chemical composition and physical specifications of the materials to be used, and check customer specifications against foundry capabilities to ensure acceptable finished castings can be produced.

The total cost of making castings is comprised of the following cost items: (1) material, (2) foundry tooling, (3) molding costs, (4) core costs, (5) machining and cleaning costs, (6) heat treatment costs, (7) inspection costs, and (8) foundry burden.

MATERIAL COSTS

To determine the material cost of finished castings, the estimator calculates finished casting weight and multiplies it by the cost per pound of the metal used in the finished castings.

Finished Casting Weight

The estimated finished casting weight (the weight of the casting as shipped to the customer) is computed from engineering drawings and is simplified when the drawings indicate stock allowances if any surfaces are to be machined. When no drawings are available, they should be prepared by the estimator and submitted to the customer or in-house requesting department for approval before proceeding with the estimate.

Finished casting weight is calculated by multiplying the volume of the casting (in cubic inches) by the weight per cubic inch of the material. While the volume of regularly shaped castings can usually be determined by the use of handbook formulas for geometrical solids, many cast parts are irregularly shaped, requiring complex calculations. A part of irregular shape and thickness should be divided into simple geometric segments, the volume of each determined as above by handbook formulas, and the total volume derived by adding the volume of each segment. For castings having irregular cross-sectioned areas, a planimeter (a precision instrument designed to assist in calculating the area of a plane surface by tracing its perimeter) can be used.

Cost of Metal in Finished Castings

Determining the cost of the metal used in finished castings involves the following steps:

1. Calculate the amount of metal charged into the furnace.
2. Make allowance for metal lossage.
3. Determine the amount of metal returned to the furnace for remelting.
4. Determine the cost/lb of metal poured from the furnace.

Furnace Charge

A shop yield factor based on previous foundry experience is used to compute the required foundry charge. Shop yield is the ratio of finished casting weight to the weight of the metal charged into the furnace. For example:

$$\frac{\text{545,000 lbs. finished castings}}{\text{1,000,000 lbs. metal charged}} = 54.5\%$$

Using a shop yield of 54.5%, and assuming a finished casting weight of 10 lbs., the furnace charge per casting is computed as follows:

$$\frac{\text{10 lbs.}}{(.545)} = \text{18.35 lbs. charged metal}$$

Because shop yield varies according to the kind of casting produced, the estimator is well advised to keep a record of casting weights such as is shown in *Table 9-1* and *Table 9-2*.

Metal Lossage

In all foundries, a certain amount of the metal charged into the furnace is lost due to oxidation, spills, overruns, and gate cutoff. A typical allowance is 10% of finished castings.

Table 9-1. Record of Weights of Gray Iron Castings.

Part	1 Pieces per Mold	2 Shipping Weight (lbs/mold) (= 4 − 3)	3 Grind Loss (lbs.)	4 Yield Weight (lbs.) (= 7 − 6)	5 Yield Weight (per cent) (= 4 ÷ 7)	6 Gate and Sprue (lbs.)	7 Pouring Weight (lbs.)	8 Rough Casting Weight (lbs.) (= 4 ÷ 1)	9 Finish Casting Weight (lbs.) (= 2 ÷ 1)
Casting	1	33.125	.104	33.229	81.2	7.709	40.938	33.229	33.125
Transmission case	1	39.156	.157	39.313	74.9	13.187	52.500	39.313	39.156
Transmission case	1	51.750	.250	52.000	78.5	14.250	66.250	52.000	51.750
Pump body	2	13.604	.334	13.938	65.2	7.437	21.375	6.969	6.802
Pump body	4	28.332	....	28.332	76.1	8.918	37.250	7.083	7.083
Carrier	1	33.896	....	33.896	67.1	16.612	50.508	33.896	33.896
Bearing cap	2	4.084	....	4.084	67.1	2.002	6.086	2.042	2.042
End bell	4	13.124	....	13.124	58.3	9.376	22.500	3.281	3.281
End bell	2	6.750	....	6.750	53.9	5.764	12.514	3.375	3.375
Housing	4	14.812	....	14.812	71.8	5.813	20.625	3.703	3.703
Distributor base	4	15.452	....	15.452	70.4	6.486	21.938	3.863	3.863
Brake drum	1	78.000	....	78.000	85.2	13.500	91.500	78.000	78.000
Flywheel	1	34.000	....	34.000	79.5	8.750	42.750	34.000	34.000
Pump rotor	8	5.248	.128	5.376	45.3	6.499	11.875	.672	.656
Oil pump	6	13.500	.186	13.686	65.2	7.314	21.000	2.281	2.250
Cover	10	12.100	....	12.100	63.7	6.900	19.000	1.210	1.210
Pressure plate	1	11.125	....	11.125	70.9	4.563	15.688	11.125	11.125
Manifold	3	30.000	....	30.000	71.0	12.250	42.250	10.000	10.000
Block	1	190.584	1.916	192.500	74.9	64.500	257.000	192.500	190.584
Drum	1	80.719	....	80.719	85.6	13.531	94.25	80.719	80.719
Block	2	392.334	.486	392.820	84.0	74.667	467.450	196.410	196.167
Housing	1	37.125	.375	37.500	77.3	11.000	48.500	37.500	37.125
Outlet	8	10.440	....	10.440	51.6	9.810	20.250	1.305	1.305
Weight	2	14.750	....	14.750	65.7	7.688	22.438	7.375	7.375

Table 9-2. Record of Weights of Malleable Iron Castings.

Part	Pieces per Mold	Shipping Weight (lbs/mold)	Grind Loss (lbs.)	Yield Weight (lbs.)	Yield Weight (per cent)	Gate and Sprue (lbs.)	Pouring Weight (lbs.)	Rough Casting Weight (lbs.)	Finish Casting Weight (lbs.)
Spacer	8	12.304	.152	12.456	79.6	3.200	15.656	1.557	1.538
Spacer	8	14.064	.184	14.248	79.2	3.752	18.000	1.781	1.758
Yoke	2	2.875	.031	2.90	43.0	3.852	6.758	2.906	2.875
Link	6	11.436	.690	12.126	56.4	9.374	21.500	2.021	1.906
Hinge	3	8.064	.063	8.127	66.7	4.061	12.188	2.709	2.688
Link	2	6.094	.062	6.156	35.7	11.094	17.250	3.078	3.047
Bearing sleeve	2	19.750	....	19.750	63.5	11.329	31.079	9.875	9.875
Spool	4	38.416	....	38.416	48.9	40.209	78.625	9.604	9.604
Spool	4	20.252	....	20.252	55.5	16.248	36.500	5.063	5.063
Washer	6	21.702	....	21.702	75.5	7.048	28.750	3.617	3.617
Wedge	10	5.030	.130	5.160	59.0	3.590	8.750	.516	.503
Casting	4	18.064	.188	18.252	80.2	4.498	22.750	4.563	4.516
Casting	1	17.834	.166	18.000	53.3	15.750	33.750	18.000	17.834
Rail block	1	30.375	.250	30.625	57.8	22.375	53.000	30.625	30.375
Rail brace	1	72.500	.500	73.000	82.0	16.000	89.000	73.000	72.500
Cap	6	16.782	.186	16.968	56.3	13.157	30.125	2.828	2.797
Bearing cap	1	27.875	.125	28.000	45.2	34.000	62.000	28.000	27.875
Clamp	5	4.570	.120	4.690	41.7	6.560	11.250	.938	.914
Clamp	12	3.132	.096	3.228	40.0	4.835	8.063	.269	.261
Gross head	1	28.800	.450	29.250	53.7	25.250	54.500	29.250	28.800
Cap	1	20.500	.094	20.594	65.9	10.656	31.250	20.594	20.500
Bearing cap	1	27.875	.125	28.000	45.2	34.000	62.000	28.000	27.875
Differential case	5	98.750	.690	99.440	63.5	57.060	156.500	19.888	19.750

For a casting weighing 10 lbs., the weight of lost metal is determined as follows:

$$10 \text{ lbs.} \times 10\% = 1 \text{ lb. of metal lost}$$

Remelted Metal

Any metal not lost or consumed in the finished casting is returned to the furnace for remelting. The percentage of the metal charged into the furnace that is returned for remelting is determined as follows:

$$\text{Remelted Metal} = \text{Metal Charged} - (\text{Shop Yield} + \text{Metal Lost})$$
$$\text{Remelted Metal} = 100\% - (54.5\% + 5.4\%)$$
$$= 40\%$$

For a finished casting weighing 10 lbs., and requiring a metal charge of 18.35 lbs., the amount of remelted metal would be calculated as follows:

$$\text{Remelted Metal} = \text{Furnace Charge per Casting} \times \text{Remelt Factor}$$
$$\text{Remelted Metal} = 18.35 \times .40$$
$$= 7.34 \text{ lbs}$$

Cost of Poured Metal

The cost of the metal poured from the furnace is the sum of: (1) the cost of the metal charged, and (2) the cost of labor and overhead to charge the furnace and melt the metal.

The cost of the charged metal is based upon the current price of the metal or metals being used, plus the value of remelted metal.

The furnace labor and overhead charges are usually based upon costs derived from a previous accounting period. For example, the cost of labor and overhead for charging the furnace and melting the 1,000,000 lbs. of metal is \$30,000. Then, \$30,000 ÷ 1,000,000 lbs. = \$.03/lb.

The \$.03 value may require adjustment if either the anticipated labor and overhead costs for the current accounting period or the amount of metal to be poured is expected to change.

The cost of the poured metal per casting is determined as follows:

$$\text{Poured Metal Cost per Casting} = (\text{Furnace Labor and Overhead} + \text{Cost of Metal Charged}) \text{ x Casting Poured Weight}$$

Where: Casting poured weight (10-lb. finished casting) = 18.35 lbs.
Cost of metal charged = .18/lb
Furnace labor and overhead = .03/lb

$$\text{Poured Metal Cost per Casting} = (\$.03 + \$.18) \text{ x } 18.35 \text{ lbs.} = \$3.84$$

Finished Casting Metal Cost

Next, the estimator determines the appropriate cost to assign the material actually used in the finished castings.

Cost of Metal in Finished Casting = Poured Metal Cost per Casting — (Amount of Remelted Metal x Value of Remelted Metal)

Where:	Weight of finished casting	= 10 lbs.
	Poured metal cost per casting	= $3.84
	Amount of remelted metal	= $7.34 lbs.
	Value of remelted metal	= $ .12 lb.

Cost of Metal in Finished Casting = $3.84– (7.34 lbs. x $.12) = $2.97

To obtain the cost per pound of metal used in the finished casting, the $2.97 value is divided by the finished casting weight of 10 lbs. The resulting material cost per pound is $.297.

FOUNDRY TOOLING

Foundry tooling includes patterns, pattern plates, blow plates, and flasks, as well as various types of core-making tooling. The cost of foundry tooling required for a particular job is estimated and the cost added to the overall estimate. A tooling cost per casting is obtained by dividing total tooling cost by the number of castings produced.

Core-Making Tooling

Core-making tooling is generally estimated separately, and the cost of these tools is used to develop a separate core estimate. The core estimate is then added to the overall casting estimate.

A *pattern* is set in the molding sand and sand is packed around it to produce the impression into which hot metal is poured to produce castings of a desired shape. The cost of patterns is assigned directly to the part being cast because patterns designed for one job are not generally usable for future orders.

A *pattern plate* separates the two halves of a pattern during molding. Composite pattern plates reduce costs by permitting the use of two or more different patterns where production quantities are low relative to the foundry production rate.

Patterns are easily removed from the composite pattern plate and can be replaced in any combination that will permit meeting the schedule for fulfilling casting orders. With such an arrangement, pattern costs may be kept at a minimum when volumes are low enough to permit making a small amount of patterns and mounting them with other patterns on existing pattern plates.

The cost of composite pattern plates should be split among the various casting orders produced with them. *Flasks*, the containers for the molding sand, are made in many different styles, types, and sizes. The size of the flask, its method of construction, and the material used in constructing it, all affect costs. When an estimate is being developed, the estimator must decide which flask is to be used. The costs of flasks designed and constructed especially for a particular job must be assigned to the castings produced for that job. The cost of permanent flasks, however, is generally included in foundry burden.

MOLDING COSTS

Molding costs include the cost of preparing sand molds and the costs of pouring the hot metal into these molds. Molding cost is generally expressed as a cost per pound of acceptable finished castings. For example, a foundry produced 545,000 lbs. of acceptable finished castings with molding costs of $81,750 during one accounting period. The cost per pound of castings would be $.15. This cost would be used during the next accounting period to estimate various production lots of castings.

The number of sand molds that can be made and poured per hour is affected by the flask size, casting weight, type of pattern equipment, and number of cores to be set. A more accurate estimate can be derived by determining how many molds can be made per hour, then converting this value into the cost per pound of casting. The number of molds per hour can be established by using standard time data or time required on similar molds.

CORE COSTS

A core is a shaped projection of sand or other material inserted into the mold to create a cavity or recess in the casting. Dry-sand cores are formed separately and inserted after the pattern is removed but before the mold is closed.

Core Tooling and Equipment

A fairly accurate plan or layout of the cores in a particular casting should be used to estimate the cost of:

1. The core box used to make the cores
2. The driers necessary to support the cores during baking
3. The blow plate which may be required for a particular core-blowing machine
4. Racks, boxes, or special containers in which to store finished cores until used in the molding process

5. Fixtures, tanks, pumps, or filters that may be required for dipping or spraying special core washes
6. Core-pasting fixtures
7. Ovens to bake cores or dry-pasted assemblies.

Estimating Methods

The cost of cores can be determined by one of three different methods, depending upon the core size and method of making the core.

One method relies upon direct labor cost per core. The number of acceptable cores made during an accounting period is divided by the cost of making the cores which is direct labor cost only. The cost per core is then adjusted by adding overhead, which includes the cost of sand, core baking, supplies, supervision, etc.

The second method is the same as the first except that sand cost is excluded from overhead and assigned to the cores on an individual basis. This method reduces the overhead percentage and takes into account the cost of material. Generally, it results in a greater cost per core for large cores and a smaller cost per core for small cores than the first method.

A third method is to determine the direct labor cost per core according to the method by which it is made, e.g., bench, blower, etc., and then add overhead and sand cost.

CLEANING AND MACHINING COSTS

Rough sand castings are generally cleaned before shipping even if no machining is required. Many casting orders call for rough or finish machining to specifications.

Cleaning and Machining

The method used to estimate cleaning costs depends upon the type of cleaning operation. Hand or table blasting costs can be estimated by using standard time data. For tumbling, it is usually necessary to estimate the cost on a per-pound basis. If the sizes and weights of the casting vary considerably, the castings may be classified into groups and a cost factor determined for each classification.

The application of direct labor costs and overhead is usually more practical than using a cost-per-pound basis. Standard time data can easily be determined for machining operations such as grinding, chipping, filing, etc., and the direct labor hours estimated from these data.

HEAT TREATMENT

For iron castings, heat treating may be specified for stress relieving or to improve machinability, and iron alloy castings may be quenched or tempered to increase their hardness and wear resistance. Steel castings may be normalized, annealed, stress-relieved, quenched, and tempered.

Heat treatment costs may be estimated on the basis of: casting weight and treatment time. Under the casting weight method, the entire cost of operating the heat treatment department is considered in conjunction with the average amount of work performed during an accounting period, and a factor developed enabling this cost to be assigned on the basis of pounds of castings treated. For example, the entire cost of operating a small heat treatment facility is $189,000 per year, and 1,512, 000 lbs. of castings are heat treated. The cost of operating this heat treating operation ($189,000) is divided by the weight of the castings treated (1,512,000 lbs.), resulting in a cost per lb. of $.12. This cost is used for estimating heat treating costs during the next accounting period.

Under the treatment time method, the total cost of operating the heat treatment facilities is divided by the total number of hours the facilities are operated. Assuming a total cost of $189,000 per year and a total annual operating time of 1,500 hours, the hourly cost of operating the facilities is $126. This hourly cost is then assigned to the total castings treated during a given time period. For example, a production lot of castings weighing 4,200 lbs. is heat treated for four hours. The heat treatment cost is divided by the weight of the castings (4,200 lbs.), giving a heat treatment cost of $.12 per pound.

The simplest method of estimating inspection and shipping costs is by the pound. In some cases, it is possible to apply direct labor costs to a job, but the operations may be so minor that this procedure is not practical. Any special handling or packaging required should be considered, however.

Foundry burden, applied on the basis of pounds of finished castings, is computed by the use of a burden factor supplied by the accounting department. For example, if 545,000 lbs. of finished castings are produced and the burden factor is $.33 per pound of finished castings, the burden cost for the production lot of castings is $179,850.

SAND CASTING ESTIMATE EXAMPLE

The part shown in *Figure 9-1* is a water outlet for a gasoline engine. the material specified is a common grade of gray iron, and the specified annual production quantity is 5,000 pieces. Accompanying the cost request for this part was a cost request for a thermostat housing for the same engine. Because each engine assembly requires one of each type of casting, the process plan calls for making an equal number (four) of each casting at one time.

The mold was made on a pin-lift molding machine in a 13-in. by 18-in. flask,

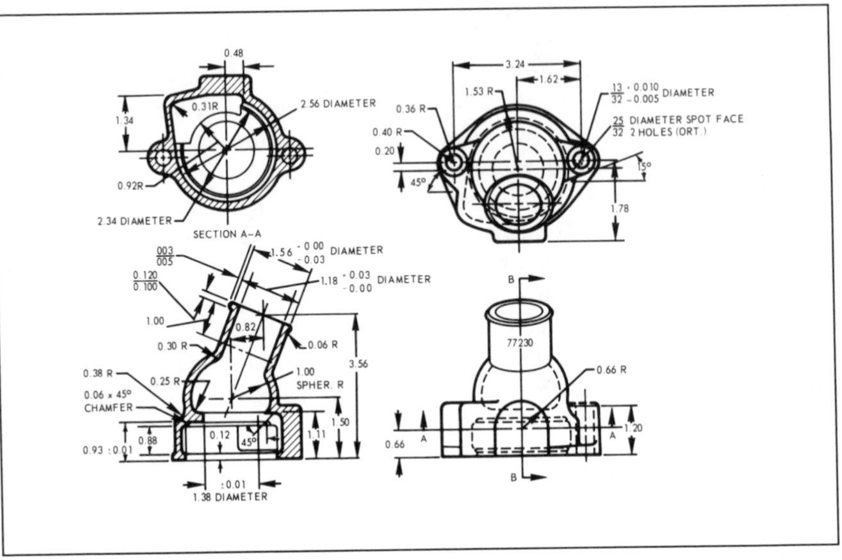

Figure 9-1. Water outlet casting.

5-in. drag and 6-in. cope, using a composite pattern with four impressions for the water outlet and four for the thermostat housing.

Material Cost

To determine material cost, the estimator multiplies finished casting weight by the cost per pound of the metal used in the finished casting.

Casting Weight

Casting weight is calculated from the engineering drawing (*Figure 9-1*) by breaking the workpiece into suitable geometric sections and obtaining the volume of each. The total weight is found by multiplying the total volume by the weight of the material per unit volume.

Section 1 in *Figure 9-1* is the cylindrical top portion of the casting with a 1.56 in. outside diameter (O.D.), 1.18 in. inside diameter (I.D.), and is 1.20 in. long. Section 2 is the spherical portion in the center of the casting. The third section is the base. The volume of the base is found by using a planimeter and Section A-A of *Figure 9-1*. *Table 9-3* shows the calculation of the casting weight.

Using the casting weight of 1.686 (as determined in *Table 9-3*), and assuming a shop yield of 54.5%, a remelt factor of 40%, and a metal lossage factor of 10% of finished casting weight, the following weights are calculated:

Table 9-3. Calculation for Weight of Water Outlet Casting.

Material: Cast iron, .26 lb/cu in
Volume of section 1.
$V = \pi h(r_1^2 - r_2^2)$
From Fig. 9-1, $h = 1.2$ in.; $r_1 = .78$ in.; $r_2 = .59$ in.
$V = 1.2\pi[(.78)^2 - (.59)^2] = 3.77(.61 - .35) = .98$ cu. in.
Volume of section 2.

$$V = \frac{4\pi}{3}(r_1^3 - r_2^3)$$

From Fig. 9-1, $r_1 = 1.18$ in.; $r_2 = 1.00$ in.; $\frac{4\pi}{3} = 4.189$ in.
$V = 4.189[(1.18)^3 - (1)^3] = 4.189(1.64 - 1.00) = 2.68$ cu. in.
For spherical segment not required

$$V = \frac{\pi h^2}{3}(3r - h)$$

For upper portion:
When $r = 1.18$ in., $h = .3$ in.

$$V_1 = \frac{\pi(.3)^2}{3}[(3)(1.18) - .3] = .0945(3.24) = .306 \text{ cu. in.}$$

When $r = 1.00$ in., $h = .2$ in.

$$V_2 = \frac{\pi(.2)^2}{3}[3(1) - .2] = .042(2.8) = .118 \text{ cu. in.}$$

$V_1 - V_2 = .306 - .118 = .188$ cu. in.

For lower portion:
Assuming the spherical segment not wanted is .40 in. below the center line, when $r =$ 1.18 in., $h = .78$

$$V_3 = \frac{\pi(.78)^2}{3}[(3)(1.18) - .78] = .64(2.76) = 1.765 \text{ cu. in.}$$

When $r = 1.00$ in., $h = .60$ in.

$$V_4 = \frac{\pi(.60)^2}{3}[3(1) - .60] = .415(2.4) = .905 \text{ cu. in.}$$

$V_3 - V_4 = 1.765 - .905 = .860$ cu. in.
Total volume of spherical portion:
2.68 − .860 − .188 = 1.628 cu. in.
Volume of section 3 (using planimeter):
Area of large section = 8.760 sq. in.
Area of small section = 5.560 sq. in.
Area of metal = 3.200 sq. in.
$V = Ah = 3.2 \times 1.2 = 3.84$ cu. in.
Total volume of part = .980 + 1.628 + 3.840 = 6.448 cu. in.
Total weight of part = 6.448 × .26 = 1.686 lbs.

$$\text{Pouring Weight} = \frac{\text{Finished Casting Weight}}{\text{Shop Yield}}$$

$$= \frac{1.686 \text{ lbs.}}{54.5\%}$$

$$= 3.1 \text{ lbs.}$$

$$\text{Remelted Metal Weight} = \text{Pouring Weight} \times \text{Remelt Factor}$$

$$= 3.1 \text{ lbs. x } 40\%$$

$$= 1.24 \text{ lbs.}$$

$$\text{Lost Metal} = \text{Finished Casting Weight} \times \text{Metal Lossage Factor}$$

$$= 1.686 \text{ lbs.} \times 10\%$$

$$= .169 \text{ lbs.}$$

Finished Casting Metal Cost

The cost of the metal used in the finished casting is computed by the use of the following formulas:

(1) Poured Metal Cost per Casting = Pouring Weight per Casting x (Labor and Overhead + Charged Material Cost)

(2) Cost of Metal in Finished Casting = Poured Metal Cost per Casting— (Amount of Melted Metal x Values of Remelted Metal)

Where: Labor and overhead = \$.03/lb.
Charged material = \$.18/lb.
Remelted metal = \$.12/lb.

(1) Poured Metal Cost per Casting = 3.1 (\$.03 + \$.18) = \$.651
(2) Cost of Metal in Finished Casting = \$.651—(1.24 lbs. x \$.12) = \$.501

Core Cost

The core-making operations are shown on the "Operation, Equipment, Tool & Gage & Standard Time Routing" sheet in *Figure 9-2*.

One each of the A, B, and C cores shown in *Figure 9-3* are made in the composite core box. The box is designed for a hand ram operation, which is the lowest-cost type of core box. No vents, screens, or blow plates are required. The cores are carefully placed on a flat plate for drying, eliminating the need for

OPERATION, EQUIPMENT, TOOL & GAUGE, & STANDARD TIME ROUTING

LEGEND	ISSUE NO 1	SHEET 1 of 1	PART NAME Water Outlet Cores	PART NO 4/10/88
	FORGING NO	ROUGH WEIGHT	MATERIAL	EFFECTIVE DATE 6/17/68
	CASTING NO	FINISH WEIGHT	REFERENCE	GROUP NO
BUDGET GROUP STD	CHANGE Orig.-Re-estimated due to diff. equip.		CURRENT GROUP STD	

TOOL & GAUGES	BUDGET STD 1961	REMARKS	OPER	OPER SEQUENCE & EQUIPMENT	STUDY	STD	NET HOURLY PROD	GROSS HOURLY PROD
	$2.31	23 PW	5	HR A, B+C core & place	Est.	$4.62	Total/100	cores
				on Conv. QR. 1.385				
				Pc. Dump core box				
Note: This is a				Wires - 0 Vents - 0			(90 boxes)	
composite core box-			see	note / box / drier				
there is an A, B + C				3/plate cores/cstg. -				
core in a box, or				1 Oper - Man				
3 cores for 1 assy.								
GT 22907-285								
	.01092	23-02		All group operations		.01638	Total	
Corebox WO 88470								
			8	Oven tenders & plate man		.01638		
			10	Tin & pack		N.T.	done w/ oper	$300
		23 PW		Core & place on			Totals/100 cores	
				O.R.	100 cores			
				Pc. Core box				
				Wires - Vents -				
				1 box / drier / plate				
				Cores/cstg - Oper -				
	.01779	23-02		All group Operations		.0798	Total	
			100	Assemble "B" to "A" using		.0714	40.0	
				2 wires, paste "C" to "A" &	Est	.00843		
				"B" assy. & mud seam	11.8%			

BOOK NOS	CHANGED STANDARD	TOOLS

Figure 9-2. Operation, equipment, tool and gage, and standard time routing sheet for water outlet casting.

special driers. Also, it was estimated that the cost of making a few extra cores to replace those damaged in drying would be less than the cost of driers. The cost estimate for the core-making equipment is shown in *Figure 9-4*; the total cost of the equipment is $786. The cost of making 100 core assemblies is $4.6998.

Molding and Cleaning Costs

The estimated cost of molding and cleaning 100 water outlet castings is $2.0694. The net hourly production is estimated as 87.2 molds. *Figure 9-5* is the routing sheet for the estimated cost of molding, cleaning, and inspection of the

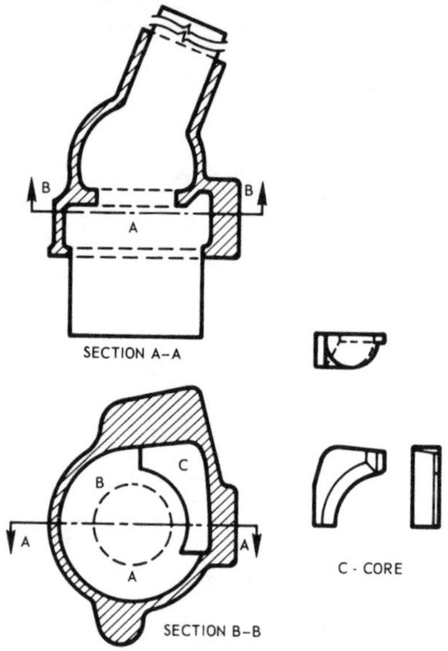

Figure 9-3. Core assembly of water outlet casting.

CORE ESTIMATE SHEET

PART NAME: Water Outlet | DATE: 6/18/88

PART NUMBER: 77230 | YEARLY VOLUME: 5,000

TO CUSTOMERS DWG. DATED: 4/22/88

TYPE OF CORE BOX: Hand Ram - Composite | MATERIAL OF CORE BOX: Alum.

OPERATIONS	WOOD	CASTING	BENCH	MILL	LATHE	KELLAR	LAYOUT	TOTAL HOURS	MATERIAL	
CORE BOX 3 IN Comp.										
MASTER	30	12						42		
BOX			30	18			6	54	$30.00	Aluminum
STEEL FACE										
VENT										
BLOW PLATE										
LAYOUT										
SETUP AND PROVING										
CORE ASSYS										
DRIERS	None									
PATTERNS	n.a.									
CAST	n.a.									
MACHINE										
SPOT FIT										
SPOTTING SLUGS										
MISCELLANEOUS										
DRILL FIXTURE										
							TOTALS	96	30.00	

LABOR ESTIMATES ARE IN HOURS 96 hrs.@ 7.86/hr. = $756.00

MATERIAL IS IN DOLLARS

DETAILS: One "A" Core; One "B" Core; One "C" Core

Figure 9-4. Cost estimate sheet for core making equipment.

TEMPORARY OPERATION, EQUIPMENT, TOOL & GAUGE, & STANDARD TIME ROUTING

	ISSUE NO. 1	SHEET 1 of 1	PART NAME Water Outlet-Molding	PART NO. 77230
	FORGING NO	ROUGH WEIGHT 12.4/Mold	MATERIAL Gray Iron	EFFECTIVE DATE 6/17/88
	CASTING NO	FINISH WEIGHT 1.686	REFERENCE	GROUP NO
BUDGET GROUP STD	CHANGE Original		CURRENT GROUP STD	

TOOL & GUAGES	BUDGET STD 1968	REMARKS	OPER	OPER SEQUENCE & EQUIPMENT	STUDY	STD	NET HOURLY PROD	GROSS HOURLY PROD
Line No. - 4	1.284	221 PW	5	Mold-Cope & drag plates		$1.284	Total 100 pcs.	
Machine No. 14 Pin Lift		OR		Pcs. per Mold - 8 4 of 77230	100 Molds	5.13	87.2	
Flask - 13 x 18				and 4 of 27573				
Drag - 5 in. Cope - 6 in.				Operators -				
Jolts -				Chaplets				
Oil -								
No. of jobs on Line	$.855		6	Set cores 1 Man	Est	$.642	Total / 100 pcs.	
Line speed -				Cores - 4 assy. - See note	100 Molds	2.565		
				Strainer -				
Note: 1-"A", 1-"B"								
and 1-"C" Core are	.01191	221-32		All group operations		.01191	Total	
pasted together to			10	Pour molds, sand	22-1	.01104		
make one assy.				clamps shakeout pins		.000822		
				and load baskets				
	.00393	241-35		All Group Operations		.00393	Total	
			15	Vib. disc, gate sort + chip	24-1	.00222		
					8%	.0001778		
			16	Barrel	24-1A	.0012		
					8%	.0001131		
			17	Load + unload 4 wheeler	24-3			
	.02028	241-36		All Group Operations		.02028	Total	
			20	Anneal + Sandblast				
				(2 men)	5%	.002238	2405	
			30	Grind	Est.	.001186		
			95	Rectify (10% 120/Hr.)		.001188	240	
Pattern Layout		29-45	100	Inspect		D.W.		
				Transfer to Shipping				
		894-17		All Group Operations	D.W.		Total	
			110					
				Credit Group Operations				
BOOK NOS. 4 (6) (2)			CHANGED STANDARD				TOOLS	

Figure 9-5. Routing sheet for the water outlet casting cost estimate.

water outlet casting. The cost of patterns for the cope and drag plates with four models of the casting is estimated at $1,392 for labor and $42 for material.

Manufacturing Cost

The manufacturing cost for the 5,000 castings is quoted as $5,063.46. Department overhead, general and administrative expense, and profit must be added to this cost to arrive at the price quoted to the customer.

10

ESTIMATING WELDING COSTS

The development of modern welding processes has provided a means of joining many different types of metal parts. As a result, castings can now be welded to castings, forgings to forgings, and forgings to castings.

EFFECT OF WELDING PROCESS SELECTION

All metals can be welded if the correct processes and equipment are used. Because the particular process chosen and means of applying it affect weld strength and costs, the welding estimator should be acquainted with the various welding methods, especially those used in his or her plant. Available processes range from the common gas or electric-arc fusion welding, to spot and seam resistance welding, to electron beam, ultrasonic, and foil-seam butt welding. The methods of applying the welding process also vary, from hand-held torches, to welding machines, to semiautomatic and fully automated welding systems. Automatic welding should be considered only when either very high volume or rigid quality requirements exist. Although any welding process can be performed automatically, automatic welding requires more equipment, better fixturing, more setup time, and closer fitup. Study is necessary to determine whether better quality and overall cost savings will justify the higher costs of automatic welding.

Workpiece thickness and composition usually determine the type of welding process that can be used. For example, the inert gas-tungsten arc (TIG) process is economical for welding light-gage material, while the semiautomatic inert gas-metal arc (MIG) process is more economical for heavier gage materials and for nonferrous materials such as aluminum.

Process Plan and Tooling List

A process plan and tooling list for the process selected is needed before estimating can begin. The process plan, usually prepared by a process planner, lists each operation to be performed. In establishing operational sequence and tooling requirements for the welding operation, the process planner considers the following factors: (1) assembly configuration, (2) quantity, (3) delivery schedule, (4) quality requirements, (5) available equipment, and (6) personnel capabilities.

COST ELEMENTS

The direct costs of manufacturing a welded part consist of material, labor, and tooling. Additional costs include quality control, packaging, shipping, and factory burden. Appropriate factors for overhead and profit are added to these costs to determine a final selling price.

Direct material

Direct material includes all the material which becomes a part of the finished product. For example, the sheet stock, castings, stampings, forgings, or extrusions used in fabricating the product. The consumable electrode or weld wire used to provide additional metal in the weld groove is another major material item. Materials are also required for finishing treatments such as painting, porcelainizing, plastic coating, rubber bonding, metallizing, etc.

The material costs of a welded product are affected by the scrap developed from the raw stock, weld rods or wires, standard component parts, and finishes. Any anticipated scrap should be considered in computing the basic material costs of each component or process.

Purchased components such as rivets, bolts, nuts, latches, and hinges are often used on the welded products. The cost of such items (plus applicable transportation charges, purchasing burden, and handling costs) is added to the direct material portion of the estimate.

The consumable electrodes used to deposit filler metal in the weld groove represent a major cost item. Excessive consumption of electrodes (or welding rods) results from:

1. Failure to use optimum amount of the electrode. Discarding electrode stubs more than 2 in. in length is generally uneconomical.
2. Poor fitup. A poorly fitted joint requires more filler metal, and may increase electrode costs as much as 500%.
3. Overwelding. Making more passes than necessary can quickly double the cost of electrodes.

For certain fusion welding processes, it is essential that an inert atmosphere surround the weld area. In some cases the welding rod has a coating which vaporizes during welding; in other cases a separate supply of inert gas must be used. Practices differ as to the method of estimating the cost of this gas; some companies include it as a part of material requirements, while others include it as overhead.

Direct labor includes are the costs of all personnel working directly upon the fabricated part. The steps involved in producing a welded part include preparation, setup, welding, postwelding operations, postmechanical operations, and finishing.

Raw stock must be prepared for welding. Preparatory operations include sizing, machining parts to print requirements, machining weld joints, and cleaning foreign material from the surfaces to be welded.

The setup for manual fusion welding, for example, includes assembling the pieces in the welding fixture, tack welding, operating the positioner, and/or preheating prior to welding. The additional step of adjusting and setting the time phase of the welding equipment is required for automatic fusion and resistance welding.

The labor used in actually making the weld is usually the largest labor cost component. However, arc time, or actual welding time, is a highly variable factor, ranging from a low of 10% to a high of 75% of the total time required to fabricate a welded product.

Factors influencing arc time include weld joint preparation, rate of weld deposit, type of welding process, and the number of passes required. The type of filler metal used also affects weld deposit time. For example, a mild steel electrode is usually deposited in two-thirds the time required for deposition of the same amount of stainless steel electrode, but it has a slower burn-off rate than iron powder electrodes.

Weld design, from the standpoint of accessiblity, shop working and safety conditions, and the amount of equipment needed also influences time requirements. Fusion position, for example, is influential. Welding in the downhand position requires the least amount of time; overhead welding the most. Shop experience indicates a 10% to 50% longer weld time for horizontal welding over downhand welding while overhead welding may require 300 to 400% more time than downhand welding.

Postwelding operations like manual or automatic fusion welds often require heat treating operations such as stress relieving, annealing, normalizing, hardening, and aging, and an appropriate amount must be added to the estimate for these operations. In the case of resistance welding, these operations are usually performed as part of the welding cycle, and are not estimated separately.

Postmechanical operations include: (1) removal of excess weld metal, slag, and weld spatter, (2) rough or finish machining to dimensional requirements of the weldment, and (3) metal conditioning processes such as peening or roll planishing to reduce cracking tendencies physically and to increase weld bead strength.

Brushing, burnishing, and other cleaning operations may be required, as may surface finishes such as painting, annodizing, or rubber coating. Each operation or process involves a labor cost.

Tooling

Special tools such as welding fixtures, machining fixtures, and machining templates are sometimes needed to complete the weld. Comparisons should be made between the cost of building tools in-plant and purchasing them from vendors.

Perishable tooling costs are generally charged directly to a specific part or product. However, durable tooling may instead be treated as a burden item. In cases of doubt, the estimator should seek a management decision.

Quality Control

Quality requirements for the welded part should be thoroughly investigated during the estimating process. Inspection and quality control are intended to assure quality at a predetermined level established by the customer and manufacturer. Meeting a high quality level may entail extensive inspection, welder testing, destructive and/or nondestructive part testing, and equipment certification. These items can add significantly to the cost of the job.

Inspection affords a simple, economical, and accurate method of identifying trouble points and determining where to take corrective action to assure conformance to contractual requirements. Making an accurate estimate requires the estimator be aware of the amount and level of inspection necessary.

One item that should always be inspected is fitup. Poor fitup can create gaps too wide to fill with the specified number of passes. Inspection prior to welding will prevent excessive corrective welding. *Figure 10-1* shows the effect of gap width on welding speed in relation to plate thickness.

The degree and amount of inspection required depends upon the type of weld, i.e., commercial, low-stress, or aircraft and missile. The types of inspection can range from visual to detailed nondestructive and destructive testing programs.

Contracts for certain types of welding, such structural welds for buildings, bridges, ships, boilers, high-pressure lines, and military programs, often require welders be tested or certified, demonstrating their ability to make satisfactory welds. Testing programs may range from an initial test to an extensive program involving continuous proficiency testing. The company is often required to keep records indicating satisfactory completion of testing and certification. The costs associated with such programs vary according to the degree of testing and the amount of required record-keeping.

Packaging, Shipping and Factory Burden

The costs for packaging and shipping of the finished article depend on the type of packaging required, shipping distance, and the method of transportation used.

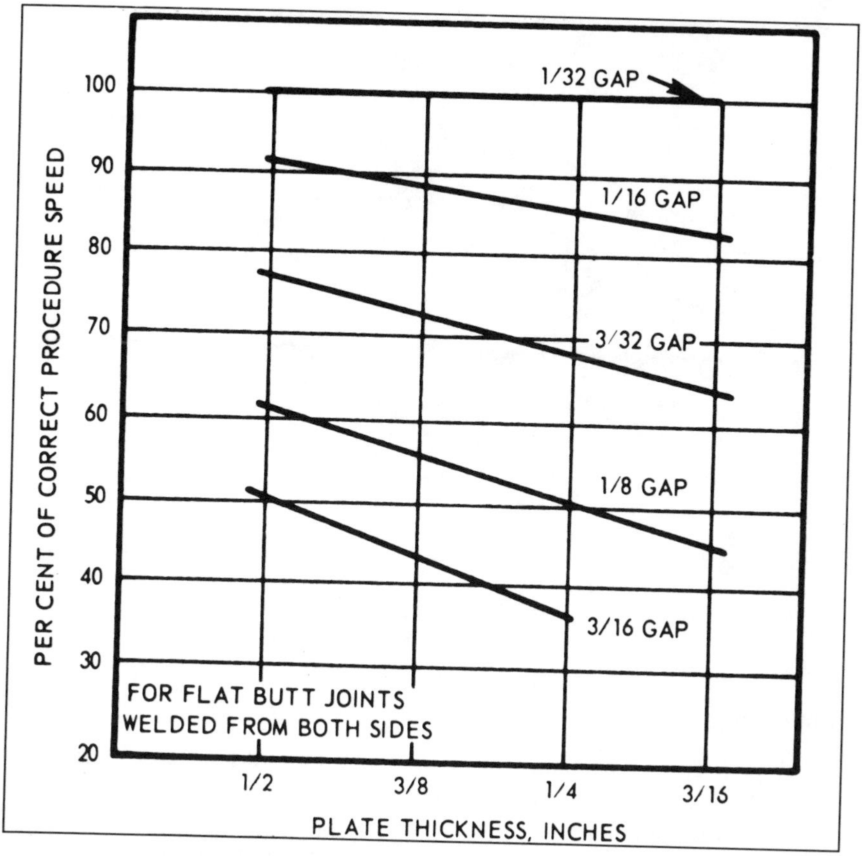

Figure 10-1. Effect of gap width on welding speed of a downhand butt joint, square or grooved.

Burden includes plant space, lighting, heating and nonperishable tooling such as welding positioners and welding equipment. When special equipment must be purchased to fabricate a part, the estimator should seek a management decision regarding what charges to apply to the part and what portion to treat as capital investment. Once completed the cost estimate is then forwarded to the accounting department. At this stage, the appropriate percentages for general and administrative costs (overhead) and profit are applied.

WELDING ESTIMATE EXAMPLE

To illustrate the foregoing costing procedure, the outlet cover shown in *Figure 10-2* will serve as an example. The outlet cover consists of 11 components and is welded by two processes; manual arc welding and resistance spot welding.

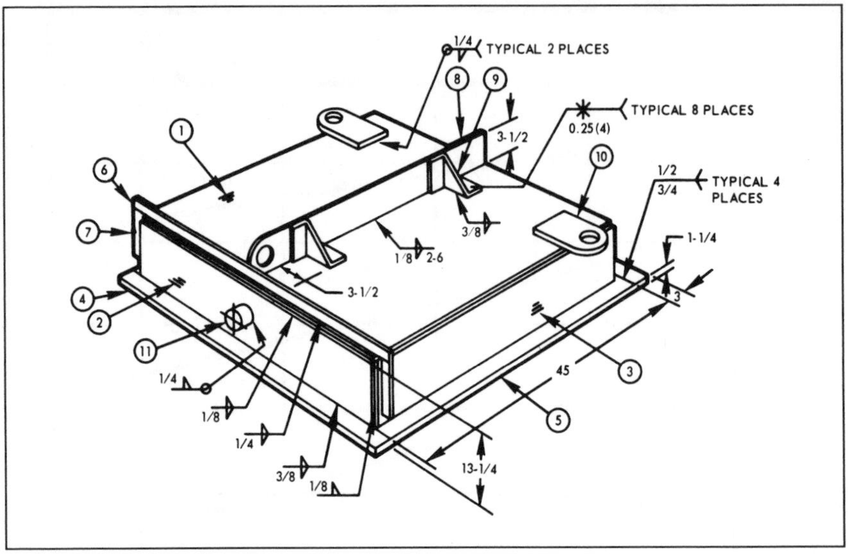

Figure 10-2. Outlet cover fabricated as a weldment.

Parameters

The parameters governing this example are; the order is for 100 units; an inspection level of 5% is required; factory personnel are well trained; and the necessary welding equipment is available. Because the customer has specified that he will pick up the finished covers, no special packaging will be needed.

Estimating Procedure

The steps involved in estimating the cost of fabricating the outlet cover are:

1. Calculate material requirements and develop total material costs (''Material Summary Sheet,'' *Figure 10-3*).
2. Determine total engineering and tooling charges (''Engineering and Tooling Summary Sheet,'' *Figure 10-4*).
3. List the welding processes necessary to assemble the outlet cover, and calculate deposited weld metal weight and welding time (''Welding Summary Sheet,'' *Figure 10-5*).
4. List the labor operations (other than those required for welding and in-house tooling) and compute the time required for each (''Labor Summary Sheet,'' *Figure 10-6*).

COST ESTIMATE
ENGINEERING AND TOOLING

CUSTOMER City Supply Company DATE 6/17/88 NO. 8302
PART NAME Outlet Cover PART NO. ESTIMATOR LMG SHEET 1 OF 1

ITEM NO	DESCRIPTION	BUY	MAKE	DELIVERY WEEKS	MAN HOURS	RATE	LABOR COST	MAT'L COST	AMORTIZED TOOL COST	NON AMORTIZED TOOL COST
1	Layout Template-8	✓		1/2						$204.00
2	Layout Template-9	✓		1/2						204.00
3	Layout Template-10	✓		1/2						204.00
4	Sub-Assy. Spotweld	✓		1						420.00
	Fixture to Locate 8 & 9									
5	Setup		✓		3.0	12.00	36.00		36.00	
6	Weldment Fixture-1,-2,	✓		1						864.00
	3, 4 and 5									
7	Setup		✓		4.00	12.00	48.00		48.00	
8	Final Assy. Fixture-Yaub	✓								633.00
	Assy.-6 & 7, -10 & 11									
9	Setup		✓		4.00	12.00	48.00		48.00	
									$132.00	$2629.00

Figure 10-3. Engineering and tooling summary sheet.

5. Summarize all costs and develop the total contract cost ("Cost Estimate Summary Sheet," *Figure 10-7*).

Direct Material

The "Material Summary Sheet," shown in *Figure 10-3*, reflects the cost of raw stock and other material used in the finished product.

For components fabricated from raw stock, the estimator must analyze the part print to determine the dimensions of each component. From these dimensions he calculates the volume of each component, and multiplies the volume times the weight per pound of raw stock to determine the weight of each component. This weight is multiplied by the cost per pound of raw stock in order to obtain the cost of the component. The resulting cost figures for each component are shown in the right-hand column of the "Material Summary Sheet" (*Figure 10-3*).

Such volume and weight calculations are not necessary for purchased parts. Note, for example, that the weight is omitted for Detail 11, a purchased pipe nipple, and that the cost of this item is simply listed under "Unit Cost," and the figure extended to the "Total Cost" column.

Finally, the total costs of the part components are added.

COST ESTIMATE
MATERIAL SUMMARY SHEET

CUSTOMER City Supply Company NO. 8302
DATE 6/17/88 ESTIMATOR J.M.D. SHEET 1 OF 1
PART NAME Outlet Cover PART NO.

DET. NO.	DESCRIPTION	QUAN.	WEIGHT	UNIT COST	TOTAL COST
1	Cover Top	1	71 lbs	@33¢/#	$23.43
2	Cover End	2	76	@33¢/#	25.08
3	Cover Side	2	76	@33¢/#	25.08
4	End Flange	2	108	@33¢/#	35.64
5	Side Flange	2	96	@33¢/#	31.68
6	Top Bar	1	5	@33¢/#	1.65
7	Side Bar	2	2	@33¢/#	.66
8	Rib	1	5	@33¢/#	1.65
9	Gusset	4	4	@33¢/#	1.32
10	Lift Lug	2	8	@33¢/#	2.64
11	1½" Pipe Nipple	1		$3.75 ea.	3.75
	Total		451#		$152.58
	1.15 scrap factor		$152.58x	1.15	175.47
	Total electrode		12.6#	@78¢/#	9.84
	Total paint		0.2 gal.	19.50/gal.	3.90
	Material Allowance				$189.21

Figure 10-4. Material summary sheet.

After determining the total cost of the part components, the estimator applies a scrap factor to allow for these losses. To keep scrap costs as low as possible, the estimator surveys raw stock vendors to determine whether material in the required sizes is commercially available. When required sizes are not available, raw stock must be purchased in larger units and cut to size, and a factor must be applied for raw stock cutoff losses. Allowance must also be made for material lossage due to machining and weld joint preparation.

The scrap factor of 1.15 used in this example was developed from previous shop experience and includes raw stock cutoff, as well as machining and weld joint preparation losses.

The amount of weld deposit (shown as "Total Electrode" on the Material Summary Sheet, *Figure 10-3*) is determined from the "Welding Summary Sheet" (see *Figure 10-5*).

The amount of paint needed is calculated on the basis of square feet of surface

COST ESTIMATE
WELDING SUMMARY SHEET

CUSTOMER City Supply Company NO. 8302
DATE 6/17/88 ESTIMATOR J.M.A. SHEET 1 OF 1
PART NAME Outlet Cover PART NO.

DET. NO.	DETAIL NAME	QUAN.	WELDING PROCESS	WEIGHT DEPOSITED METAL, LB.	TIME, MIN.
1	Cover Top	1			
2	Cover End	2	3.6 ft. 1/8 / 1/8 ▶ @ 0.027#/ft.	0.40	21.6
3	Cover Side	2	3.6 ft. 1/8 / 1/8 ▶ @ 0.027#/ft.	0.40	21.6
			1.88 ft. 1/8 ▶ @ 0.027#/ft.	0.10	5.7
4	End flange	2	3.6 ft. 3/8 / 3/8 ▶ @ 0.239#/ft.	3.44	86.0
5	Side Flange	2	3.75 ft. 3/8 / 3/8 ▶ @ 0.239#/ft.	3.58	89.7
			0.25 ft. 1/2 / 3/4 ▶ @ 0.425# / 0.957#/ft.	1.38	27.1
6	Top bar	1	3.75 ft. 1/4 / 1/4 ▶ @ 0.106#/ft.	.80	20.0
7	Side bar	2	0.75 ft. 1/4 / 1/4 ▶ @ 0.106#/ft.	.32	7.9
			0.125 ft. 1/8 / 1/8 ‖ @ 0.027#/ft.	.015	0.8
8	Rib	1	3.75 ft. 1/8 / 1/8 ▶ 2 @ 0.027#/ft.	.05	3.0
			0.125 ft. 1/8 / 1/8 ▶ @ 0.027#/ft.	.01	.4
9	Gusset	4	.25 —✕—		2.2
10	Lifting lug	2	1.75 ft. 1/4 / 1/4 ◀ @ 0.106#/ft.	.38	9.3
11	1½" pipe nipple	1	0.5 ft. 1/4 ◀ @ .106#/ft.	.06	1.3
			Total	10.935	296.6 min
			1.15 scrap factor	1.64	or 5 hrs.
				12.575	
			use	12.6#	

Figure 10-5. Welding summary sheet.

area to be covered. For this example, it has been determined that one gallon of paint will cover five units.

Tooling

The "Engineering and Tooling Summary Sheet," shown in *Figure 10-4*, covers the cost of the required fixtures, templates, and setups, as well as the labor costs for those items produced in-plant.

Fixtures and templates made in-plant require a separate estimate. (For the purpose of this example, it is assumed that any special tools will be purchased from an outside vendor. Bids are normally taken, and the best price received from a reliable vendor is applied to the estimate).

Welding fixtures should be designed to accommodate welding methods that are the most effective and economical for the job. The dimensional accuracy to which components have to be welded must also be taken into consideration. The

COST ESTIMATE
LABOR SUMMARY

CUSTOMER City Supply Company NO. 8302
DATE 6/17/88 ESTIMATOR J.M.D. SHEET 1 OF 1
PART NAME Outlet Cover PART NO.

DET. NO.	DESCRIPTION	QUAN.	SIZE	OPERATION	TIME-MIN
1	Cover Top	1	1/8 x 44 3/4 x 44 3/4	Shear	11.9
2	Cover End	2	1/4 x 12 x 44 1/2	Shear	18.4
3	Cover End	2	1/4 x 12 x 44 1/2	Shear	18.4
4	End Flange	2	1 1/4 x 3 x 51	Cut	5.0
5	Side Flange	2	1 1/4 x 3 x 45	Cut	5.0
				Machine	9.0
6	Top Bar	1	1/4 x 1 1/2 x 48	Shear	7.4
7	Side Bar	2	1/4 x 1 1/2 x 9	Shear	2.5
8	Rib	1	1/8 x 3 1/2 x 44	Shear	7.8
				Drill	.4
9	Gusset	4	1/8 x 7 1/2 x 8 (makes 2)	Shear	10.0
				Mark + Form	8.0
10	Lift Lug	2	1/4 x 6 x 9 1/2	Shear	4.2
				Drill	.8
				Total	108.8
					1.8 hr.
	Outlet Cover	1		Clean for paint	.4 hr.
				Paint	.3 hr.
				Total	2.5 hr.

Figure 10-6. Labor summary sheet.

fixtures used should be of no higher quality than necessary to obtain the required dimensional accuracy so that their cost can be held to a minimum.

Setups

Setup time includes the cost of labor required to assemble the fixture, check for the dimensional characteristics, and install the positioners.

Welding Operations

The "Welding Summary Sheet" shown in *Figure 10-5* is used to develop costs directly related to the welding operations. To avoid overlooking any required welding, the estimator lists each part component on the summary sheet. Welding time and filler metal quantity is based on the size and length of the weld.

In calculating the weight of deposited metal, the first part component is

COST ESTIMATE
SUMMARY SHEET

CUSTOMER City Supply Company NO. 8302
DATE 6/17/88 ESTIMATOR J.M.A. SHEET 1 OF 1
PART NAME Outlet Cover PART NO.

MATERIAL ALLOWANCE $189.21 WASTE FACTOR 1.15
LABOR ALLOWANCE REJECTION FACTOR 1.03
MACHINE & FINISH 2.5 hr. BURDEN FACTOR 2.15
WELDING 5.0 hr. G & A FACTOR 1.07
OFF STANDARD FACTOR 1.90 PROFIT FACTOR 1.11
TOOL & ENGINEERING ALLOWANCE LABOR RATES
AMORTIZED $132.00 WELDER $8.40/hr.
NON-AMORTIZED $2,529.00 MACHINE & FINISH $8.25/hr.

TOOL DELIVERY 3½ weeks
PART DELIVERY 7 per week beginning the fifth week.

QUANTITY	REJECTION ALLOWANCE	MATERIAL SELLING PRICE	LABOR SELLING PRICE	ENG'RG & TOOL SELLING PRICE	TOTAL SELLING PRICE
100	1.03	$231.48	$100.29 Mach.	$1.56	$552.36
			203.76 Weld		
			15.27 Insp.		
			$319.32 Total		

(1) 189.21 x 1.03 x 1.07 x 1.11 = 231.48
(2) 2.5 x 8.25 x 1.90 x 2.15 x 1.07 x 1.11 = 100.29
5.0 x 8.40 x 1.90 x 2.15 x 1.07 x 1.11 = 203.76
7.5 x .05 x 8.40 x 1.90 x 2.15 x 1.07 x 1.11 = 15.27
(3) 44 ÷ 100 x 1.07 x 1.11 = $10.52
Cost 100 pieces $552.36 x 100 = $55,236.00
Non Amortized Tooling $2529 x 1.07 x 1.11 = 3,003.69
Total Estimated Price $58,239.69

Figure 10-7. Welding cost estimate summary sheet.

considered only as a starting piece because no joining weld is required. For the second piece, only the amount of welding needed to join it to the first piece is estimated and entered on the summary and, for each additional piece, only the amount of welding required to join it to the preceding parts is listed.

The weld lengths are entered in feet, and weld sizes are indicated by standard symbols with the weight per foot of each different weld size. *Table 10-1* shows average arc time in minutes per foot and weight of deposited metal in pounds per foot for different sizes of fillet and 45-deg. bevel welds using mild steel electrodes. Deposited metal weight for different type welds may be calculated by multiplying the cross-sectional area of the weld by 12 inches. The product (cu in/ft) is then multiplied by the weight of a cubic inch of weld metal (a deposited steel electrode weighs .238 lb/cu in). The result is weight per foot of deposited weld metal.

Table 10-1. Data for Fillet and 45 Degree/Bevel Welds*.

Weld Size (in.)	*Weight (lb/ft)*	*Time (min/ft)*
1/8	.027	1.5
1/4	.106	2.65
5/16	.166	4.15
3/8	.239	5.98
7/16	.325	7.40
1/2	.425	9.06
5/8	.664	13.10
3/4	.957	18.00
7/8	1.300	23.70
1	1.700	30.40
1 1/8	2.150	37.80
1 1/4	2.640	46.00

*Based on average 45 to 50 per cent arc time and welding deposition rates of 2.4 lb/hr for welds 3/8 in. and under; 3.6 lb/hr for 3/8 in. and over.

For manual welding, the total weight of deposited weld metal is converted to an estimated weight of required electrodes by dividing by a factor of .55. This value is based on the assumption that the actual deposited weld metal is 55% of the electrode's original weight.

Estimates for spot welding are normally based on charts such as that shown in *Table 10-2*. This shows typical point-closing to point-opening times for various thickness of material. These will vary slightly form one material to another and from one type of welder to another. The contact time for spot welding is taken as approximately 50% of total weld time on thicker-gage materials. The remainder is required for fixture loading, etc. Contact time will be a slightly smaller percentage for thinner materials.

Labor

Labor costs for operations other than in-plant tooling and welding are summarized on the "Labor Summary Sheet." shown in *Figure 10-6*.

To determine machining and cutting costs, the parts are itemized, and the time for each operation is calculated by using the company's standard accumulated data.

The cost of labor for painting and plating preparation is computed by use of standard time data.

Inspection labor costs can be handled either as standard time data for each inspection operation, or as a percentage of the standard labor hours for manufacturing the part if a correlation can be developed. In this example a factor of 5% of direct labor hours is used for inspection.

Total Contract Cost

The cost data and labor hours computed on the preceding summary sheets (*Figures 10-3, 10-4*, and *10-6*) are transferred to the "Estimate Summary Sheet" (*Figure 10-7*) prior to developing a total estimated selling price.

Table 10-2. Data for Spot Welding.

Material Thickness (in.)	*Time (sec.)*
.025 to .025	1
.031 to .031	1
.042 to .042	1
.050 to .050	1
.062 to .062	1.5
.093 to .093	3
.125 to .125	4

First, the estimator computes separate selling prices for: (1) material, (2) labor, and (3) amortized engineering and amortized engineering and tooling. This is done by applying the predetermined company rates and factors shown in the upper portion of *Figure 10-7* to the following formulas:

1. Material Selling Price = Material Allowance × Rejection Factor × G and A Factor × Profit Factor
2. Labor Selling Price = Labor Allowance × Labor Rate × Off-Standard Factor × Burden Rate × G and A Factor × Profit Factor
3. Amortized Engineering and Tooling Expense = Engineering and Tooling Allowance ÷ Quantity × G and A Factor × Profit Factor.

For the actual computations, see the lower portion of *Figure 10-7*. The values determined by these formulas are added to arrive at the total selling price minus nonamortized engineering and tooling per unit. The unit price is multiplied by the desired quantity (100 in this case) to determine the total selling price (again excluding nonamortized engineering and tooling).

Next, nonamortized engineering and tooling must be determined. The formula used is:

Nonamortized Engineering and Tooling = Engineering and Tooling Allowance × G and A Factor × Profit Factor.

Total estimated contract price is then determined by adding the total selling price to the nonamortized engineering and tooling cost.

11

ESTIMATING FORGED PARTS

Forging, one of the oldest known methods of metalworking, is still widely used. Forged parts offer high strength and good fatigue-life characteristics.

Almost any forging can be made using in one of several methods unless a definite restriction, like grain flow position, eliminates one or more of them. The technique used depends upon individual shop practices and the type of equipment available.

The use of a drop hammer or forging press for a specific part, for example, often depends on which machine is available. Some types of forgings can be produced on either class of equipment. However, certain forgings are best suited for a particular piece of equipment. Generally, parts suited to the forging machine cannot be made satisfactorily by either the drop hammer or the forging press.

KINDS OF FORGINGS

Forgings are usually classified into four general groups according to their method of fabrication: (1) smith forgings, (2) drop forgings, (3) machine or upset forgings, and (4) press forgings. Smith forgings are also referred to as open-die forgings, while drop forgings, machine forgings, and press forgings are known as closed-die forgings.

Open-Die Forgings

Smith forgings are classified as open-die forgings because flat dies are used to make them instead of impression dies. Open-die forgings are selected for large or irregularly shaped parts that are impractical to produce with impression dies, or for short production runs where quantities are too small to justify the cost of impression dies.

Closed-Die Forgings

Drop forgings, machine forgings, and press forgings are classified as closed-die forgings because they are made from impression dies. The advantages of closed-die forgings are: (1) lower operator skill requirements, (2) accelerated production rates, and (3) holding of closer tolerances. Because of the extra cost of the impression dies, closed-die forgings are more likely to be selected for long production runs.

ESTIMATING PROCEDURES

Until three or four decades ago, when forging materials and shapes were less complex, estimating procedures were simpler. Estimating departments were new and the work was usually done by the plant superintendent or the sales department. One method of estimating forging costs involved using a chart listing pound prices for easy, medium, and difficult forgings, along with several grades of material, and then multiplying the net weight by a suitable pound price to obtain the estimated cost. Another method was to figure the cost of the forging stock needed and multiply its cost by a suitable factor. For example, if the forging stock cost $1.50, it would be multiplied by a factor (perhaps 2 1/2) and the estimated cost would be $3.75. A third method was to use estimated man-hours multiplied by a material factor.

Today, with many simple to highly complex materials, a greater variety in forging equipment, closer tolerances, metallurgical requirements and restrictions, it has become necessary to develop detailed cost estimates in a consistent manner. The estimating procedures set forth in Chapter Four are generally applicable to forgings; specialized procedures are outlined in the following sections.

Estimating Forms

Many standard shapes of forgings can be estimated from a price list after the weight has been calculated. If additional work like rough machining, testing, or special inspection is required the cost is totaled on a simple estimate form.

Specially developed estimating forms are invaluable in detailing and presenting the various forging cost elements. Although commercial forging companies generally design their own forms to suit individual need, most forms call for the same basic information.

Estimating Data

The availability of standard data from previous jobs greatly facilitates forging estimates. Helpful data include net and gross weights, production sequences, production rates, die life, scrappage rates, and tooling and die costs. Such data permit quick estimates on parts comparable to those produced previously.

In many cases the new parts can be estimated by comparison with parts previously forged, making adjustments for slight variations in size, shape, material, quantity, etc.

When forging is considerably different in shape or other specification from those previously produced, a basic study should be made of detailed sketches, or even a model, to work out all production details.

COST ELEMENTS

Direct material, dies and special tooling, machining operations, scrappage, and labor are the most significant cost elements of the forging estimate. The cost of special items such as torch cutting, bending, and other auxiliary operations must also be computed. All of these costs must be analyzed carefully in preparing the detailed cost estimate.

Direct Material

Direct material is the largest single cost element for forged parts. In a typical cost estimate for a closed-die forging made of carbon or low-alloy steel in medium to high-production quantities, 40% to 60% of the total factory cost is direct material when the forging is produced on a drop hammer or mechanical forging press. For parts made in a forging machine, the direct material percentage is sometimes higher.

Quantity

To determine direct material cost, the estimator first calculates the quantity of forging stock required for the desired production run, making appropriate allowances for material loss.

Information from previous jobs permits quick computation of material allowances for comparable forgings. For example, filed data indicates that on a previous job a material allowance of 6.6 lbs. was required to fabricate a finished smith forging estimated to weigh 5.3 lbs. in its finished condition.

The estimator establishes a material allowance/finished weight ratio (6.6 lbs. :5.3 lbs. = 1.25:1) and applies this ratio to the finished weight of the casting being estimated. A comparable smith forging with a finished weight of 7.2 lbs., for example would have a material allowance of 9 lbs. (7.2 lbs. × 1.25).

When data from previous jobs are not available, the estimator must compute the material allowance. First, the shape weight (a theoretically correct weight as computed from engineering drawings or sketches) is calculated by dividing the part into geometric sections and obtaining the volume of each section. The total shape weight is found by multiplying the total volume by the weight of the material per unit volume.

It is difficult to divide the part into sections to obtain shape weights if the

Table 11-1. Density of Metals (lb/cu in).

Metal	*Density*	*Metal*	*Density*
Aluminum	.098 to .101	Nickel alloys, A	.321
Beryllium	.067	Low carbon	.321
Beryllium copper	.298	Duranickel[2]	.298
Brass, forging	.305	Monel[3]	.319
Bronze, aluminum	.269 to .274	K Monel[2]	.306
Nickel aluminum	.273	Inconel[3]	.304
Tobin[1]	.304	Inconel X[3]	.298
Manganese	.282 to .302	Steel (cast)	.283
Bearing alloy	.292 to .299	Carbon	.284
High silicon	.308	Alloy	.284
Aluminum silicon	.278	18-8	.285
Phosphor	.311	13% Cr	.283
Copper	.325	14% W	.312
Duralumin	.102	22% W	.321
German silver	.306	Tantalum	.600
Lead	.409	Titanium	.160
Magnesium	.063	Tungsten	.700
Molybdenum	.368		

[1]TM Anaconda American Brass Company
[2]TM International Nickel Company, Inc.
[3]TM Huntington Alloy Products Division, The International Nickel Company, Inc.

contours are comprised of irregular fillets, oddly shaped ellipsoidal sections, or other peculiar shapes. On such sections, the estimator should make an accurate layout of the section and use a planimeter to find the area of the irregular surface. This area is multiplied by the section thickness and material density to find the weight of the section. *Table 11-1* shows the density of metals commonly used for forgings.

Next, the *net weight* (the average actual weight of finished castings) is determined by multiplying the shape weight by a factor based upon data from previous shop experience. The net weight of most forgings exceeds the shape weight by 3% to 5%.

Gross Weight (the weight of the forging stock required to make a forging) is determined simplest by multiplying the net weight by a factor developed from previous shop experience. For closed-die forgings, the multiple may be as high as 60% to 70%.

When the appropriate multiple is not known, gross weight must be determined by adding to net weight the material loss due to factors such as: (1) flash, (2) scale, (3) tonghold, (4) sprue, and (5) cut waste.

First, a *flash weight* loss is added to the net weight. (Flash is the excess metal extruded as a thin plate surrounding the forging at the die parting line to assure that all impressions are properly filled). Flash is removed by shearing in a power press, while the forging is still hot or after it has cooled. Average flash width and

Table 11-2. Approximate Flash Thickness and Width on Forgings.

Net Weight (lbs.)	*Thickness (in.)*	*Width (in.)*	*Weight of Flash (lb/in)*
	Cold-Trimmed Forgings		
Up to 1	1/16	3/4	.0133
1 to 5	1/16	1	.0177
5 to 10	3/32	1 1/4	.0333
10 to 15	1/8	1 3/8	.0487
15 to 25	5/32	1 1/2	.0668
25 to 50	3/16	1 3/4	.0937
50 to 100	1/4	2	.1425
	Hot-Trimmed Forgings		
Up to 1	1/8	3/4	.0266
1 to 5	1/8	1	.0354
5 to 10	5/32	1 1/4	.0553
10 to 15	3/16	1 3/8	.0730
15 to 25	7/32	1 1/2	.0941
25 to 50	1/4	1 3/4	.1250
50 to 100	5/16	2	.1790
100 to 200	3/8	2 1/2	.2670

thickness varies with the weight of the forging, though hot-trimmed forgings have thicker flash sections than cold-trimmed forgings. Approximate flash dimensions for both types of forgings are shown in *Table 11-2*.

Allowance must also be made for flash or punchout slugs from holes in the forging. Punchout slugs vary with the dimensions of the punched hole and the thickness of the section through which the hole is punched. In many cases, the punchout slug may be considered having approximately the same thickness as the flash.

Scale is the material lost due to surface oxidation in heating and forging. The amount lost is a function of surface area, heating time, and type of material. Scale loss is generally computed as a percentage of forging net weight. For forgings under 10 lbs., 7.5% of the net weight is added for scale loss; for forgings from 10 to 25 lbs., 6% is added, and for forgings over 25 lbs., an addition of 5% is a close approximation.

Scale loss becomes increasingly important as the surface area increases in relation to the shape weight, or where the sections are forged with very small flash allowance, as in press forging or upsetting work. Scale loss also becomes greater with reheating.

The tonghold is a projection, 1/2 in. to 1.0 in. long at one end of the forging which is used to hold the forging. The sprue (the connection between the forging and the tonghold) must be strong enough to permit lifting the workpiece out of the impression without bending. Sprue loss, approximately 7.5% of forging net weight, must be added to net weight. Some estimators provide for tonghold and sprue loss through a liberal flash allowance.

After gross weight is determined, an allowance must be made for cut waste. Cut waste consists of: (1) stock consumed as sawdust when bar stock is sized by saw cutting, and (2) bar end loss resulting from purchased bar length variations and short ends resulting from cutting the forging stock to an exact length. An allowance of 5% of total gross weight is often used.

Cost

Direct material cost is calculated by multiplying total gross weight (plus cut waste allowance) by the cost per pound of forging stock. Direct material cost per forging is then obtained by dividing the resulting sum by the number of finished forged parts of acceptable quality.

Dies and Special Tooling

The cost of dies and tooling varies,depending upon the type of forging produced. These costs differ according to whether open-die or closed-die forgings are used.

Open-die forgings are produced without the use of impression dies. The part is forged between lower-cost flat dies and possibly given some of its shape by using stock hand tools on the flat dies.

The cost and life of the dies and tooling are computed, with appropriate allowances for maintenance and repair, and the total cost is distributed evenly across the production run. Impression dies and special tooling are necessary for closed-die forgings. For small quantities, the cost of dies and other tooling can be a substantial factor.

The cost of impression dies depends upon the kind of forging being made and the forging stock specified. A simple closed-die forging made from conventional material usually requires a set of dies and a set of trimming tools to shear away the flash.

As a general rule, as the cost of the forging stock goes up because of higher alloy content, it forges with greater difficulty and the die impressions tend to wear faster, increasing the die factor cost increment. This rule applies to the copper-base alloys and to the aluminum-base alloys.

In some instances, it may be more economical to use simple dies at a nominal cost and a small amount of additional forging material because of a small number of forgings and low-cost material. With more expensive forging stock, it may be best to reduce the material used and add a forging step.

Once the general sequence has been established and the size of the forging unit determined, the size of the die blocks the cost of the dies can be estimated.

Small parts, where quantity permits, may be forged two, three, four, or six at a time.

The increment of die maintenance or die replacement in closed-die forgings is developed by estimating the total cost of a set of dies, including any resinkings, and dividing this total cost by the estimated number of pieces than can be produced from the dies. The cost and life of other tooling must be computed to develop a tooling replacement or repair factor. Data concerning die life and die and tooling costs from previous forging estimates assists in making these computations.

Machine Operations

Various types of forging equipment are available. The machine selected for a specific forging depends upon the size of the forged part, the availability of the machine, and economic factors related to machine operation.

Costs are developed for the various types of equipment by assigning an hourly rate to each item such as forging hammers, forging presses, forging machines, forge heating furnaces, trimming presses, and other types of production equipment. The hourly cost of operating a small drop hammer with its furnace and trimming press but without the production crew may be $75 per hour; one of the larger ones might cost $450 per hour. Much of the other supplementary equipment might be given an hourly rate. Usually, each forging plant develops its own machine-hour rates from its own experience through recognized cost accounting procedures. *Table 11-3* lists some representative machine hour rates. Not all the items of cost are on the basis of machine hours. It's impractical to cover shearing, steel handling, cleaning, production material handling through the plant, shipping, heat treating, and certain other cost items on a machine hour basis. These operations are generally estimated on a gross or net pound basis such as listed in *Table 11-3*. These cost increments are usually smaller than the production increments but reflect a necessary part of the total cost.

Setup and Labor

Previously accumulated data also establish setup costs for the various types of available forging equipment. See the applicable column in *Table 11-3*.

Next,the estimator adds labor costs to the estimate. Because the cost of labor varies with the type of machine used, it is convenient to summarize these costs as shown in *Table 11-3*.

Scrappage Allowance

The expected allowance for spoilage or scrap is normally taken as a percentage of the factory cost. On small quantities, or special compositions, the scrap percentage will be higher than for large production quantities.

Table 11-3. Typical Forge Shop Estimator's Chart.*

Machine	*Rate per Hour*					*Setup Cost*
	Machine	*Furnace*	*Trim Press*	*Operators and Helpers*	*Total*	
2,000-lb. board drop hammer	$ 45	$ 27	$ 9	$ 36	$117	$ 195
3,000-lb. board drop hammer	63	36	15	36	150	270
5,000-lb. board drop hammer	102	42	18	45	207	420
3,000-lb. steam drop hammer	108	42	15	48	213	420
6,000-lb. steam drop hammer	150	54	27	69	300	600
12,000-lb. steam drop hammer	225	69	36	105	435	1200
20,000-lb. steam drop hammer	300	105	60	135	600	2400
3-in. forging machine	60	30	....	45	135	450
6-in. forging machine	165	75	....	90	330	900
1,500-ton forging press	120	45	24	66	255	450
3,000-ton forging press	225	60	10	90	405	750
1,000-ton coining press	60	....	....	30	90	150
Snagging or grinding	18	....	....	12	30	....
Special inspection	12	....	....	15	27	....
Magnetic inspection	$ 18	$....	$....	$ 12	$ 30	$....

Shearing and steel hammer	7.50/gross cwt
Shipping and product handing	9.00/net cwt
Conditioning and inspection	3.00/net cwt
Normalize	3.00/net cwt
Anneal	6.00/net cwt
Heat treat (quench and temper)	12.00/net cwt
General, administrative, and selling	9%

*The figures shown are fictitious and are given for purposes of illustration only. These figures are subject to occasional variation. An extra press or an extra man may be required for some types of forgings, and this would change the total.

OVERHEAD AND PROFIT

General and administrative costs (overhead) are usually calculated as a percentage of total manufacturing cost. If sales commissions or royalties are paid, they are added as separate items. The markup necessary to provide the desired profit is added to the total cost derived to arrive at the actual selling price.

FORGING ESTIMATE EXAMPLE

A cost estimate for the gear blank shown in *Figure 11-1* has been requested in the production quantities of 1,000, 5,000, 10,000, and 20,000 forgings. The estimated life of each die sinking is 8,000 forgings, with a maximum die life of 40,000 forgings. The forging stock to be used is AISI C1045 steel. The forge shop operations will include pancaking (flattening), blocking, forging, trimming, and normalizing. A 3,000-ton forging press and 1,000-ton coining press are to be used to forge the blank. The numerous items comprising the estimate

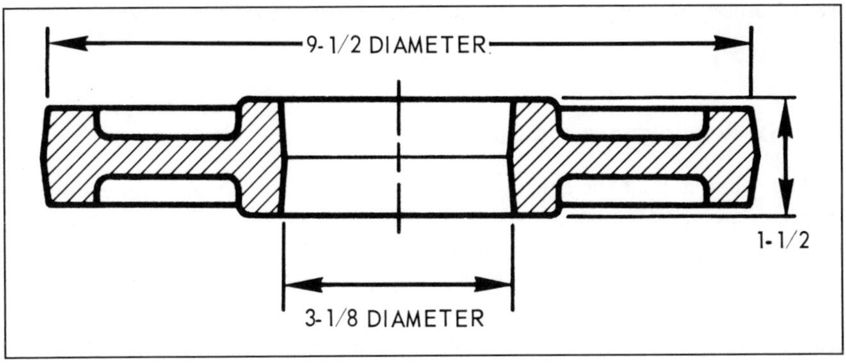

Figure 11-1. Forged gear blank.

Table 11-4. Calculation for Weight of Gear Blank.

Section 1:

$9\frac{1}{2}$ in. diameter = 20.08 lb/in

$8\frac{1}{4}$ in. diameter = 15.15

4.93 lb/in × $1\frac{1}{4}$ in. = 6.17 lbs.

Section 2:

$8\frac{1}{4}$ in. diameter = 15.15 lb/in

$4\frac{1}{2}$ in. diameter = 4.51

10.64 lb/in × $\frac{1}{2}$ in. = 5.32 lbs.

Section 3:

$4\frac{1}{2}$ in. diameter = 4.51 lb/in

$3\frac{1}{8}$ in. diameter = 2.17

2.34 lb/in × $1\frac{1}{2}$ in. = 3.51 lbs.

Shape weight 15.00 lbs.
Plus 5% shape allowance .75

Net weight 15.75 lbs.

Flash allowance:

From Table 11-3, for a 16-lb. hot-trimmed forging, flash width = $1\frac{1}{2}$ in.; $\frac{7}{32}$ in. thickness; weight per inch = .0941 lb.

For a ring, the center of gravity is .707 times the width from the I.D. The weight of the outer ring of flash is:

$2(.707 \times 1.5) + 7.5 = 11.6$ in. diameter

$11.6\pi \times .0941 = 3.42$ lbs.

The slug in the hub is 2.173 lb/in for $3\frac{1}{8}$ in. diameter × $\frac{7}{32}$ in. = .48 lb.

Scale loss: .075 × 15.75 = 1.18 lbs.

Gross weight: 15.75 + 3.42 + .48 + 1.18 = 20.83 lbs. or 21 lbs.

are recorded and summarized on the forging estimate form shown in *Figure 11-2*.

Material Requirements and Costs

The gear blank can be conveniently divided into three sections for estimating the shape weight. Section one is the rim which is 9 1/2 in. O.D. by 8 1/4 in. I.D. by 1 1/4 in. thick. Section two is a disk, 8 1/4 in. O.D. by 4 1/2 in. I.D. by 1/2 in. thick. Section three is the hub, 4 1/2 in. O.D. by 3 1/8 in. I.D. by 1 1/2 in. long. *Table 11-4* shows the calculations used to derive the shape weight, net weight, and gross weight of the forging. As shown, net weight is usually 3% to 5% greater than shape weight.

To the net weight is added an allowance for flash around the outside of the blank and within the hub, scale loss and for most forgings, a tonghold and a sprue between the forging and the tonghold. However, for this gear blank, tonghold and sprue are not required. *Table 11-2* lists typical flash allowances for hot and cold trimmed forgings.

The material costs shown on the cost estimate in *Figure 11-1* include the mill price plus extra charges for grade, size, and freight. Not shown on the estimate, but often applicable, is a "quantity extra." For small quantities not available from the mill, the forger may often be required to purchase the metal from a warehouse at a higher price which is called a "quantity extra."

These estimated costs are based on the forging weight. The charges for each operation per hundredweight are shown in *Table 11-3*.

Die Costs

Tooling costs are shown in the "Blocks & Material" column at the top of the estimating form (*Figure 11-2*). The basic die and tooling cost, as shown, is $8,010. Because die life is estimated at 8,000 forgings, $8,010 is the total die cost for the 1,000 and 5,000 production quantities.

After 8,000 forgings, additional labor is required to machine the forging and trimming dies, resink the forging die, and recondition the trimming die so they will produce forgings within the required tolerances. The time required for this series of operations (68 hrs.) is multiplied by the hourly rate ($30) to arrive at a cost of $2,040. For 10,000 forgings, the cost of one machining, resinking, and reconditioning operation (or $2,040) is added, making a total of $10,050. For 20,000 forgings, another series of operations is required, making a total die cost of $12,090. The tooling cost is a separate item on the quotation and is not included in the quoted forging price. Examples of these costs are given in *Table 11-3*. On the estimate form (*Figure 11-2*) the setup costs and production costs are prorated per piece.

FORGING ESTIMATE

CUSTOMER *J. R. V. Company* DATE *6/17/88*

ADDRESS *Detroit, Mich.*

PART NAME *Gear Blank* PART NO.

MATERIAL *c 1045* SIZE *4" H.R.S.* GR. WT. *21#* NET WT. *16.0#*

MAT. COST	ITEM	WGT.	RATE	COST	ITEM	HRS.	RSK.	BLOCKS & MATERIAL	
BASE 21.00	C & H	21	7.50	1.59	PLANE			2-11½ Φ × 4½ } 900#	
GRADE 1.50	SHIP.	16	9.00	1.44	TURN	80	30	2-16 Φ × 5 } @ 2.10	1890.00
SIZE	CLEAN	"	3.00	.48	TEMP.	12		Trim. Mat. 400# @ .90	360.00
FGHT. .45	COND.	"	3.00	.48	SINK			192 hrs @ 30.00	5760.00
	NORM.	"	3.00	.48	DOWEL			Total dies	$8010.00
	ANN.				TRIMS.	90	30	RSKS	
	H.T.				COMB.			68 hrs. @ $30.00	2040.00
	BRIN.							Die life 8000 pcs	
					MISC.	10	8		
	D.M.			1.14					
TOTAL 8.15	TOT. FIXED COST			5.61	TOTAL	192	68	DIE COST $6210	

	OP.	HLP.	RATE				
QUANTITY				1000	5000	10000	20000
PRODUCTION pcs./hr.				100	150	170	190
UNITS	OP.	HLP.	RATE				
SETUP 3000 T Press			750.00	.750	.151	.075	.039
" Coin Press			150.00	.150	.030	.015	.009
FORGE " "	1	4	405.00	4.050	2.700	2.385	2.13
" ✓							
TRIMS (H) (C)							
Coin - 250/Hr.	1	1	90.00	.120	.120	.120	.120
TOTAL FIXED COST				5.610	5.610	5.610	5.610
MATERIAL 21 × 1.05 × 0.0815				5.400	5.400	5.400	5.400
SUB-TOTAL				16.32	14.25	13.845	13.548
SPOILAGE 3%				.48	.42	.42	.402
FACTORY COST				16.8	14.67	14.25	13.95
SALES & ADMINISTRATION 9%				1.5	1.32	1.29	1.26
COMM. OR ROYALTY							
TOTAL COST				18.30	15.99	15.54	15.21
MARKUP OR PROFIT 10%				1.83	1.59	1.56	1.53
QUOTING PRICE				20.28	17.68	17.10	16.74
LB. PRICE				1.26	1.11	1.08	1.50

SEQUENCE	REMARKS
Pancake	
Block	
Forge	
Comb. Trim	
Normalize	

Figure 11-2. Forging estimate for gear blank.

Quoting Price

The costs recorded on the upper portion of the form are summarized on the lower portion to determine the quoting price. When calculating the material cost, a 5% scrap allowance is made, and 3% is added for spoilage, while 9% goes for sales and administration costs, and 10% for profit. As mentioned previously, the quoted price does not include the tooling cost.

12

ESTIMATING METAL STAMPING COSTS

Assume that the sales department has requested a cost estimate for the stamped lever shown in *Figure 12-1*. The customer's initial order is for 500 parts, to be followed by an order for 5,000 parts per month for one year, for a total of 60,500 parts.

PROCESS PLAN

The cost estimate request should be accompanied by a process plan specifying the stamping process to be used. When the process plan is not included, the estimating coordinator either requests one from the manufacturing engineering department or develops it personally. In either case, the person preparing the process plan must analyze the part design and be aware of the desired production quantity. Data available from previous stamping jobs greatly facilitates selecting the most efficient and economical processes and methods available in the plant.

Because no process plan was provided in this case, the estimator must determine the most economical method of manufacturing the lever to specifications. Three stamping processes commonly used in the plant are considered:

1. Pierce and blank in a compound die from hand fed strip second die.
2. Blank, pierce, and form with three separate dies from hand fed strip stock.
3. Pierce and blank in a compound die from coil stock and form in automatically fed forming die.
4. After evaluating each of these processes, the estimator selects the first as the most efficient and economical.

The second process was examined in detail but rejected because its slight reduction in material cost does not offset the increased cost of using three separate dies. Although the company owns automatic feeding equipment, the estimator determines that the third process would not be economical for production quantities less than 100,000 parts.

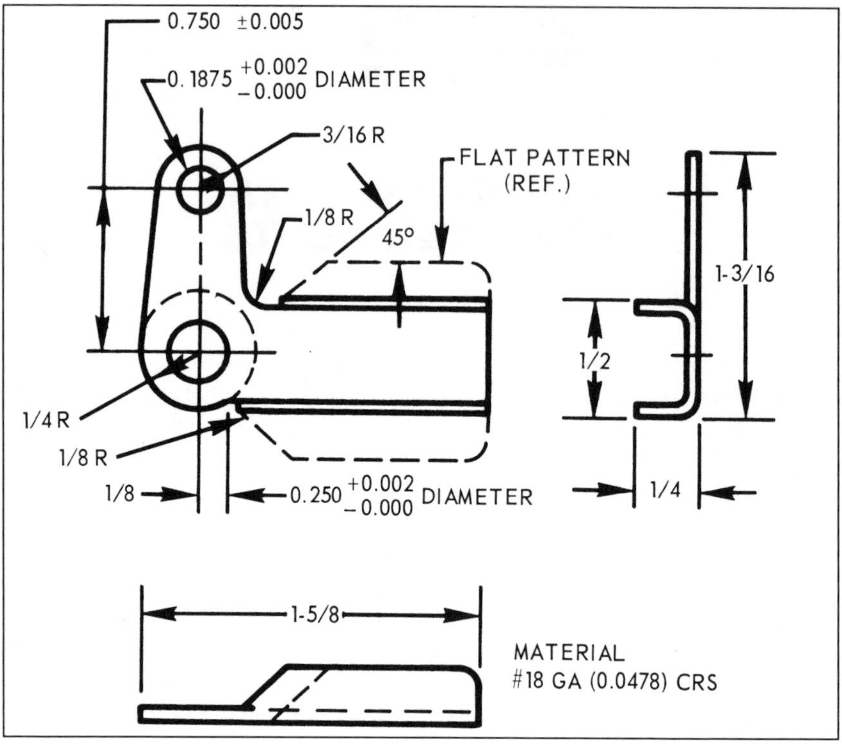

Figure 12-1. Lever made by pressworking operations.

Estimating Procedure

After carefully analyzing the selected process, the estimator calculates the manufacturing cost for the stamped part. First, the cost of material is computed in the top portion of the estimating form (*Figure 12-2*). Next, die cost, die repair, die set, labor, and burden costs are calculated in the "Operations" portion of the form, and appropriate amounts are entered in the "Partial Minor Costs" section of the form for miscellaneous operations such as shearing, handling, inspection, salvage, and shipping. The labor and burden costs are then added to "Partial Minor Costs" to arrive at "Conversion L & B" (labor and burden).

All costs are summarized in the bottom left portion of the form to develop a cost per hundred pieces. First, die repair, die set, and "Conversion L & B" are added to arrive at "Total L & B." To this cost, the estimator adds the material cost and an allowance for spoilage to obtain a manufacturing cost per hundred pieces.

Finally, the estimator sends the completed estimate to the accounting or sales department to determine the selling price.

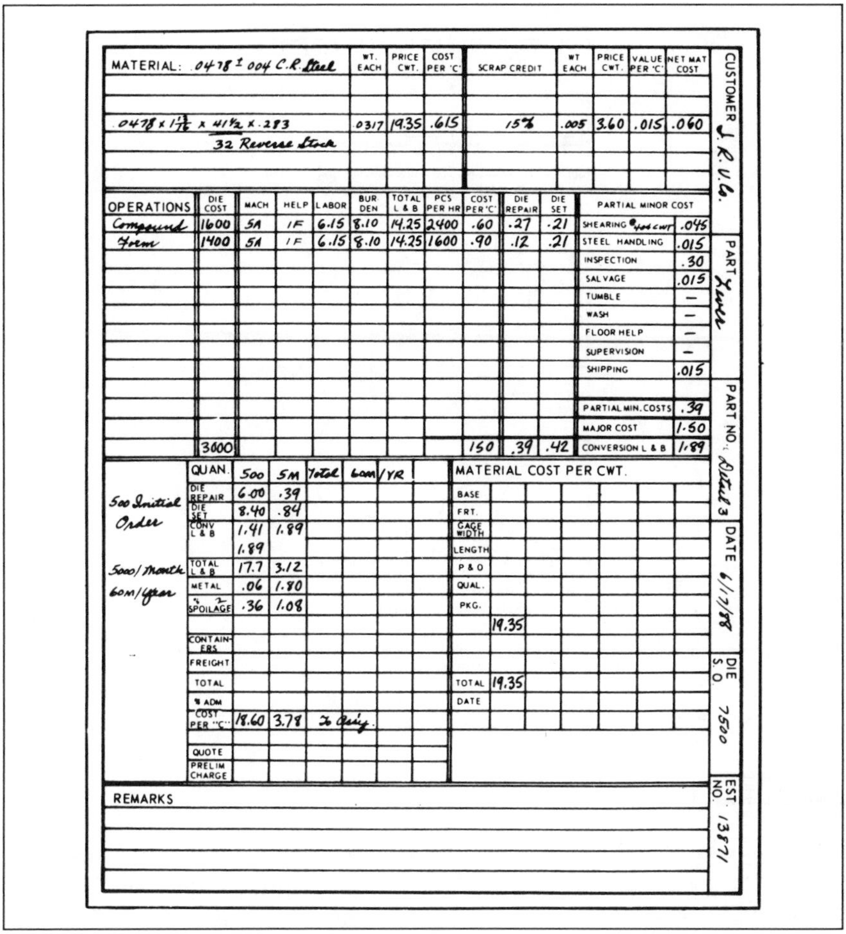

MATERIAL: .0478 ± 004 C.R. Steel | WT. EACH | PRICE CWT. | COST PER 'C' | SCRAP CREDIT | WT EACH | PRICE CWT. | VALUE PER 'C' | NET MAT COST

.0478 x 1 7/16 x 41½ x .283 | .0317 | 19.35 | .615 | 15% | .005 | 3.60 | .015 | .060

32 Reverse Stock

OPERATIONS	DIE COST	MACH	HELP	LABOR	BUR DEN	TOTAL L & B	PCS PER HR	COST PER 'C'	DIE REPAIR	DIE SET
Compound	1600	5A	1F	6.15	8.10	14.25	2400	.60	.27	.21
Form	1400	5A	1F	6.15	8.10	14.25	1600	.90	.12	.21
	3000							1.50	.39	.42

PARTIAL MINOR COST	
SHEARING @ .40 CWT	.045
STEEL HANDLING	.015
INSPECTION	.30
SALVAGE	.015
TUMBLE	—
WASH	—
FLOOR HELP	—
SUPERVISION	—
SHIPPING	.015
PARTIAL MIN. COSTS	.39
MAJOR COST	1.50
CONVERSION L & B	1.89

500 Initial Order

5000/Month

60M/Year

QUAN.	500	5M	Total	60M/YR
DIE REPAIR	6.00	.39		
DIE SET	8.40	.84		
CONV L & B	1.41	1.89		
	1.89			
TOTAL L & B	17.7	3.12		
METAL	.06	1.80		
% SPOILAGE	.36	1.08		
CONTAINERS				
FREIGHT				
TOTAL				
% ADM				
COST PER "C"	18.60	3.78	To Quay.	
QUOTE				
PRELIM CHARGE				

MATERIAL COST PER CWT.

BASE

FRT.

GAGE WIDTH

LENGTH

P & O

QUAL.

PKG.

19.35

TOTAL 19.35

DATE

REMARKS

CUSTOMER J. R. U. Co.

PART Lever

PART NO. Detail 3

DATE 6/17/88

DIE S.O. 7500

EST. NO. 13871

Figure 12-2. Cost estimate sheet for Figure 12-1 using two dies and layout.

Material

Material is one of the most important considerations in producing stamped parts. In checking engineering specifications and the process plan, the estimator pays close attention to material requirements. Alternative materials are suggested to effect cost reductions when possible without loss in product quality or functionality. The estimator also considers the form in which the material is available (sheets, strips, etc.),because the stamping process selected determines the form that must be used. For example, strip stock must be used for automatic equipment.

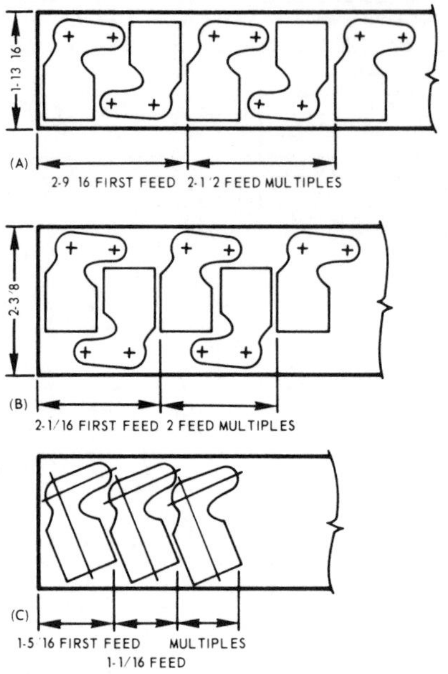

Figure 12-3. Three strip layouts for Figure 12-1.

Stock Utilization

When the material has been determined, the estimator considers stock utilization. The positioning of the blanks on the coil or strip is studied and the layout that produces maximum stock usage and minimum scrap is selected. This procedure, sometimes called "blank nesting," requires careful and intricate planning. Data from past estimates are seldom of any assistance because of the variations in part shape and stock size.

If bending or forming operations are required, the grain direction of the stock may be of importance. To aid in positioning the part on the strip, the estimator makes a template of the blank pattern of the part. Since there are flanges on the part, the bend lines cannot be more than 45 ° to the grain direction of the metal. In this case, the grain direction is parallel to the edge of the strip or coil. *Figure 12-3* shows three possible strip layouts. Views *A* and *B* represent layouts for strips 41.5 in. long which are fed through the die twice. View *C* represents a layout for a strip 41.5 in. long which is fed through the die once, or for coil stock fed by an automatic stock feeder.

The strip layout shown in *Figure 12-3 (a)* allows 32 blanks to be cut from each strip of stock. The strip layout shown in *Figure 12-3 (b)* provides 40 blanks per strip. Each strip is fed through the die at the feeding increment indicated, then reversed and fed through the second time. The weight of stock per blank for the layout of view *A* is .0317 lb.; for view *B*, .033 lb.; for view *C*, .0304 lb. When using coil stock, the weight per piece for the strip layout of view *C* is .0296 lb. since there is less waste stock at the end of each coil than for strip stock. Computations for determining material weight are made in the ''Material'' section of the cost estimate sheet (see *Figure 12-2* for computations for view *A*).

The use of the layout shown in view *C* would result in a lower material cost, but this layout is rejected because of the extra cost of automatically-fed forming dies. The layout shown in view *A* is selected as being best for the hand-fed process selected.

Material Cost

Material cost is computed in the ''Material'' section of the estimate form (*Figure 12-2*). To determine material cost per hundred parts, the weight per hundred pieces (3.17 lbs.) is multiplied by the material cost per pound ($1,935/cwt or $.1935), and the resulting cost ($.615) is modified by the subtraction of an allowance for scrap.

To determine the scrap allowance, weight per piece (.0317 lb.) is multiplied by the scrap credit factor of 15%. The scrap weight per 100 pieces (.50 lb.) is multiplied by scrap value per pound ($.036/lb.) to obtain the scrap allowance per hundred pieces which is $.018 (rounded off in the ''Value per 'C''' column to $.015).

''Net Material Cost'' is determined next by subtracting scrap credit per hundred ($.015) from material cost per hundred ($.615), and the resulting cost of $.60 is entered in the appropriate column.

MACHINE OPERATIONS

In the ''Operations'' section of the estimate form (*Figure 12-2*), the estimator enters the cost of the dies including tryout and engineering costs, computes the labor and burden costs associated with the stamping machine operations, and enters amounts for die repair and die sets.

Die Cost

The cost of the compound and forming dies, and the tryout and engineering costs associated with them are entered and totaled as $3,000. These are permanent dies, and because their cost is nonrecurring, it remains the same regardless of the production quantity.

Labor and Burden

Under the appropriate columns, the estimator enters hourly costs for labor and burden and adds these under the "Total L & B" column. These costs are then divided by the production rate per hour and the resulting figure multiplied by 100 to arrive at a labor and burden "Cost per 'C'."

Die Repair and Die Set

This is the cost of repairing and resetting the compound and forming dies. These costs are entered for both operations and totaled.

Minor Costs

Next the estimator computes the costs of the labor and burden involved in miscellaneous operations such as shearing, steel handling, inspection, salvage, shipping, etc. The cost of each of these items is determined from a study of data developed from previous stamping operations and entered in the appropriate place under the section entitled "Partial Minor Costs."

Conversion Labor and Burden

This is determined by adding the labor and burden cost from the "Operations" section and the "Partial Minor Costs" section. Conversion labor and burden in this case is $1.89.

Total Manufacturing Cost

The total manufacturing cost for the stamped part is determined by adding all the applicable costs in the lower left section of the estimate form. An additional amount is included for spoilage. The total cost for a production lot of 500 pieces is $18.60 per hundred; for production lots of 5,000 pieces the cost per hundred decreases to $3.78.

Quotation

The price quoted to the customer is determined by adding percentages for general and administrative costs (overhead) and profit. Assuming an overhead factor of 10 percent of total manufacturing cost and a profit factor of 15 percent, the computations necessary to develop a quotation may be summarized as follows:

Total Manufacturing Cost per Hundred	$3.78
Overhead (10% of $3.78)	.38
Profit (15% of $3.78)	.56
Total Cost per Hundred	$4.72

The quotation for 65,000 pieces (initial order of 5,000 plus 5,000 pieces per month for one year) would be $3,068 plus $3,000 for dies.

13

ESTIMATING PLASTIC PARTS

This chapter presents a general orientation of plastic parts estimating, with specific application included for a molded plastic tank.

PLANNING AND ANALYSIS

The processes available for fabricating thermoplastic products include: injection molding, blow molding, thermoforming, slush molding, extrusion, and casting. For thermosetting materials, the available processes include; compression molding, transfer molding, matched metal molding, premix molding, pressure laminating, filament molding, spray molding, and casting. These are commonly used techniques; special shapes and problems often necessitate variations.

Process Planning

Ordinarily, the cost estimate request is accompanied by a process plan. When the process plan is not provided, the estimator requests this item from the process planning department or prepares it personally.

Fabricating Methods

The person preparing the process plan must be aware of plant capabilities and equipment. In any plant, the choice of molding methods may be limited by the available equipment. Where there is a variety of equipment, the estimator may be responsible for selecting the most suitable and economical process. Each fabricating method has advantages that may make it the proper choice for a particular product. Tooling costs, cycle time, labor, and overhead vary according to the method selected.

Part Analysis

The person preparing the process plan works from drawings of the part and other specifications received from the customer. The drawing or specifications should establish dimensional tolerances, surface condition, color, as well as the mechanical, chemical, electrical, or thermal properties of the material or product.

The process planner reviews only the general design characteristics of the part, not the physical and chemical stresses the part will be subjected to once placed in use by the customer. The estimator should note dimensional tolerances because these directly affect labor and tooling costs.

Plastic Fabrication Practices

The part design should be reviewed for good plastics fabrication practices such as:

1. Generous use of fillets because square corners concentrate stresses and increase mold costs.
2. Use of thin cross sections to speed up cycle time.
3. Use of stiffening ribs on large flat surfaces.
4. Holes through the section wherever possible which permit support of the core pin in both halves of the mold (blind holes should not be more than 2D deep).
5. Hole spacing sufficient to permit the material to flow smoothly.
6. Draft allowances where necessary to facilitate removal of the part from the mold.

Labor and Burden Costs

Labor and burden costs for both major and secondary operations are assigned on the basis of machine operation time. The costs per piece may be reduced by having the operator tend more than one machine and/or by using multiple cavity dies.

Cycle Times

The molding cycle times for thermosetting plastics are determined by curing rate and section thickness. Preheating the thermosetting plastics reduces cycle time. Unless kept within prescribed tolerances, a change in moisture content of the material will result in improper curing.

Secondary Operations

After fabrication, it may be necessary to trim, drill, tap, or otherwise finish a plastic part.

PROCESSES

Filing

Flash, sprue, and gate marks are usually removed by filing or by abrasive methods.

Drilling

Plastics should be drilled with a 60-to 90° included angle point drill with highly polished flutes. Speeds of 100 to 300 sfpm are used for most plastics. The speed may be reduced to about 75 sfpm for plastics with abrasive fillers. Holes may be tapped at 40 to 50 sfpm. Water is usually a good coolant for these types of jobs. Holes with threads larger than 1/4 in. diameter should be molded. Threaded inserts should also be considered for additional strength.

Turning

Feed rate and depth of cut for turning operations are a function of the material's physical properties. Turning speeds using high-speed steel tools range from 200 to 600 sfpm. For carbide tools, the speed ranges from 500 to 1,500 sfpm.

Milling

The speed for milling with high-speed steel cutters is approximately 400 sfpm. For carbide cutters, the range is 1,200 to 1,600 sfpm.

Material

The estimator must be concerned with the moldability and fabrication characteristics of the plastic to be used, and must know if it is thermoplastic or thermosetting, since fabricating procedures and tool costs are affected.

Part Weight

The volume or weight of the finished part must be known to estimate material requirements. This may be determined by one of three ways:

1. Weighing a sample of the part being estimated.
2. Immersing a model of the part in water and using the weight of the displaced water to calculate the weight or volume of the finished part.
3. Dividing the part into basic geometric forms and calculating the volume.

Scrap Allowance

Depending upon the fabricating process used, an allowance for shrinkage, flash, trim stock, process loss, sprues, and runners is added to the weight of the finished part. It is usually expressed as a percentage of the finished weight, and determined from past performance.

Direct Material Cost

Material cost is determined by multiplying the cost per pound of raw material by the finished part weight after an allowance has been made for scrap.

Indirect Material

Indirect materials such as release agents, mold cleaners, vacuum bleeder liquids, and packaging supplies are usually considered as overhead. This simplifies the estimating procedure, and is sufficiently accurate to distribute these costs.

Tooling Costs

These costs vary with the process to be used. In the manual layup of laminated plastics, a form block must be made. The cost of these blocks varies with their size and complexity. Pressure laminating may require the construction of a die similar to that for metal forming.

The cost of injection, compression, and transfer molds varies with the complexity of the part, the number of cavities in the mold, and whether the cavities are in inserts or machined directly into the die block. The transfer molding of thermosetting materials permits the use of thinner die sections and increased die life over compression molding.

Cost Estimate Example

The estimate request form shown in *Figure 13-1* was prepared by the sales department and sent to the estimating coordinator. Because part drawings were not supplied by the customer, the estimator drew the sketch shown in *Figure 13-2* for guidance in the estimate. The drawing assists in visualizing possible manufacturing difficulties such as sharp radii, reverse flanges, negative draft, and the inaccessiblity of some areas of the part. These difficulties affect labor costs, and should be called to the customer's attention for appropriate design modifications.

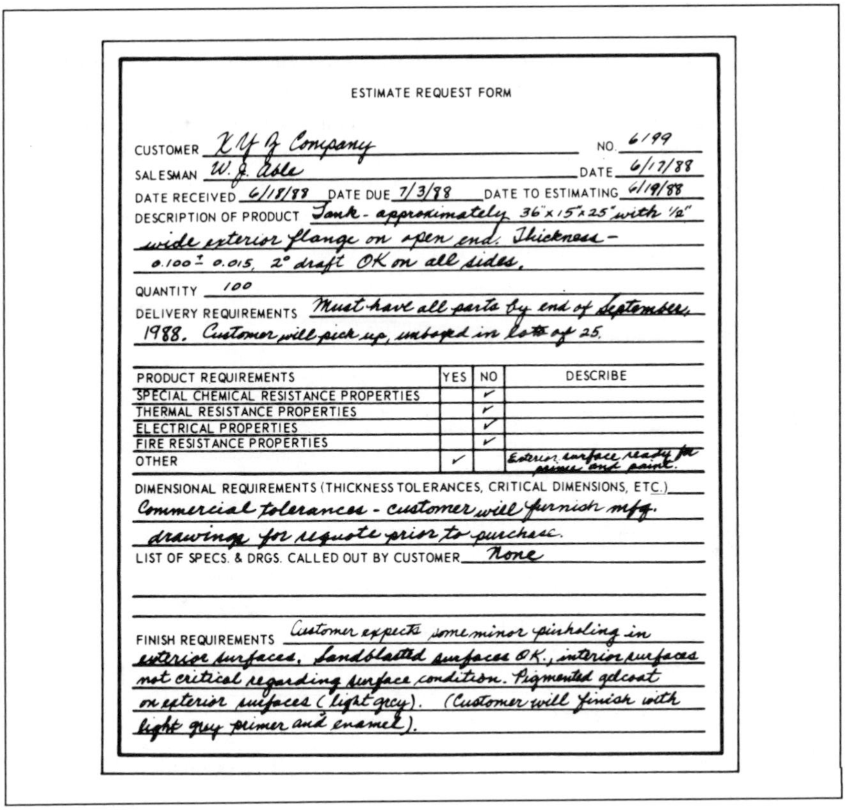

ESTIMATE REQUEST FORM

CUSTOMER XYZ Company NO. 6199
SALESMAN W. J. Able DATE 6/17/88
DATE RECEIVED 6/18/88 DATE DUE 7/3/88 DATE TO ESTIMATING 6/19/88
DESCRIPTION OF PRODUCT Tank - approximately 36" x 15" x 25" with 1/2" wide exterior flange on open end. Thickness - 0.100 ± 0.015, 2° draft OK on all sides.

QUANTITY 100

DELIVERY REQUIREMENTS Must have all parts by end of September, 1988. Customer will pick up, unboxed in lots of 25.

PRODUCT REQUIREMENTS	YES	NO	DESCRIBE
SPECIAL CHEMICAL RESISTANCE PROPERTIES		✓	
THERMAL RESISTANCE PROPERTIES		✓	
ELECTRICAL PROPERTIES		✓	
FIRE RESISTANCE PROPERTIES		✓	
OTHER	✓		Exterior surface ready for primer and paint.

DIMENSIONAL REQUIREMENTS (THICKNESS TOLERANCES, CRITICAL DIMENSIONS, ETC.) Commercial tolerances - customer will furnish mfg. drawings for requote prior to purchase.

LIST OF SPECS. & DRGS. CALLED OUT BY CUSTOMER None

FINISH REQUIREMENTS Customer expects some minor pinholing in exterior surfaces. Sandblasted surfaces OK., interior surfaces not critical regarding surface condition. Pigmented gelcoat on exterior surfaces (light grey). (Customer will finish with light grey primer and enamel).

Figure 13-1. Cost estimate request form.

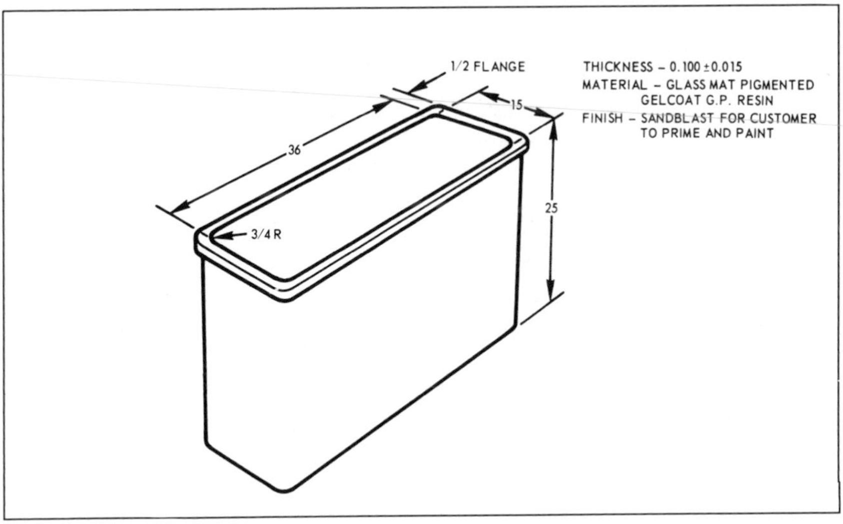

Figure 13-2. Reinforced plastic tank with flanges.

Material Requirements

The calculations for determining material requirements are shown in *Figure 13-3*. The form shown in *Figure 13-4* includes a checklist of the materials the estimator must consider when making the estimate. The volume of the laminate and gelcoat were computed. Using the density of each, the total weight of the tank was calculated. The estimator also calculated the waste factors for the glass cloth, resin, and gelcoat. These variables were included when estimating the gross material requirements listing in *Figure 13-4*.

COST ESTIMATING CALCULATION FORM

CUSTOMER XYZ Company NO. 6199

DATE 6/17/88 ESTIMATOR W.A.K. SHEET 1 OF 1

SHOW ALL CALCULATIONS

Ref. dwg A6-199-A

AREAS Flange 2(15+36)½ = 51 sq. in.

sides 2(15×25)+2(36×25) = 2550

bottom 15×36 = 540

3141 sq. in.

21.8 sq. ft.

TRIM PERIMETER (37+16)2 = 106 in.

THICKNESS 0.100 in. = 0.090 laminate + 0.010 gelcoat

VOLUME laminate 3141 × 0.090 = 282.7 cu. in.

gelcoat 3141 × 0.010 = 31.4

314.1 cu. in.

DENSITY laminate 0.05563 lb/cu. in. (51% glass, 49% resin

gelcoat 0.05054 lb./cu. in.

Total 0.05563 × 0.9 + 0.05054 × 0.1 = 0.0551

WEIGHT (282.7 × 0.05563) + (31.4 × 0.05054) = 15.7 + 1.6 = 17.3 lb.

WASTE FACTORS

GLASS (4 plies of 1.5 oz. mat 38" wide — resin & gelcoat

2 pcs. 90×19 = 3420 sq. in. — $W_{LAM} = 1.11 \times \frac{\Delta+1}{\Delta}$

2 pcs. 70×38 = 5320

4 pcs. 28×19 = 2128 — $\Delta = \frac{3141}{106} = 29.6$ sq in/in

4 pcs. 28×38 = 4256

total 15124 sq. in. — $\frac{\Delta+1}{\Delta} = 1.034$

$W_{LAM} = 1.034 \times 1.11 = 1.148$ lb.

gross glass weight: $\frac{15124}{144} \times \frac{1.5}{16} = 9.85$ lb.

net glass weight 15.7 × 0.51 = 8.01 lb.

$W_E = \frac{9.85}{8.01} = 1.23$

PVA bag: 14 ft. of 3 mil by 52 in. sheet × ½ lb./ft. = 1.17 lb.

Figure 13-3. Calculation sheet for plastic tank with flanges.

COST ESTIMATING
BILL OF MATERIAL

CUSTOMER XYZ Company NO. 6/99
DATE 6/17/88 ESTIMATOR W.A.K. SHEET 1 OF 1

1	CLOTH		8	FINISH		15	CATALYST	✓
2	MAT & ROVING	✓	9	HARDWARE		16	PROMOTED	✓
3	GELCOAT	✓	10	PVA	✓	17	PIGMENTED	
4	RESIN	✓	11	VENDOR		18		
5	CORE		12	PACKAGING				
6	ADHESIVE		13	BLEEDER				
7	FILLER		14	BINDER				

CODE	MATERIAL DESCRIPTION	NET AMOUNT	WASTE FACTOR	GROSS AMOUNT	MAT'L COST/LB	COST
2	1.5 oz. mat. (38 in. wide)	8.01#	1.23	9.85#	$ 1.80	17.73
3	light grey Gelcoat	1.60#	1.148	1.84#	1.47	2.70
4	general purpose resin	7.69#	1.148	8.83	1.035	9.15
10	14 ft. of 3 mil x 52 in PVA	-	-	1.17#	5.10	5.97
15	MEK peroxide (2%)	0.15#	1.148	0.17#	5.40	.93
16	cobalt naphthenate (1%)	0.08#	1.148	0.09	.159	.15
		18.17#		21.95#		36.63

Figure 13-4. Material estimate sheet.

Labor

The time needed to fabricate the laminated plastic tank is shown in *Figure 13-5*. A labor operations checklist is provided to remind the estimator to include all the necessary items. The labor operations are described in sequence, and the number of workers, time in minutes, and worker-minutes for each operation are listed.

Tooling

The tools involved in making the part and the data pertaining to their design and manufacture are shown in *Figure 13-6*. This form does not provide spaces for itemizing the labor and materials necessary for each tool. If this cost data is required, the forms shown in *Figures 13-4* and *13-5* may be used.

Cost Estimate Summary

A summary of the cost estimate is shown in *Figure 13-7*. The form contains space for summarizing the dimensional data compiled during the initial calculations, and important processing information like prices for different quantities should the customer request it.

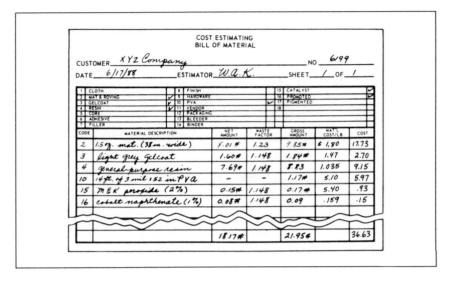

COST ESTIMATING
LABOR REQUIREMENTS

CUSTOMER XYZ Company NO. 6199
DATE 6/17/88 ESTIMATOR W.A.K. SHEET 1 OF 1

1 MATL. PREP.	✓	6 MACHINE		11 SAND SURFACE	✓	16 HANDLING	
2 LAYUP	✓	7 ROUGH	✓	12 PRIME		17 UNASSIGNED TIME	
3 INSPECTION	✓	8 BOND		13 PAINT		18 SUPERVISION	✓
4 TRIM	✓	9 MECH. ASS'Y		14 NEOPRENE COAT		19	
5 HOLES		10 SALVAGE		15 PACKAGE		20	

CODE	SEQUENCE OF OPERATIONS	NO. MEN	TIME, MIN.	MAN MIN.
1	Cut set of patterns	1	8	8
1	make 100 x 84 in. bag	1	5	5
2	mix resin	1	3	3
2	clean mold	1	4	4
2	spray mold release	1	3	3
2	spray gelcoat	1	6	6
2	layup part	1	14	14
2	bag	1	7	7
2	remove part	1	5	5
3	inspect	1	2	2
4	trim part	1	20	20
7	sandblast outside surfaces	1	8	8
11	sand out inside bag wrinkles	1	10	10
3	final inspection	1	3	3
18	supervision	1	12	12

AVERAGE PRODUCTION RATE
1 man makes 6 pcs. per day plus mat preparation, inspection and supervision.

TOTAL LABOR, MAN MINUTES 110
MAN HOURS 1.84

Figure 13-5. Labor estimate sheet.

COST ESTIMATING
ENGINEERING AND TOOLING

CUSTOMER XYZ Company NO. 6199
DATE 6/17/88 ESTIMATOR W.A.K. SHEET 1 OF 1

1 ENGINEERING		5 MOLDS	✓	9 DRILL JIG		13 SETUP	✓
2 DESIGN		6 SCREEN		10 TRIM JIG	✓	14 TESTING	
3 DRAWINGS		7 CUTTING TEMP	✓	11 MACH FIXT		15 HANDBOOKS	
4 PATTERNS	✓	8 INSP FIXT		12 ASSEMBLY FIXT		16	

CODE	DESCRIPTION	BUY	MAKE	DELIV WEEKS	MAN HOURS	RATE	LABOR COST	MAT'L COST	AMORTIZED TOOL COST	NON-AMORTIZED TOOL COST
4	male wood pattern		✓	1	80	$12.00	$960.00	$165.00		$1125.00
	(inside)									
5	female epoxy laminate		✓	1	70	12.00	840.00	471.00		1311.00
	bag mold with									
	hold down ring									
7	mat cutting temp.		✓	½	4	12.00	48.00	6.00		54.00
10	trim jig (for rad. saw)		✓		12	12.00	144.00	18.00		162.00
13	tool setup		✓		2	12.00	24.00		$24.00	

ESTIMATED DELIVERY 2½ weeks TOTAL $24.00 $2652.00

Figure 13-6. Engineering and tooling form.

COST ESTIMATING SUMMARY SHEET

CUSTOMER XYZ Company NO. 6199
DATE 6/17/88 ESTIMATOR W.A.K. SHEET 1 OF 1

AREA, SQ. IN.	3141	MATERIAL ALLOWANCE	$ 36.63
AREA, SQ. FT.	21.8	LABOR ALLOWANCE, MAN MIN.	110
THICKNESS, IN.	0.100 ± 0.015	TOOL & ENGINEERING ALLOWANCE	
DENSITY, LB CU. IN.	0.0551	AMORTIZED	$ 24.00
WEIGHT OF LAMINATE, LBS.	17.3	NON-AMORTIZED	$2652.00
WEIGHT OF FITTINGS, LBS.	–	OVERHEAD FACTOR	215
TOTAL WEIGHT, LBS.	17.3	G & A FACTOR	1.07
TRIM PERIMETER, IN.	106	PROFIT FACTOR	1.11
\ SQ. IN., PER IN.	29.6	LABOR RATE, PER MIN.	$ 0.09
WR	1.14		
WL	1.148		

TOOL DELIVERY 2½ weeks from acceptance of order
PART DELIVERY 25 per week starting 4 weeks from acceptance of order

QUANTITY	REJECTION ALLOWANCE	MATERIAL SELLING PRICE (1)	LABOR UNITS	LABOR UNITS QUANTITY	LABOR SELLING PRICE (2)	ENGRG. & TOOL SELLING PRICE (3)	TOTAL SELLING PRICE (4)
100	1.03	$44.85	2.04	2.04	$ 51.66	$0.27	$96.78

(1) MATERIAL SELLING PRICE EQUALS MATERIAL ALLOWANCE TIMES REJECTION FACTOR TIMES G & A FACTOR TIMES PROFIT FACTOR.

(2) LABOR SELLING PRICE EQUALS LABOR ALLOWANCE TIMES LABOR RATE TIMES LABOR UNITS DIVIDED BY QUANTITY TIMES OVERHEAD FACTOR TIMES G & A FACTOR TIMES PROFIT FACTOR.

(3) FOR AMORTIZED ENGINEERING AND TOOLING EXPENSE ONLY: ENGINEERING AND TOOLING ALLOWANCE DIVIDED BY QUANTITY TIMES G & A FACTOR TIMES PROFIT FACTOR.

(4) TOTAL SELLING PRICE = 1 + 2 + 3.

(5) FOR ENGINEERING AND TOOLING NOT AMORTIZED: ENGINEERING AND TOOLING ALLOWANCE TIMES G & A FACTOR TIMES PROFIT FACTOR $3150.00
ESTIMATED COST FOR 100 PIECES = 100 × $96.78 = 9678.00
MAXIMUM TOTAL ESTIMATED COST 12,828.00

APPROVED
ESTIMATING C.N. 6-12-88 PLANNING O.R. 6-13-88

Figure 13-7. Cost estimate summary sheet.

14

ESTIMATING TUMBLING AND VIBRATORY FINISHING COSTS

A wide range of surface improvement operations are made economically possible by using tumbling and vibratory machines. Deburring, cleaning, polishing, mirror finishing, and honing processes are accomplished by proper selection of equipment, abrasives, lubricants, and ratio of volume of work as well as volume of batch and barrel.

To accurately assess part or product manufacturing costs, the estimator must determine the cost of any surface finishing operations that might be needed. This requires accurate data concerning abrasives, compounds, loading and unloading time, and machine time.

EQUIPMENT

The estimate should include a comparison of the efficiency of machines in the plant. Accurate cost records on previous operations assist in making sound estimating decisions.

Finishing Costs per Piece

Performance is the most important factor in determining finishing costs per unit. Accurate shop performance costs require close study of labor rates and times, material costs, and overall processing operations.

ESTIMATING PROCEDURES

Several methods can be used to calculate the cost of finishing parts through the use of tumbling or vibratory equipment. *Figure 14-1* shows the estimating form one company uses to estimate finishing. The costs incurred in barrel finishing are: (1) floor space, (2) depreciation and maintenance, (3) power, (4) media (abrasive), and (5) labor.

The assignment of these cost elements to an individual piece part requires the following five-step procedure:

TUMBLING BARREL FINISHING COST CALCULATOR

	COSTS $ PER YEAR	COSTS $ PER HOUR	COSTS $ PER PIECE
FLOOR SPACE COSTS			
ADD ALL THESE COSTS PER YEAR FOR A DEPARTMENT FLOOR AREA IN WHICH MACHINE IS LOCATED			
RENT $ ____			
HEAT ____			
LIGHT ____			
INSURANCE ____			
GEN. OVERHEAD ____			
SUPERVISION ____			
TOTAL (A) $ ____ X (____ SQ. FT NEEDED FOR OPERATION / ____ SQ. FT. IN DEPARTMENT)	$ ____		
DEPRECIATION AND MAINTENANCE			
TOTAL COST OF TUMBLING BARREL & ACCESSORIES . . . $ ____			
DIVIDED BY YEARS OF DEPRECIATION ALLOWED . . . . ____ YRS =	$ ____		
MAINTENANCE COST PER YEAR	$ ____		
TOTAL (B) . . .	$ ____		
MACHINE HOURLY COST RATE			
TOTAL (B) ABOVE $ ____ + ____ HOURS USED PER YEAR		$ ____	
POWER COSTS PER HOUR (1, 2, 3, 5, 10HP USE $ 02 PER HP PER HOUR)		$ ____	
MEDIA COST PER LOAD			
____ LBS PER LOAD X $ ____ PER LB X ____ % ATTRITION RATE . . . . (SEE CHART ON OTHER SIDE)		$ ____	
TOTAL (C)		$ ____	
COST PER LOAD			
COMPOUND USED PER HOUR ____ LBS X $ ____ PER LB			$ ____
TOTAL (C) HOURLY RATE $ ____ X ____ HOURS PER LOAD			$ ____
DIRECT LABOR RATE (+ FRINGES) $ ____ PER HOUR X ____ HOURS PER LOAD . . . . (WORKER NEEDED FOR ONLY PART OF LOAD CYCLE TIME)			$ ____
TOTAL (D)			$ ____

TOTAL (D) $ ____ ÷ ____ PIECES PER LOAD = $ ____ PER PIECE

Figure 14-1. Cost estimate form for parts finished using tumbling barrel equipment.

1. Determine floor space costs. The costs of rent, heat, light, insurance, general overhead, and supervision for the department using the barrel finishing equipment are totaled and multiplied by the ratio of space needed for finishing equipment space in the entire department.
2. Compute annual depreciation and maintenance costs. This figure is added to "Total *A*, Floor Space Costs," on the form illustrated to give "Total *B*."
3. Calculate the hourly machine rate. "Total *B*" (the sum of floor space costs and depreciation and maintenance), shown in *figure 14-1*, is divided by annual hours of operation. To this figure is added power costs per hour, and media costs per load. Determining media cost per load involves the use of attrition rates for finishing media. These rates

Table 14-1. Media Attrition Data for a Tumbling Barrel Finishing Machine*.

Slide Systems (Surface FPM)	*Random Shape, Alum. Oxide ($\frac{1}{2}$" × $\frac{9}{16}$")*	*Preformed Cylinder, Silicon Carbide ($\frac{3}{8}$" diam. × $\frac{3}{4}$" long)*	*Preformed Triangle Alum. Oxide ($\frac{5}{8}$" × $\frac{3}{16}$")*	*Preformed 45° Angle Cut Cylinder Alum. Oxide ($\frac{1}{2}$" diam. × $\frac{7}{8}$" long)*	*Ceramic Cones*	*Random Shape, Red Granite Size 2*
25	.08	.07	.05	.02	.03	.02
50	.19	.15	.11	.05	.06	.04
75	.32	.24	.18	.08	.10	.06
100	.45	.34	.26	.11	.15	.08
125	.59	.45	.34	.15	.19	.10
150	.74	.56	.42	.18	.24	.12
175	.87	.66	.50	.21	.28	.14
200	1.02	.77	.59	.25	.33	.16
225	1.15	.87	.67	.28	.37	.18
250	1.29	.98	.75	.31	.42	.20

*Per cent of media consumed per hour.

Table courtesy of J. F. Rampe, Rampe Manufacturing Company, Cleveland, Ohio

are shown in *Table 14-1*. The total of these items (''Total *C*'') results in an hourly cost for operating the machine.

4. Determine cost per load. The cost of the compound used per hour is computed first, followed by the machine rate per load. The labor cost per load is then calculated and the three cost items per load are totaled to give cost per load (''Total *D*'').
5. Determine finishing costs per piece. The cost per load is divided by pieces per load.

15

ESTIMATING MULTIPURPOSE JIGS AND FIXTURES

This chapter discusses estimating costs for jigs and fixtures. It is taken from William E. Boyes' SME book *Low Cost Jigs, Fixtures and Gages for Limited Production*.

In spite of the tool engineer's best efforts to reduce the costs of individual jigs and fixtures for limited production operations, it may be found that the total cost still exceeds the desirable level and cuts into profits that might otherwise be made. When this problem occurs, the tool engineer may often be able to combine the features of two or more tools into a single jig or fixture. Such a tool, designed to be used for more than one operation or part configuration, is called a multipurpose jig or fixture. This chapter examines the applications of multipurpose jigs and fixtures, points our their limitations, and provides a method of estimating their costs and the savings they may provide.

MULTIPURPOSE TOOL APPLICATIONS

Before the tool engineer decides to tool up for limited production, the operations involved and the parts to be produced should be analyzed first to determine if a multipurpose tool would actually be practical and economical.

As a rule, multipurpose jigs and fixtures should be given serious consideration whenever the parts to be produced or the operations to be performed are similiar, and when production time schedules and quantity requirements permit.

SIMILARITIES IN PARTS AND OPERATIONS

The various parts to be made, and the operations involved in making them, should be carefully studied for any points of similarity. Similar parts or operations should then be segregated and examined to determine the features of their designs that can be worked with a single, cheaper jig or fixture. Radically different parts or operations are seldom suitable for multipurpose tooling; multipurpose tools that are complex enough to accommodate unlike parts or operations are usually impractical because of their high cost.

SCHEDULES AND PRODUCTION QUANTITIES

If the tool engineer finds similar operations that multipurpose tools can perform, a thorough study of production requirements should be made to see if the multipurpose tooling will be compatible with time schedules and quantity requirements. Multipurpose jigs and fixtures should be used only when production commitments can be handled through part-time or interrupted operations, not when operations must be run continuously or simultaneously.

For example, assume that Part A and Part B are similar and a multipurpose tool is being considered for their production. Eighty units of each part are needed. Part A requires 1 hr/unit and Part B requires .8 hr/unit for production. Part A can then be produced in 80 hours and Part B in 64 hours.

If only 80 hours total production time can be allowed for both parts, however, it is obvious that the operation for Part A must be run continuously, and that the operation for Part B must be run simultaneously in order to meet the production deadline. In this case, a multipurpose tool probably could not be used unless it was overly complex and costly.

If, on the other hand, the total production time for the two parts is not limited, then a multipurpose tool could be used to produce all units of A followed by all units of B or, if necessary, lots alternating A-B-A-B-A-B. Total production time for the two parts would then equal 144 hours plus the amount of time required to convert the tool from the Part A operation to the Part B operation and back, if necessary.

Each process of converting a multipurpose jig or fixture from one use to another is called changeover, and the amount of time that process requires is called changeover time. Changeover has an important bearing on estimating the applicability and cost of a multipurpose tool.

MULTIPURPOSE TOOL COST ESTIMATING

Though multipurpose tooling may, at first, appear to offer cost advantages, the costs of setups or changeovers for different parts may cancel out many of those gains. Maximum savings are only possible when a complete lot of parts can be machined in a single setup. Each additional changeover subtracts from those savings. Before capital is invested on multipurpose tools, a simple cost study should be made.

A multipurpose tool cost estimate requires that the following data be known:

- The cost of the multipurpose tool, including its design costs.
- The total cost of all the single-purpose tools that the multipurpose tool will replace, including their design costs.
- Estimated changeover time.
- The number of changeovers, as determined from production schedules.
- The hourly labor and burden rate of changeovers.

The formulas to be used in the cost estimate are:

$$A = B \times C$$
$$D = A \times E$$
$$F = G - (H + D)$$
$$J = \frac{G - H}{A}$$

Where:

A = Estimated cost of each changeover, including labor and burden
B = Estimated changeover time
C = Hourly labor and burden rate for changeovers
D = Estimated total cost of changeovers to complete the order
E = Number of changeovers necessary to complete the order
F = Estimated savings using the multipurpose tools
G = Total cost of all replaced single-purpose tools, including design
H = Cost of the multipurpose tool, including design
J = Maximum number of changeovers up to the break-even point (If the number of changeovers is greater than J, then single purpose tools should be used).

Consider the following example. For a certain machining operation on two similar parts, two separate drill jigs can be designed and fabricated at a cost of $475 for one and $325 for the other-a total of $800. A multipurpose drill jig for both parts can be designed and constructed for an estimated $620. Production schedules call for five lots to be produced of each part. Five lots of two parts each will require 10 operations-nine tooling changeovers. Changeover time is estimated as .6 hours at a cost of $16.00/hr (labor and burden). Consider the following questions:

- What is the estimated cost of each changeover (A)?
- What is the estimated total cost for changeovers (D)?
- What are the estimated savings using the multipurpose tool (F)?
- What is the maximum number of changeovers up to the break-even point (J)?

The calculations for the estimated cost of each changeover (A) are:

$$A = B \times C$$
$$= .6 \times \$16.00$$
$$= \$9.60$$

The estimated total cost for changeovers (D) are:

$$D = A \times E$$
$$= \$9.60 \times 9$$
$$= \$86.40$$

The calculations for the estimated savings using the multipurpose tool (F) are:

$$F = G - (H + D)$$
$$= \$800 - (\$620 + \$86.40)$$

$$= \$800—\$706.40$$
$$= \$93.60$$

The calculations for the maximum number of changeovers up to the break-even point (J) are:

$$J = \frac{G - H}{A}$$
$$= \frac{\$800 - \$620}{\$9.60}$$
$$= \frac{\$180}{\$9.60}$$
$$= \$18.75$$

The results of this cost analysis indicate an estimated savings of $93.60 in favor of the multipurpose drill jig. If more than 18 changeovers were necessary, however, the advantage of lower cost would be with the two separate, single-purpose jigs.

It is important to know the changeover break-even point before a decision on the type of tools to be used is made because production schedules can often be adjusted to lower tooling costs by reducing the number of changeovers. Also, the break-even point may determine whether multi- or single-purpose tools should be used if future reorders are possible.

BIBLIOGRAPHY

Ahlemeyer, C. H. "Economic Justification," ASTME Paper No. MM63-648 (1963).

Anderson, E., and Weitz, B. A. "Make or Buy Decisions: Vertical Integration and Marketing Productivity," *Sloan Management Review*, Spring 1986, pp. 3-19.

Bangasser, R., and Tonini, J. "Nomography--An Estimating Tool," ASTME Paper No. MM66-144 (1966).

Benkelman, W. D. "A Re-Evaluation of Production Processes for Plastic Parts," ASTME Paper No. MM66-140 (1966).

Beutel, M. L. "New Code Simplifies, Expands Cost Estimating by Computer," *Engineering*, May 14, 1964, pp. 30-32.

Boothroyd, G. and Dewhurst, P. *Material Selection and Cost Estimating for Injection Molding, Software*, Wakefield, RI: Boothroyd Dewhurst Inc. 1988.

Boyes, W. E. *Low Cost Jigs, Fixtures and Gages for Limited Production*, Dearborn, MI: Society of Manufacturing Engineers, 1986.

Brescka, R. S. "Tool Room Cost Control," ASTME Paper No. MS65-714 (1965).

Brown, C. F. "ABC's of Weld Estimating," *Welding Engineer*, October 1958.

Camps-Campins, F. M. "Cutting Costs with Value Analysis," *The Tool and Manufacturing Engineer*, April 1965, p. 39.

Chang, T. C. and Wysk, R. A. *An Introduction to Automated Process Planning Systems*, Englewood Cliffs, NJ: Prentice Hall, 1985.

Clark, F. D., and Lorenzoni, A. B. *Applied Cost Engineering*, New York: Marcel Dekker, 1985.

Cocker, R. "Cost Comparison Determines Machining Method," *The Tool and Manufacturing Engineer*, October 1967, pp. 20-22.

"Computerized Cost Estimating" *The Tool and Manufacturing Engineer*, November 1966, p. 13.

Conn, H. "Economic Justification of Equipment for Short Runs," ASTME Paper No. MM66-575 (1966).

Corker, R. "Machining Cost Comparison—Milling, Grinding, Planning," ASTME Paper No. MM66-173 (1966).

Doyle, L. E. "Cost Estimating, How To Minimize the Dangers of Chance," *The Tool Engineer*, June 15, 1959.

Dudick, T. S. *Cost Controls for Industry*, Englewood Cliffs, NJ: Prentice-Hall, 1962.

"Estimating with a Computer," *American Machinist*, November 21, 1966, pp. 115-117.

Fleming, R. A. "Facilities Planning," ASTME Paper No. MS66-907 (1966).

"For Your Operating Management—Unprecedented Control Over Key Costs!" *Modern Materials Handling*, October 1967, pp. 43-50.

Gallagher, P. F. *Project Estimating by Engineering Methods* New York: Hayden Book Companies, 1964.

Gillespie, C. *Standard and Direct Costing, Revised Edition of Accounting Procedures for Standard Costs*, Englewood Cliffs, NJ: Prentice-Hall, 1962.

Gladstone, J. *Mechanical Estimating Guidebook*, New York: McGraw Hill, 1970.

Gould, A. F. "Operations Research Case Studies," ASTME Paper No. MM62-103 (1962).

Graham, C. F. *Work Measurement and Cost Control*, New York: Pergamon Press, 1965.

Graham, G. A. *Automation Encyclopedia: A to Z in Advanced Manufacturing*, Dearborn, MI: Society of Manufacturing Engineers, 1988, pp. 163-167, 445-446.

Hammerton, J. C. "Cost Determinants in Designing Production Control Systems," *Automation*, November 1967, pp. 92-97.

Harig, H. "Accurate Pricing of Dies," ASTME Paper No. MS65-121 (1965).

Heineke, J. M. "Notes on Estimating Experience Curves: Econometric Issues," *IEEE Transactions on Engineering Management*, May 1986, pp. 113-119.

Henrici, S. B. *Standard Costs for Manufacturing*, Third Ed., New York: McGraw Hill Book Company, 1960.

Hill, L. S. "Towards An Improved Basis of Estimating and Controlling R & D Tasks," *Journal of Industrial Engineering*, August 1967, pp. 482-488.

Howell, R. A. and Soucy, S. R. "Capital Investment in the New Manufacturing Environment," *Management Accounting*, November 1987, pp. 26-32.

Industrial Engineering Technology, Atlanta: Industrial Engineering and Management Press, 1983.

Jacobs, H. J. "Estimating Short Run," ASTME Paper No. MM65-606 (1965).

Jelen, F. C., and Black, J. H. *Cost and Optimization Engineering*. New York: McGraw Hill, 1983.

Kellee, L. W. "The Use of a Computer in Cost Estimating," ASTME Paper No. MM67-680 (1967).

Leenders, M. and Nollet, J. "The Gray Zone in Make or Buy," *Journal of Purchasing and Materials Management*, Fall 1984, pp. 10-15.

Malstrom, E. M. *What Every Engineer Should Know About Manufacturing Cost Estimating*. New York: Marcel Dekker, 1981.

Mamer, J. W. "Discounted and Per Unit Costs of Product Warranty," *Management Science*, July 1987, pp. 916-930.

Matthews, L. M. *Estimating Manufacturing Costs*, New York: McGraw Hill, 1983.

McNeil, T. F. and Clark, D. S. *Cost Estimating and Contract Pricing*, New York: American Elsevier Publishing, 1966.

Morgan, J. "Software in the World of Make-Buy Decisions," *Purchasing*, September 12, 1985, pp. 77-82.

Naujoks, W. and Fabel, D. C. *Forging Handbook*, The American Society for Metals, Cleveland, Ohio, 1939.

Nelson, L. "How to Estimate Dies, Jigs, and Fixtures From a Part Print," *American Machinist*, September 4, 1961, pp. 185-201.

Nichols, W. T. "Capital Cost Estimating," *Industrial And Engineering Chemistry*, October 1951.

Nicks, J. E. *Manufacturing Cost Estimating, Software*, Big Rapids, MI: MiCAPP, 1986.

Nicks, J. E. *Tool and Die Quoter, Software*, Big Rapids, MI: MiCAPP, 1989.

Ostwald, P. F. *Cost Estimating*, Fourth Ed., New York: McGraw Hill, 1988.

Ostwald, P. F. *Cost Estimator, Software*, Cleveland: Penton Publishing, 1985.

Ostwald, P. F. *Cost Estimating*. Englewood Cliffs, NJ: Prentice Hall, 1984.

Ostwald, P. F. *Manufacturing Cost Estimating*. Dearborn, MI: Society of Manufacturing Engineers, 1980.

Parkinson, C. N. *Parkinson's Law*, Boston: Houghton Miffin, 1957.

Petruschell, R. L. "Project Cost Estimating," *Royal Aeronautical Society Journal*, November 1967, pp. 737-744.

Porteus, E. L. "Optimal Sizing, Process Quality Improvement and Setup Cost Reduction," *Operations Research*, January-February 1986, pp. 137-144.

Quartarone, R. "The Economic Considerations of Numerical Control," ASTME Paper No. MM63-666 (1963).

Reichert, D. I. "Estimating for Short Run Production of Electronic Systems," ASTME Paper No. MM66-701 (1966).

Sheffler, F. W. "Estimating for Reinforced Plastics," *Modern Plastics*, May 1957.

Sluhan, C. A. "How Cutting and Grinding Fluids Effect Value Analysis-Manufacturing Cost Reduction," ASTME Paper No. MM63-565 (1963).

Smith, L. A. and Mandakovic, T. "Estimating: Input Into Good Planning," *IEEE Transactions on Engineering Management*, November 1985, pp. 181-185.

Stewart, R. D. *Cost Estimating*. New York: John Wiley & Sons, 1982.

Stewart, R. D. and Wyskida, R. M. *Cost Estimator's Reference Manual*. New York: John Wiley & Sons, 1987.

Stewart, R. D. and Stewart, A. L. *Microestimating for Mechanical Engineers*, New York: McGraw Hill, 1987.

Veilleux, R. F. and Petro, L. W. *Tool and Manufacturing Engineers Handbook*, Fourth Edition (Volume 5: Manufacturing Management), Dearborn, MI: Society of Manufacturing Engineers, 1988, 4-1—4-14.

Walker, G. and Weber, D. "A Transaction Cost Approach to Make-or-Buy Decisions," *Administrative Science Quarterly*, September 1984, pp. 373-391.

Wallis, B. J. "The Economies of Transfer Dies," ASTME Paper No. MF66-133 (1966).

Williams, R., Jr. "Why Cost Estimates Go Astray," *Chemical Engineering Progress*, April, 1964, pp. 15-18.

Winn, L. J. "Selecting of Optimum Proposals From Various Value Engineering Alternatives," ASTME Paper No. MM64-597 (1964).

Zeyher, L. R. *Cost Reduction in the Plant*, Englewood Cliffs, New Jersey: Prentice-Hall, 1966.

INDEX

D

E

F

G

H

I

J

K

L

M

N

O

P

Q

R

S

T

U

V

W